JANUA LINGUARUM

STUDIA MEMORIAE
NICOLAI VAN WIJK DEDICATA

edenda curat

C. H. VAN SCHOONEVELD

Indiana University

Series Minor, 98

A SURVEY
OF
PSYCHOLINGUISTICS

by

SUSAN H. HOUSTON

1972

MOUTON

THE HAGUE · PARIS

LIBRARY OF CONGRESS CATALOG CARD NUMBER: 73-154526

Printed in The Netherlands by Mouton & Co., Printers, The Hague.

PREFACE

A Survey of Psycholinguistics is planned as a beginning text in socio-behavioral linguistics, surveying the field in breadth rather than in depth and introducing the student to a wide selection of the topics most often studied by psycho- and sociolinguists. The text presupposes no knowledge of psychology and only a beginning knowledge of linguistics, the latter including generative grammar theory. It is the chief intent of this work to reveal for the student some of the many research possibilities open to him in sociobehavioral linguistics. Thus, no single topic is treated exhaustively, but the reader is throughout the text referred to numerous advanced works in the various fields discussed so that he may pursue newly discovered interests on his own. For the same reason, the book literature in psycho- and sociolinguistics is given strong precedence over article literature. I have here tried to cover only the fundamental theory in many areas, rather than discussing the many small studies elaborating upon each area.

The treatment of the material in this text is essentially diachronic, at least in regard to child language acquisition theory, the central concern of much current psycholinguistic work. I wish to show the reader what he is expected to figure out himself in most extant psycholinguistics texts, namely the logical progression which has taken place in the development of psycholinguistic theory over time. Approaches to language acquisition postulated by learning theorists have thus been granted as much space as more current models, because I feel it is of paramount importance – especially to the student just beginning the field – to understand what prompted construction of older theories, in what respects they proved inadequate to the demands of new data, and how more recent work grew from and superseded them.

Much of the material in this text is the standard theory of sociobehavioral linguistics. Occasionally I have added an elaboration or a counter-argument to accepted theory, as for instance in the chapters on Osgood and Whorf; since such discussions represent my own hypotheses and are so labeled, they may be considered as asides for interested readers rather than as essentials for the student to learn. But particularly in the material on modern developmental psycholinguistics, I have included chiefly that information currently considered as the basis of the field, and have avoided presenting the reader with unnecessary theoretical debate where possible.

Some of the material included in *Survey of Psycholinguistics* tends not to be generally thought of as belonging to this field, for example the discussion of foreign language learning or of animal communication. On the other hand, I see no reason not to define the limits of the field rather broadly in an introductory work, and I have found that these topics are of especial interest to students in my own beginning psycholinguistics courses.

Finally, although I intend this work as a survey of the field even for those students majoring in other areas of linguistics or psychology and wishing merely to learn the groundwork of psycho- and sociolinguistics, it is of course my hope that readers may become sufficiently interested in the several areas treated that they want to continue working therein. For these as well as other readers, I have attempted to indicate as candidly as possible how little is yet considered fact rather than hypothesis in psycholinguistics, and how much remains to be discovered. I hope that the relative newness of the field and the tremendous research opportunities in it may encourage readers to participate in such discoveries.

CONTENTS

CONTENTS

ABBREVIATIONS

S-R . . . . stimulus-response
CS . . . . . conditioned stimulus
CR . . . . conditioned response
US . . . . unconditioned stimulus
UR . . . . unconditioned response
S_D . . . . . discriminative stimulus
S^Δ . . . . . stimuli to which learning organism is not to respond
GSR . . . . galvanic skin response
SD . . . . Semantic Differential
SAE . . . . Standard Average European
LAD . . . Language Acquisition Device

1

INTRODUCTION TO PSYCHOLINGUISTICS: S-R LEARNING THEORY

1.1. As any discipline develops, areas of study within it wax and wane in prominence, and aspects of the field previously considered minor frequently may receive sudden emphasis. The growth and subdivision of knowledge is particularly open to witness within the social and behavioral sciences: these disciplines are of relatively recent origin, at least in codified form, and thus their genesis has been compacted into a brief modern span readily susceptible to analysis, much as the rapid life-cycle of the fruitfly arrays itself before the biologist.

Of these disciplines, one of the youngest and most volatile is linguistics, the scientific study of language. Although language has been inspected and described since earliest times (cf. Pedersen, 1931; Robins, 1951 and 1967; Lyons, 1968, pp. 4 ff.), linguistics as such is not older than the present century. The bent of scholars within the field has changed, and changed again; before the late 1920's most language study tended to center around intuitive psychology-based examination of speech, the connections between language and thought, and similar topics (although to be sure this trend was coeval with rigorous and scientific phonetic work, especially in Europe). As is well enough known, the advent of structuralism brought scientific formalism and rigor of procedure to descriptive linguistics, and additionally tended to preclude general psychological theories of language. Structuralism carried as a basic tenet the concentration upon observable phenomena of language behavior, and concomitant refusal to speculate upon the hidden processes of language acquisition and production. It should be noted that linguistics is of course a behavioral science, and as such shared its main precepts of development with, for example, psychology and sociology; the former especially, under the influence of Thorndike and his contemporaries, underwent during this same period a pronounced move toward objective and formalistic thought, so that one may see in this not a trend innovated by linguistics so much as a general process taking place within all the social sciences.

If social science theory may be conceptualized as a machine operating with feedback from the most extreme trends within the field, one may be able to predict with fair accuracy in what direction the next swing of emphasis will proceed. From extreme mentalism, the area as a whole shifted to rather extreme formalism. Under such circumstances a good cybernetic mechanism should correct for the overreaction, and this is precisely what is taking place at present. By the late 1940's, linguists were once again turning to psychology for answers to some general questions concerning language acquisition, perceptual cognates of linguistic units, the differences between comprehension and production, and the like. Such topics are clearly of overwhelming importance to any general theory of language, but just as clearly they are outside the demesne of standard descriptive linguistics. By the early 1950's, therefore, committees on interaction between linguistics and psychology were being formed, guided by linguists such as Thomas Sebeok and psychologists such as Charles Osgood (cf. Osgood and Sebeok, 1965). The result of this interaction has been a gradual coalescing of the two fields into a new discipline, and this discipline is called psycholinguistics.

As will become evident, there is much common ground between these subjects. Laboratory studies of verbal conditioning have been performed for years, arising from standard theories of learning. Although such studies did not (perhaps could not) take into account parallel work in linguistics, nevertheless their results, producing as they do valuable information about verbal behavior, are of obvious importance to the linguist attempting a comprehensive description of language production (cf. e.g. Dixon and Horton, 1968). And likewise, from modern psycholinguistic speculation on the language learning mechanism have come hypotheses of general interest to the learning theorist. Psychologists studying language are for all practical purposes indistinguishable from linguists studying learning, concept formation or other major problems of psychology. Psycholinguistics is an interdisciplinary area, and is in fact more than a mere sharing between the two fields composing its name: the psychology of language leads naturally to concern with the sociology of language, or the linguistics of group interaction; with anthropological linguistics, or the interrelationships between language and cultural variation; with educational psychology, insofar as concerns second language learning and teaching, and so forth. Again we may see in the interdisciplinary nature of this extremely significant new field the opportunity to generalize about behavioral science: typically in modern social and behavioral science as a whole, boundary lines between disciplines merge and dissolve quite readily. Despite the specialization of all current knowledge, there is increasingly less tendency to differentiate between related areas in social or in physical science – perhaps because a single piece of information may relate many apparently diverse sets of data. Psycholinguistics, our present concern, is not only significant because of its intrinsic concerns with basic problems of language and thought; it is in addition prototypic of the modern, interdisciplinarily organized social science, taking from and contributing to an entire field of human inquiry.

1.2.   There are both advantages and disadvantages to newness in a field; sometimes it may be rather difficult to determine whether a condition is the former or the latter. Psycholinguistics, for example, suffers – or benefits – from the extremely broad and inclusive approach characteristic of all young sciences. The psychology of language appears, at least on the surface, to subsume all of linguistics and all of psychology, at the very least. Of course one does not seriously advocate disorganization; but since there are distinct advantages to allowing any related topic to offer its contribution to the major area of concern, we shall take a fairly liberal approach to the content of this work. This will be especially beneficial since the present work is intended as a survey of psycholinguistics, an in-breadth rather than in-depth introduction to all areas representing the intersection between linguistics and the other sociobehavioral sciences. Following are the approximate general topics we shall hope to cover:

1.2.1. *General learning theory.* – As stated in the preface, we do not presume a specialized background in psychology in this survey; but we are not planning a comprehensive discussion of learning studies either. There are certain basic precepts of standard learning theory necessary to understanding of, and meaningful contribution to, language acquisition theories. For this reason a very brief investigation of the area is included.

1.2.2. *Verbal behavior and conditioning.* – This is material of psychology proper, not usually contributed to by linguistic thought. Since there have been some recent works devoted exclusively to this area (e.g., Deese, 1965), we shall treat it only in passing.

1.2.3. *Major standard theories of language learning.* – There are only three or four which have historical significance, all of which predate the inception of modern psycholinguistics.

1.2.4. *The relationship between language and cognition.* – Often areas which have been investigated for many years are suddenly found to belong within the domain of a new field. Benjamin Lee Whorf and his contemporaries produced well known material on language and thought, in the late 1930's and early 1940's. Although the Whorfian approach is rather distant from modern psycholinguistics, the problem of the relationship between language and cognition is central to the discipline, and it would not be an error to classify Whorf himself as an early psycholinguist. However, linguistics has not utilized the work of Whorf to so great an extent as have other disciplines, for instance anthropology and social psychology. Nevertheless his hypotheses have some significant implications for a general theory of linguistic structuring.

1.2.5. *The nature of linguistic universals.* – In the structuralist period of American linguistics this topic would not have been discussed at length in a work on linguistic science. But there are now several entire works devoted to universals of language (e.g., Greenberg, 1963, 1966; Bach and Harms, 1968). This is partly because the intent of the term 'universal grammar' has altered considerably, as will be shown.

1.2.6. *Bilingualism*; and

1.2.7. *Second language learning.* – The latter two topics are phases of the same problem, namely acquisition and coexistence of two languages spoken by one individual. Those interested in second language teaching should find a theoretical background in this area most useful, especially because most extant work on second language instruction provides only the barest heuristics for the prospective teacher.

1.2.8. *Miscellaneous.* – Under this topic will be included such subjects as animal communication, paralinguistics, aphasia; these areas, although marginal to psycholinguistics, nevertheless draw on the work of the latter for their basic precepts.

1.3.   The diversity of the above topics is one of surface rather than of deep structure, so to speak. As within any field, there are a number of fundamental questions in psycholinguistics which all contributing areas work toward answering. Although it may not be comprehensive, an overview of questions posed by those in a particular field may often provide a rapid overview of the goals of the field. Following are a number of basic problems which concern modern psycholinguists:

1.3.1.   How does a child acquire his native language?

An important facet of this question concerns how much of language is innate and how much learned. Psychologists have tended to view language as chiefly learned, whereas linguists have tended to view it as having a sizeable innate component at least in reference to the origins of basic linguistic patterns and hierarchies. There are a number of reasons for this diversity of opinion, which will be examined presently.

1.3.2.   What are the essential differences between child language and adult language, and how does the former gradually develop into the latter? Why do children learn language at all?

Despite appearances, the answer to the latter question is far from self-evident. In the strictest sense, language is not necessary for survival, as demonstrated by the mere fact of speech-delayed children (and cf. Lenneberg, 1962). Since language learning is universal among all normal members of the species, however, one must inquire not only how this learning proceeds but also why. It is after all not a sufficient explanation to note that children learn language because they are exposed to it.

1.3.3. What is the relation between linguistically created and perceptual units of language?

This question has long remained unsolved, although structuralists used to debate various aspects of it (e.g., the existence of the phoneme and of the word). Most modern psycholinguists would probably be inclined to affirm the reality of both these units, although the essential problem remains (cf. Miller, 1962; Fodor and Bever, 1965).

1.3.4. How are sentences understood and produced?

Language specialists are currently approaching a solution to this problem; the whole of modern generative grammar theory is the best answer now known. There are many levels at which such a question can be posed, and present linguistic technology is directed primarily toward creation of a schematic diagram of the ideal sentence-producing system.

1.3.5. What is the perceived relationship between a word and its referent, and between related words? Can it be measured?

Interword and word-referent relationships have been troublesome largely because they seem to be the products of hidden or unobservable processes. But the psychologist Charles Osgood (1957) has developed a tool called the Semantic Differential, which gives a consistent representation of some connotative relationships between words.

1.3.6. What are the biological bases of language?

Current opinion holds this to be among the most vital problems in the discipline. Once some knowledge is attained of the biological foundations of language, many of the other problems cited here will be readily soluble. In a very real sense neurophysiology is at the core of all psychological and linguistic theorizing. The mechanisms postulated by the psychologists and by the technical descriptive linguist (especially in dealing with generative grammar), are 'clean' mechanisms, behavior-generating machines with self-contained structure, operating *in vacuo*. But finally all such postulated devices must correspond to real physiological processes (cf. Peters, 1969). This is the case, of course, even in reference to learning theories which regard most or all nonmolecular behavior as learned; the learning mechanism itself is necessarily innate and must correspond at some level to theoretical descriptions.

1.3.7.   What is the range of language pathologies?

There is a wide range of language pathologies, central and peripheral, temporary and permanent. Examples are stuttering, deaf speech, mutism, aphasia, cleft-palate speech. Only the range of neurologically based disorders classed as aphasia and related problems will be examined here. Again the discussion will of necessity be brief, in the nature of a survey of current thought. There have been many volumes written about aphasia, a disorder which still largely defies organized analysis and treatment.

1.3.8.   Do animals have language or approximations to language, and if not, what is the nature of their communication?

Animal language has received much scientific and popular attention. Although discussion on the subject is frequently speculative, a number of approaches to animal language will be reviewed here.

1.3.9.   How can the relationships among language, culture and personality best be discussed?

Since this question subsumes most remaining inquiry into the nature of the universe, it must necessarily be the final one offered.

1.4.   The problem at the focal point of much current psycholinguistic attention is how and why the child learns his first language. Although it is often unwise to dichotomize, one may identify two basic ways of approaching this problem, which may be labeled as learning-theory psycholinguistics and developmental psycholinguistics. The force of this two-way division is most obvious from a diachronic standpoint. Language acquisition was not neglected during the reign of American structural linguistics. Rather it was chiefly the province of contemporaneous psychology, which was for the most part dominated by adherents of the varieties of standard learning theory known as behaviorism. As we shall see presently, behaviorism is just what the name implies, a descriptive framework for human behavior. An important although largely implicit axiom of behaviorism is that major forms of observable human behavior, including language, are established through a few relatively simple learning operations. Further, the significance of language to the totality of human behavior and thought is empirically so clear that no non-trivial theory of language can neglect this aspect of behavior. As a result, from behaviorist psychology alone, uninfluenced by linguistics, have come a number of complex and purportedly comprehensive theories of language learning. Learning-theory psycholinguistics, the older of the two types, is in fact responsible for all important attempts at an inclusive description of the language acquisition process.

It will be clear to the historian that the learning-theory approach flourished before the advent of psycholinguistics proper, before any union and thus any accessible communication channel between linguistics and psychology had been established. Now, learning theory, especially behaviorism, is by no means obsolete as a school of psychology, and there are modern behaviorist and other stimulus-response models of language learning (cf. Braine, 1963 and 1965). But because of its traditions, even modern behaviorist work shows little influence from other fields. Within the last decade or so, developmentalism has become prominent, arising from new methods of investigating language acquisition and from the information produced by these new investigatorial techniques. The inability of learning-theory psycholinguistics to take such new information into account has resulted in its relegation to a distinctly minor position, particularly by those psycholinguists trained in modern descriptive linguistics.

Despite the rechannelling of the modern field, there is every reason for the young psycholinguist to become familiar with learning-theory explanations of language acquisition and production. Perhaps the most compelling reason is that, had there been no learning-theory psycholinguistics, there would be no developmentalism either, since the very flaws of the former approach served to indicate new directions of search to modern investigators of language (cf. e.g. Chomsky, 1964). In order to advocate any position intelligently, within any field, it is necessary to understand both the strong points and the inadequacies of other possible views. The developmental psycholinguist must know why conditioning theory fails to account for major portions of the language acquisition process, if he is to make any headway in finding new theories which remedy this failure. This is not to say that total rejection of antecedent work is always, or even usually, essential; there is much in behaviorist psychology which the modern language-acquisition specialist can utilize.

As has been indicated, language should according to the behaviorist be explicable in terms of those learning hypotheses devised for general learning behavior. From this it follows that some familiarity with general learning theory is necessary before one can deal with behaviorist-based descriptions of language acquisition. The remainder of this section and that following will present a brief overview of some basic learning theory principles and terms, in order that those unacquainted with these areas of psychology might better be able to proceed with language-specific material. This presentation will concentrate on a general description of learning models on which specific theories are based; a good survey of theories themselves is presented in Hilgard (1956) or Hill (1963). Most language learning material is understandable from the standpoint of the major learning models alone.

There are two main learning models on which most learning theories are built. These have many different names; a useful pair are stimulus-response (S-R) and cognitivism. S-R theories, especially those classifiable as behaviorism, are by far the more important group for the psycholinguist. (For an early pioneering work in behaviorism, cf. Watson, 1930.) They consider learning as an orderly and predictable series of observable behavior patterns; a key S-R concept is 'habit'. Cognitive theories, on the other hand, tend to view learning as the development of a series of cognitions about the environment and its organization. 'Perception' and 'insight' are typical concepts of this school.

S-R theory recognizes two major classifications of learning, namely classical conditioning and instrumental or operant conditioning. The name of Pavlov is frequently associated with discussions of classical conditioning; this Russian psychologist was among the first to formulate the conditioned-response principle which lies at the core of standard psychology (cf. Pavlov, 1960). The conditioned response, or CR, principle stems from the possibility of exploiting natural tendencies of an organism to respond in certain ways to stimuli, a stimulus being anything which elicits or calls forth a response of observable behavior. The stimulus of a light flashed in the eyes causes the response of blinking; the stimulus of food presented to some animals causes or elicits the response of salivation. Since such natural 'reflexes' or responses are present without prior training or conditioning, they are called unconditioned responses (UR), and the stimuli which elicit them are called unconditioned stimuli (US).

Classical conditioning theory stems from the discovery that if a second stimulus, not originally leading to a response, is frequently presented slightly before or accompanying the unconditioned stimulus, then this second stimulus presently comes to elicit the response also. The new stimulus is called a conditioned stimulus (CS), since the organism's reaction to it must be conditioned or learned; the response to it is a conditioned response (CR). In the familiar Pavlovian experiments, a dog was presented food (US) and responded by salivating (UR). Then each time the food was presented a buzzer was sounded (CS). Eventually the buzzer elicited the response of salivation (CR) as the food alone originally had. The dog had become conditioned to respond to the buzzer tone by salivating, even when no food was present.

The appearance of a CR takes place through reinforcement, one of the most important concepts in psychology. In classical

conditioning, 'reinforcement' refers to the following of the conditioned stimulus by the unconditioned stimulus, as in Pavlov's
work the presentation of food following the buzzer tone was a
reinforcement. When the CS is not followed by the US – e.g., if
the buzzer were presented to the dog but not followed immediately by food – then the conditioned response is said to be non-
reinforced. Under conditions of non-reinforcement, the conditioned response tends to grow weaker or less probable, and ultimately to disappear altogether. This is known as extinction of the
response. Extinction is not equivalent to total annihilation of the
organism's tendency to respond; after a response has been experimentally extincted, it often may reappear spontaneously after a
rest period, usually at a lesser strength or probability of occurrence than formerly.

Two more concepts important in this connection are generalization and discrimination. Hilgard explains the former thus:

A new conditioned stimulus, not previously reinforced, may elicit a
conditioned response the first time it is presented. The probability that
it will do so is increased if it is similar to the conditioned stimulus
which has been reinforced. Thus if a conditioned stimulus is obtained
to one tone, another tone, at a slightly different frequency, will also
produce a conditioned response, with lesser magnitude the further
the separation of the tones. This process whereby a novel stimulus
produces a response learned to another similar stimulus is known as
generalization (p. 51).

The key to generalization is the notion of stimulus similarity.
Verbal stimuli may be similar enough to prompt generalization
also (cf. Phillips, 1958). Thus one responds correctly to foreign
pronunciations of English words, perhaps to the degree that such
pronunciations represent good approximations to the standard.
In some sort of way it is possible to think of generalization as
occurring when the organism in question does not know that two
stimuli are different, although this is most applicable to human
learning.

Discrimination may be considered as representing the opposite
end of the continuum from generalization. Reactions to a new
stimulus may range from the organism's behaving as though it

were identical to a previous CS, to recognizing that is is a different stimulus altogether and one for which the previously learned conditioned response would not be appropriate. The latter process is discrimination. Discrimination of this type is not experimentally produced. There is, however, conditioned discrimination, which occurs when an organism is presented with two possible stimulus situations which are somewhat alike, but is reinforced for responding to only one of the two. For a child learning to name objects, for example, the presence of a horse is the proper occasion for the child to say 'horse', whereas the presence of a cow is not the occasion for such behavior. In this case there is an entire pattern of stimuli which set the occasion for the proper CR, rather than just one single stimulus. The concept of stimulus discrimination has many applications. The psychologist B. F. Skinner (cf. Chapters 3 and 4 of the present work) has employed it in his system of programmed instruction, an educational technology based upon behaviorist learning theory. Skinner refers to the stimulus which 'sets the occasion' for a response as the discriminative stimulus, abbreviated S^D; this is contrasted with stimuli to which the learning organism is not supposed to respond, called $S^\triangle$ (read S-D and S-Delta). In the above example, the presence of a horse would be an S^D with regard to the verbal response 'horse', while the presence of a cow would be an $S^\triangle$ (cf. Holland and Skinner, 1961).

A somewhat more recent and more widely applicable conditioning theory is that termed instrumental or, more frequently, operant conditioning. Operant conditioning principles were largely developed by Skinner, and they represent to some extent a break from the classical stimulus-response models described above. Rather than one type of response, Skinner proposes two, namely elicited responses and emitted responses. Responses elicited by known stimuli, or elicited responses, Skinner calls 'respondents'; responses merely emitted without direct reference to known stimuli, or emitted responses, he calls 'operants'. The operant is postulated as more significant in human learning than the respondent (cf. Skinner, 1938).

In respondent conditioning, which is equivalent to classical conditioning, the reinforcement is correlated with the stimuli. In the Pavlov experiments, for instance, the reinforcement was the presentation of food to the dog subsequent to the buzzer tone, but the food was also the unconditioned stimulus. In respondent or classical conditioning, then, the US serves as reinforcement. In operant conditioning, on the other hand, the reinforcement is correlated with the response. Operant conditioning does not deal with reflexes or UR's. Another way of putting this is that stimulus conditions are 'irrelevant' to emitted or operant behavior. The reinforcement follows the response. When an operant has been emitted, for whatever reason, it can then be reinforced by reward. Skinner notes that the stimulus conditions preceding or eliciting an operant cannot always be identified (cf. Skinner, 1953, pp. 64-66). In operant conditioning, the experimenter waits for the organism to emit the desired behavior naturally and then reinforces it, thus strengthening the tendency of the organism to emit the behavior again. The experimenter does not elicit the behavior, in other words, by presenting a stimulus to which the behavior occurs as an unconditioned response or reflex.

Operant conditioning, which in practice is essentially a process of shaping behavior, is the standard method of training animals, quite probably in use for the last 1500 years at least. Suppose, for example, that one wishes to train a bear to dance in a figure-eight pattern. This is clearly not reflex behavior, or an unconditioned response to some stimulus situation, so that operant conditioning rather than classical is applicable here (cf. Skinner, 1957, p. 29). One must work at shaping the behavior of the animal, and bringing this behavior under the control of some artificially selected stimulus such as a command. One starts out by waiting until the bear, in the course of its natural lumbering about its cage, happens to make a right turn, say; then one immediately reinforces this behavior by rewarding the animal, probably with food. (It will also become important not to reward such behavior unless it follows the trainer's command, for instance a whistle, since one does not wish the bear to emit the behavior ceaselessly.) The reward will reinforce the bear's tendency to make right turns. After a while, the trainer will reward not merely right turns following the command to perform, but only right turns followed by left turns in the pattern desired. In this way the behavior is shaped little by little. Finally only the completed pattern is reinforced. By this method of reinforcing successive approximations to the desired terminal behavior, the conditioning is accomplished. Although the behavior is brought under the functional control of a stimulus selected by the trainer, the stimulus only comes to elicit the CR, it does not do so naturally – there is no US involved. The conditioned response in operant conditioning does not equate with the response to the reinforcing stimulus, as in classical conditioning. Rather the organism must perform or emit the CR in order for the reinforcement to appear, since the reinforcement is contingent upon the response. This is the major difference between classical and operant conditioning.

Another well-known example of operant conditioning methodology is the following: there is a device invented by Skinner and commonly called the Skinner Box, which is used to train animals by operant conditioning. It consists of a darkened, soundproofed box in which there is a lever, such that when the lever is pressed, a food pellet is dropped through a slot into the box. If a food-deprived rat, for instance, is placed in the Skinner Box, the rat will run about and eventually stumble onto the lever by accident, thus obtaining a food pellet. This will most likely happen repeatedly, and result in the rat's gradually becoming conditioned to pressing the lever in order to obtain food. An observer might note that the time interval between lever presses gradually diminishes as the rat learns to press the lever in order to get fed. The lever press is an operant, since the original stimulus conditions causing the rat to bump into the lever are irrelevant; the food is the reinforcement, contingent upon the rat's emitting the operant of lever-pressing. The basic law of operant conditioning upon which this description is based is, if the occurrence of an operant is followed by presentation of a reinforcing stimulus, the strength (that is, probability of occurrence) of the response is increased.

It is Skinner's contention that nearly all human behavior is based upon this type of learning. The principle involved, namely that reward increases the probability of occurrence of a behavioral item, is both simple and highly useful.[1] It is most important to understand the role of reinforcement in operant as contrasted with classical conditioning. A concept frequently mentioned in connection with operant conditioning is secondary reinforcement (cf. Hilgard, pp. 94-96). The principle of secondary reinforcement is that a stimulus which is not originally reinforcing can become so through repeated association with a stimulus which is reinforcing. Money is an esteemed secondary reinforcer; money does not satisfy any drives in itself, it is merely used to obtain food, etc., but through association with many naturally reinforcing objects it has become reinforcing for many kinds of behavior (this is actually an example of a generalized reinforcer, a subcategory of secondary reinforcer). A secondary reinforcement serves to

---

[1] Among the most interesting and significant recent applications of this principle is the technique known as behavior modification or behavior modification therapy, a method of effecting alterations in performance applicable to a wide variety of undesirable behaviors ranging from childhood autism and adult schizophrenic behavior to alcoholism and classroom problems. In its applications to abnormal psychological states, the theory behind this technique is approximately as follows: Rather than regarding, e.g., autism or catatonic schizophrenia as disorders of a theoretical organ called 'the mind', one can regard them purely as collocations of symptoms, or behavior disorders; thus the trouble with an autistic child would be diagnosed not as psychosis or severe maladjustment characterized by withdrawal, but rather as a set of aberrant and socially unacceptable behavior patterns. Behavior modification uses the principles of behavior shaping and instantaneous reinforcement to change these behavior patterns, for example gradually reinforcing more and more social-contact-oriented activity on the part of an autistic child, perhaps by luring him closer to people by giving him candies when he turns his head toward the experimenter or approaches him. In the classroom, the child who 'acts up' is rewarded instantly and consistently for such good behavior as he shows, even if it is only the absence of bad behavior, and is ignored when he is misbehaving, so that he is conditioned to acceptable modes of conduct. Although the theory as well as the technique of behavior modification remains repugnant to many people, who regard it as overly mechanistic and unanalytical, there is good evidence to suggest that it is highly successful in many types of situation. For more on this, cf. Lent (1968), Ferster (1968), Ullmann and Krasner (1966), Bandura (1969).

strengthen the response with which it is correlated, and may in fact be used to reinforce other forms of behavior also once it has become established.

The secondary reinforcer is frequently used in animal training, particularly when working with rather inaccessible animals such as aquatic mammals. With animals especially, it is necessary that reinforcement immediately follow the CR in order that the animal know for what it is being rewarded. But it is not always practical to present the animal with food, for instance, directly after it has emitted a piece of behavior. Typically the trainer will begin in this manner: he will give a command, the animal will perform, then the trainer will blow a whistle (for instance) and present the food. Through repeated association with the reinforcement of food, the whistle will acquire secondary-reinforcement properties, signalling to the animal that it has performed correctly and serving as a reward in exactly the same manner as the food itself. It is presumed that in all cases a secondary reinforcement will lose its reinforcing properties when not followed ultimately by the primary reinforcer; in such circumstances the response in question may become extinct. This is a rather controversial subject, however, especially when dealing with somewhat mysterious animals such as dolphins – one suspects that the difficulty lies in insufficient knowledge of what is a primary reinforcer to the animal in question, rather than in the theory itself. Most human training or teaching is performed through secondary reinforcement, at least in the period after infancy. As we shall see presently, Skinner presumes operant conditioning to be the process behind language learning, and thus he bases his entire theory of language acquisition and operation upon this learning model.

2

COGNITIVE LEARNING THEORY

2.1. Because stimulus-response-based theories have dominated the field of psychology during this century, it is not surprising to find them at the foundation of most language-acquisition work as well. However, there is another important psychological school which has had a profound effect on psycholinguistic thinking: cognitive theory forms the second theoretical framework on which a number of learning models have been built.

Cognitivism has proved less satisfactory than the S-R theory as an explanation for learning, for several reasons. Whereas S-R hypotheses are fairly molecular in nature, that is, concerned with very small units of behavior or learning, cognitivism deals with molar behavioral units, or entire complexes of events on a more abstract level. This is a difficulty because the molecular nature of S-R theory allows postulation of correspondence between the essential hypothetical unit of learning, namely the stimulus-response bond, and a physiological event, namely neuronal connections. In cognitivism, on the other hand, there is no such clear-cut learning unit, a situation which has led some psychologists to question the explanatory power of this model in relation to real neurological processes. Another phase of this same problem is the tendency of cognitivists to be rather empirical and intuitive, and discuss hidden processes rather than measurable or at least observable forms of overt behavior. The S-R theorist deals with good data such as response strength and latency of response, while the cognitivist tends to discuss perceptions, insights and other purely theoretical constructs of a nonrepeatable or nonobservable character.

But there are areas in which cognitive theories excel. For

example, cognitivism is well suited to the study of perception and concept formation, topics for which stimulus-response explanations are either weak or lacking. Cognitive theory, and Gestalt theory in particular, has produced what seems to be a valid and useful set of principles describing the development of perceptions, the role of insight in learning, and especially the nature of our intrinsic structuring of the environment. It may be readily seen that this is a different order of phenomenon than that treated by most S-R oriented work, and thus one need not regard the 'choice' of a school of psychology as an all-or-none proposition – both S-R and cognitive notions are blended in any realistic description of the learning process.

The relevance of cognitive theory to modern psycholinguistics may not be immediately apparent from the above indication of typical cognitive concerns. But, although cognitive theory has not played an active part in the discipline of psychology for some years, it is in one sense at least very much akin to current psycholinguistic thought. We have indicated that in general the S-R theorists are concerned with learning and the cognitivists with perception. The ability to learn, or to form stimulus-response associations, may properly be regarded as universal to all creatures with a nervous system (as well, apparently, as to some dubious cases such as the earthworm). The only significant endogenous[1] component of this kind of learning is precisely the ability to associate a response with a stimulus. Very little, then, need be postulated as innate in such a system, nor is there any pressing need to assume different neural equipment for *homo sapiens* than for other relevant species.

Perception, however, does not appear to depend to the same extent as S-R learning on directed exogenous stimuli, nor can it usually be described as any simple association between one unit

---

[1] 'Endogenous' means developing from within, internal to; the opposite term is 'exogenous', which means developing from outside, or external to. One might say, for example, that the developmental psycholinguist presumes formal linguistic universals (such as grammatical categories) to be endogenously developed, rather than being learned or exogenous to the individual.

of environment and one unit of behavioral response. Whereas it is often possible to observe and replicate the learning of particular behavior, it is rarely possible to isolate the process of acquisition of perceptual patterns, or to specify precisely what in the environment may have been responsible for this acquisition process. Further, although S-R theory postulates only a few basic learning procedures, clearly every organism has a different repertoire of behavior. But it is not at all clear that every organism has a different repertoire of perceptual patterning, especially within a single species (cf. Vernon, 1962). And the lack of perceptual diversity does not seem dependent upon environmental conditions.

Gestalt psychology does not speak of the learning of perceptions. Instead, the Gestalt laws of perception describe a framework assumed to be present at the start of any learning or conceptualizing activities. The Gestalt perceptual framework is either innate or maturationally caused, and it is species-specific, at least to the extent that the human species is postulated as able to operate differently with the environment than can most animal species. Thus the innate component assumed by the cognitivist is far more extensive and complex than that of the S-R psychologist. In this regard, the cognitive learning model is of some interest to the psycholinguist: modern developmentalism breaks with standard learning-theory psycholinguistics in this same area, namely the assumption of a built-in underlay to language and related behavior. Whereas perceptual universals are not equivalent to linguistic universals, there is every reason to suppose that the two are related – and in any case, since current psycholinguistic thought is very much concerned with the notion of an inherent and species-constant substrate of linguistic behavior, it will be of interest to the new psycholinguist to understand the school of psychology most in accord with this view.

2.2. The best-known and most important learning model within the cognitive school is Gestalt psychology. *Gestalt* is a German word, generally left untranslated; it means 'figure' or 'configuration', and is used to refer to any unitary perception, even though the unit may be complex or composed of several parts.

Gestalt theories appeared first in the early part of this century, originally constituting a reaction toward the contemporary trend toward strict experimentalism instituted by Thorndike and his followers (cf. Thorndike, 1898 and 1913). Previous to the inception of Gestalt theory, learning was generally described as a trial-and-error process, in conjunction with which the introduction of higher-level decision-making and other such notions constituted a needless complication. The cognitive school viewed this description of human behavior as overly deterministic and rigid, and felt that the omission of 'consciousness' from a theory of learning is a gross error.

The first major publication of Gestalt theory was by Max Wertheimer, in 1912; it was he who established the basic laws of perception which characterize Gestalt psychology. In contrast to the behaviorists, who favored concentration on observables and rejection of introspective notions such as the mind, Wertheimer felt that a meaningful learning theory is possible only if consciousness is included as intrinsic to perception and learning. Wertheimer said that we view the universe not as a set of serial associations or chains without inner structure, but rather as meaningful wholes which can only be broken down by structural analysis of an artificial type (cf. Wertheimer, 1923 or 1938). This concept is highly relevant to the psycholinguist, since an important developmentalist precept is that linguistic behavior cannot be adequately described in terms of associative chains either (cf. Chomsky, 1962, pp. 18-25; cf. also Lashley, 1960, p. 506 f.).

2.2.1. Although Wertheimer's publication was the first to appear in Gestalt theory, he is not generally regarded as most instrumental in the growth of the school. Two of his colleagues, Wolfgang Köhler and Kurt Koffka, are better known than Wertheimer as the co-founders of Gestalt psychology. Koffka's first work, entitled *Growth of the Mind*, appeared first in London in 1924. Portions of this work still seem startingly modern in approach, although in part it treats of arguments no longer at issue. Koffka's position on consciousness was much the same as Wertheimer's; *Growth* contains a specific attack on the concept of trial-and-error learning, and explains the Gestalt attitude toward consciousness thus:

The behaviorist is right in denying the existence of conscious criteria wherever the method of experimental observation is inapplicable; but in spite of this we shall refuse to accept his position, for the simple reason that there is a consciousness, reports of which can only be made by the experiencing individual, and which is therefore not subject to the control of others. Science can not refuse to evaluate factual material of any sort that is placed at its disposal. Furthermore, what appear to be two cases of the same objective behavior may prove to be fundamentally different when the accompanying phenomena of consciousness are taken under consideration (pp. 16-17).

Of course, there are other ways of explaining the latter phenomenon; the S-R explanation would be simply that the same response could be associated with two separate stimuli, a situation which one might conceptualize as behavioral redundancy. But to Koffka, the important factor would be the different underlying ideas or thought processes at the root of the behavior. As we have indicated, Koffka takes a more liberal position on the role of heredity in learning than do the S-R proponents. He states that the brain is physically incomplete and immature at the time of birth, and that subsequent development is due to both learning and maturation, with the latter providing the capacity for the former to take place (pp. 54 ff.; cf. also Kessen, 1965, for further discussion of this point). Koffka feels that the human infant has far more sensory organization, even in the neonatal period, than many psychologists had previously thought (cf. Pines, 1966).

2.2.2. Wolfgang Köhler, the other leading Gestaltist, pioneered in the study of insights, or sudden 'flashes of understanding' of the environment. Insight or insightful learning presents several problems to the learning theorist. This form of learning appears not to be directly based on experience or on habit; it is not predictable from environmental factors; it does not occur in the same manner throughout a species. But Köhler felt that animal as well as human behavior can display insights, and that it is possible to design experiments in which animal behavior is highly likely to show insight and in which such insight may be differentiated from solution of problems by luck or chance.

Köhler's main experiments were performed with chimpanzees, as detailed in his *Mentality of Apes* (1925). The experimental design was suggested by his observation that insight is likely to occur in problem situations in which the direct path to solution is blocked, but in which indirect paths are left open, and in which overview of the entire situation is potentially possible (Köhler, 1917, p. 5; Koffka, 1959, p. 199). Should the solution be hit upon by chance in such experiments, its attainment will display a different character than if it were due to insight: there is no organized, goal-directed activity in the former case, but rather more blundering about, trying a solution, abandoning it and trying something else, thus creating a particular type of learning curve. Contrariwise,

A true solution is quite different; for the animal proceeds by a single continuous curve from its original position to the attainment of the goal. To be sure, a true solution often follows after a perplexed period of trial and error; but in this case the difference is even more striking, for the animal suddenly gives a start, stops a moment, and then proceeds with a single impulse, in a new direction, to the attainment of the goal (Koffka, 1959, p. 200).

With these concepts in mind, Köhler designed a series of some seventeen experiments. Each experimental situation contained a goal toward which the ape was motivated, namely a banana, and a problem which had to be solved before this goal could be attained.[2] The experiments ranged from situations easy for the

---

[2] In order to obtain some prior notion of the abilities of the chimpanzees, and of what sort of situation to construct that might be challenging to them, Köhler constructed the following pre-experimental situation: he suspended a basket containing a banana from a cord which passed through an iron ring at the top of the ape's cage. The other end of the cord was looped over a branch of a tree, also within the cage, so that the loop hung at the same height as the basket (about two metres above the floor). It was intended that the chimpanzee recognize that the fruit could be obtained by removal of the looped end of the cord from the tree-branch, thus letting the fruit-basket fall to the floor of the cage. The ape tested, Sultan by name, was the clever-

animals to solve, in which some connection between the animal and the fruit was already established and had only to be utilized, to extremely complicated situations in which an element had to be removed from one grouping or configuration (or Gestalt) by the animal and put to an entirely unrelated use in another. In a simple experiment, for example, the fruit was placed outside the animal's cage out of its reach, but was attached to a string the end of which could be reached and pulled by the animal. A slightly more complex situation likewise contained fruit outside the cage, but this time the ape had to rake the fruit in with a stick placed in its cage. Alternatively, the fruit might be in a basket on the roof of the cage, and could only be reached by the ape's swinging from a nearby rope to grasp it.

---

est of Köhler's chimps. The results, although most informative, were quite other than had been anticipated, since the ape proceeded to yank the entire apparatus from its moorings.

Since the description of this experiment appearing in Köhler's original papers on ape mentality (1917, p. 9) is both enlightening and charming, we shall quote it here as given: "Sultan, der die Vorbereitung nicht gesehen hat, wohl aber das Körbchen vom Füttern her gut kennt, wird auf den Platz gelassen, während der Beobachter ausserhalb am Gitter Stellung nimmt. Das Tier betrachtet zunächst den hängendem Korb, beginnt aber bald lebhafte Unruhe (wegen des ungewohnten Alleinseins) zu zeigen, donnert nach Schimpansenart mit den Füssen gegen eine Holzwand und sucht an den Fenstern des Affenhauses und wo es sonst Ausblicke gibt, mit den andern Tieren, am Gitter mit dem Beobachter in Verbindung zu kommen; jene sind unsichtbar, dieser verhält sich gleichgültig. Nach einer Weile geht Sultan plötzlich auf den Baum zu, steigt schnell hinauf bis zur Schlinge, bleibt einen Augenblick ruhig, zieht dann, auf den Korb blickend, an der Schnur, bis der Korb oben am Ring (Dach) onstösst, lässt wieder los, zieht ein zweites Mal kräftiger, so dass der Korb oben klippt und eine Banane herausfällt. Er kommt herab, nimmt die Frucht, steigt wieder hinauf, zieht jetzt so gewaltsam, dass die Schnurr reisst und der ganze Korb herabfällt, klettert hinunter, nimmt Korb und Früchte und geht damit ab, um zu fressen."

It is clear from this that the experiment can in no wise be described as a failure: the animal did recognize the connection between the rope and the basket (cf. Koffka, 1959, pp. 200-02). Moreover, when the experiment was repeated, the ape simply replicated its performance despite more secure fastenings employed by the experimenter. One would not hesitate in calling this a 'true solution', even though it was not the solution intended by the designer. It must be borne in mind too that the task put to Sultan was not a simple one.

All the above-described experiments were characterized as requiring, on the part of the chimpanzee, mere employment of available tools. A second group of tests in this series required in addition the setting aside of obstacles (Koffka, 1959, p. 203). A typical example of this group consisted of a banana outside the cage, able to be reached by an available stick; but in order to reach the banana with the stick, the ape had first to move a heavy box placed inside the cage directly opposite the fruit.

This latter group of experiments, although somewhat more complex for the animals than the first, was still similar to the first in that both groups required working only with materials directly at hand. As we have noted, in the most complicated experiments in the series, the ape was required to supply or fabricate a tool from a source external to the nuclear problem-situation. For instance, in one such experiment the fruit was placed outside the cage. In order to reach it, the ape had to break a branch off a dead tree at the rear of its cage and use this as a tool. In another, the ape had to use a rope as a climbing or swinging device to reach the fruit, but first had to uncoil the rope from a horizontal bar. Similar to this was the only experiment which proved impossible for all animals tested, in which it was necessary for the ape to re-hang a swinging-rope which had been removed from its hook and placed on the floor of the cage. Perhaps the most interesting of the so-called 'stick problems' was one in which the fruit was placed outside the cage in a square three-sided box, lacking a top and a rear wall. In order to obtain the fruit, the chimpanzee was required to turn the box with a stick provided it, until the opening in the box faced the cage permitting the fruit to be pulled in with the stick. Although this does not sound especially difficult, it requires the animal to begin by pushing away the fruit, which at first is quite near to it and directly visible, in the course of turning the box. Typically an animal's goal-directed behavior does not permit of a change in orientation such as that displayed here, and in fact the need to push the banana away temporarily created a strong conflict for the animals and proved very difficult to solve. Only one animal performed the experiment correctly, and that only after beginning to turn the box in the right direction, pausing and turning it the other way, and then returning once again to the proper course of action. These results were rather unexpected, since one would assume that apes in their natural habitat are forced to take detours to reach their goals fairly frequently.

In addition to the stick problems and rope problems, there were also a number of box problems, in which the goal, placed in a basket on the cage roof, could be reached only after the ape had stacked and climbed one or more boxes placed in its cage. Here the problem was not only to figure out how to reach the fruit, but also to construct the actual stack of boxes required in the multiple-box problems. Chimpanzees are apparently categorically unable to build stable two- or three-box structures, a fact masked somewhat by their ability to climb and leap from extremely flimsy and ill-stacked structures. Köhler considered the problem to lie with the basic visual perception of the apes, since experience with boxes even over a year's time did not improve the animal's stacking ability.[3]

From these experiments, Köhler was able to draw certain conclusions about the conditions under which insights are likely to occur, and the form these insights should take. The most signifi-

---

[3] From such experiments as these one is led to speculate upon the differences of visual perception between ape and human. The apes had notorious difficulty with the thrice-coiled rope which had to be uncoiled and swung on in order to reach the fruit. Most of the animals merely pulled on the free end of the rope, although the resulting length could only be used to swing from by the most able gymnasts among the apes. Koffka remarks, "The nature of this behaviour with respect to a coiled rope leads one to think that apes see these simple orderly coils, not as we do, but rather as a confusion of strands like a snarl; and we, too, are apt to attack a snarl without any definite plan, by grasping a strand at random and pulling at it. Though objectively a simple construction, a coil of rope seems to be something that a chimpanzee is incapable of apprehending as a clear-cut visual form; instead it seems to appear to him as a more or less chaotic figure, and this indicates a certain limit to his capacity for achievement" (Koffka, 1959, pp. 216-17). But at a later date one or two of the animals proved able to solve the problem, due, presumably, to better capacity for 'visual articulation'.

cant experiments were those in which the ape was required to remove an object from one setting and employ it in another. In order for the animal to carry out the proper action in these tests, an alteration had to occur in the object of perception (Koffka, 1959, p. 209). An object which had been merely 'something to bite on', perhaps, or 'something to play with', had to become 'something to rake in fruit with'. A problem situation is likely to be most difficult, for animals or for humans, when it involves the necessity of transferring an object from one stable configuration or Gestalt to another, even if the transfer is theoretical, i.e., consists in realizing a new use for a familiar object, rather than physical (cf. Maier, 1930). Where insights occur, they will frequently be characterized by the sudden realization that the components of a familiar situation may be viewed as something other than their accustomed nature, and that one structure may be able to take on multiple functions.

Köhler emphasizes that there is nothing mysterious or mystical in the attainment of the insight needed to solve a problem (Köhler, 1947, p. 200). Whether for apes or for humans, it is necessary only to have the proper inclusive overview of the situation and understanding of how its component elements fit together, plus freedom from what modern efficiency engineers term 'functional fixedness' or the inability to see objects as having more than their accustomed function or use. Of course, familiarity with the general type of situation in which the problem exists is also a desideratum, since insight depends in part upon the possibility of analogizing from past experience. There are also factors which facilitate insight-achievement in apes which would not be necessary for humans; for example, Koffka notes, in relation to Köhler's stick experiments, that

if a stick is so placed that it is not visible when the animal's gaze is on the goal, or in the course of a wandering glance which is limited to the region of the goal, its employment may be prevented. Even if the animal occasionally looks at the stick, it does not necessarily employ the tool, because it can not see both the stick and the goal at the same time. In this respect, one might say that the chance of a stick becoming a tool is a function of a geometrical constellation (Koffka, 1959, p. 209).

Proximity of the crucial element to the goal is not vital to humans in the achievement of insight, although to be sure it is probably a factor here as well. Proximity ceases to play so vital a role once the animal is used to the experimental situation and 'knows enough' to look around for a key object to manipulate, however.

2.2.3. It was mentioned above that past experience facilitates insightful learning or problem-solving. The role of past experience in learning was a source of much controversy during the early years of Gestalt psychology. Contrary to common opinion, both at the time and since, Gestalt theory did not postulate that all problem-solving involves insight, nor that past experience is of no importance in present learning. Nor did Gestaltists ever attempt to deny the existence of trial-and-error learning, the reality of which has been demonstrated countless times. Gestalt theory recognizes several possible ways of solving problems. A major difference between early S-R and Gestalt theories of learning is that the former felt that the possession of the necessary past experience guarantees the solution to the problem, or in other words that organisms always learn from their mistakes and, once having performed correctly, will perform correctly on the next occasion as well. Gestaltists, on the other hand, postulate that although experience clearly facilitates solution, organization must also be taken into account, since more is generally required than mere information. The following are the main principles of insightful learning, as characterized by Gestalt psychology (Hilgard, 1956, pp. 234-36):

2.2.3.1. "A more intelligent organism is more likely to achieve insight, just as it is more likely to be successful at other forms of complex learning." This point is seldom touched upon in standard behaviorist learning-theory writings. It creates a difficulty, however, in determining exactly what 'more intelligent' means – especially since intelligence in animals is typically determined by performance in experimental problem-situations, thus creating a circular definition. But the point seems empirically valid, especially insofar as concerns humans, for which species our notions of intelligence are at least informally somewhat more codified (cf. e.g., Bayley, 1955).

2.2.3.2. "An experienced organism is more likely to achieve insightful solution than a less experienced one", although this is not always borne out. Past experience must first be seen by the organism to be applicable in the present situation. In other words, the internal structure of the situation and its similarity to that of previous situations must be recognized, and only then the method of application may be figured out and utilized.

2.2.3.3. "Some experimental arrangements are more favorable than others for the elicitation of insightful solution. Organization is contributed both by processes inherent in the organism and by structural patterning in the environment, and, of course, basically through the interaction of organism and environment." Pattern overview is essential if insight is to be achieved; the organism incapable of, or prevented from, seeing the total structure of the situation, is not going to achieve a meaningful insight into its resolution. Note that here as always, the Gestaltist recognizes that any organism in a learning or problem-solving situation must work with its own inherent capacities to structure the environment in meaningful ways – learning is never wholly or even mainly exogenously motivated (cf. Wertheimer, 1945).

2.2.3.4. Finally, Gestalt theory notes that "trial-and-error behavior is present in the course of achieving insightful solution." The learner may make many false starts before achieving insight, as indeed Köhler's chimps did, and when or if he will achieve it is not completely predictable. But the Gestaltist does not interpret trial-and-error behavior as randomized fumbling about and running off of previously acquired habit. Rather it is intelligent searching, in which each new trial is based on the results of the last. The more intelligent and practiced the organism, the more likely its behavior will be to show intelligent and reasoned attempt at solution rather than blundering around and repeating the same mistakes again and again. Where this latter form of non-functional behavior is found, it may be caused by lack of pattern overview or by functional fixedness on the part of the learning organism. It is not relevant, by the way, whether or not the organism's judgments about the results of its last trial are correct: it is quite conceivable to misconstrue or misinterpret the effect of one's behavior upon the environment while still behaving in a rational manner.

2.3. The greatest success of Gestalt-theory behavioral explanations has been in the area of perception. Gestalt hypotheses demonstrate the roles of background and organization in perception, memory and forgetting, and postulate a number of 'laws' by which our tendencies in these areas may be predicted. Although psychologists of this school traditionally relegated problems of learning to a secondary position, Koffka at least felt that the laws of organization in perception are in fact applicable to learning in general. These laws, described originally by Wertheimer, are five in number: there is one basic guiding principle, called the Law of Prägnanz, and four subordinate laws, namely those of Similarity, Proximity, Closure and Good Continuation (from Hilgard, 1956, pp. 227-29).

2.3.1. The Law of Prägnanz states that psychological organization tends to move toward the state of Prägnanz, or toward the so-called 'Good Gestalt'. A good Gestalt is simple, regular and stable, and represents for the individual a maximum structuring of events or objects. This Law has been compared to the second law of thermodynamics, that dealing with entropy or physical equilibrium. Theoretically, the individual seeks the good Gestalt in any situation, and has a tendency to regularize the environment both in perceiving it for the first time and in remembering it. Operating from analogy is one way of effecting this regularization: in an environment in which many events are structured according to the same underlying pattern, there is clearly a high degree of organization and regularity, thus rendering the individual more capable of dealing with any randomly selected event from this environment. The process of analogy is familiar to the language specialist, and its function in child language is well known (cf.

McNeill, 1966). The Law of Prägnanz acts as a levelling tendency in remembering as well as in initial learning, in linguistic as well as nonlinguistic spheres. For instance, a speaker asked to repeat an utterance in his native language, spoken by someone else, typically will do so using relatively standard and 'most colorless' intonation, omitting any peculiar prosodic and paralinguistic features of the original: the individual tends not to notice, or to forget, those features which ruin the good Gestalt.

2.3.2. The Law of Similarity (or of Equality, as it is sometimes known), was initiated by Wertheimer to determine the principle of grouping in perception, exemplified by perception of line or dot patterns. The law states as follows: "Similar items (e.g., alike in form or color) or similar transitions (e.g., alike in the steps separating them) tend to form groups in perception" (Hilgard, 1956, p. 227). Köhler found that similar pairs of nonsense syllables or of drawings were more readily associated and learned than dissimilar pairs. It is necessary for those working with this law to have some prior notion of what constitutes similarity, and whether it is a property of the words or objects concerned or rather of the individual perceiving them. This becomes a problem since, for example, the pair of words 'boy/girl' is more closely associated and more easily learned than either 'boy/man' or 'boy/toy' (for a relevant discussion, cf. Cofer and Foley, 1942).

2.3.3. The Law of Proximity states that "perceptual groups are favored according to the nearness of the parts" (p. 228). If a number of parallel lines are spaced unevenly on a page, those with narrower spaces between them will be seen as groups. This law is the Gestalt equivalent of the behaviorist principle of association by contiguity, which states that two objects or events which often appear together will tend to become associated. Thus objects or events perceived as related because of proximity will be more easily learned or associated with one another than those seen as belonging to different groups, as unrelated. The Law of Proximity also holds true temporally: events which occur within a short time of one another are associated. In this version the principle becomes a Law of Recency. Hill notes that the

Morse Code uses this principle by employing silences of different lengths to separate letters and words, making sound groups stand out as units (Hill, 1963, p. 97).

2.3.4. The principle stated by the Law of Closure is that "closed areas are more stable than unclosed ones and therefore more readily form figures in perception" (p. 228). This law too has its equivalent in association theory: the Law of Effect, first postulated by Thorndike, states that when a connection (as between stimulus and response) is followed by a satisfying state of affairs, its strength is increased; when by an annoying state, its strength is decreased. The direction of behavior is said to be toward an end-situation which brings closure or a feeling of completion with it.

In regard to the Law of Closure, Koffka states,

So long as the activity is incomplete, every new situation created by it is still to the animal a transitional situation; whereas, when the animal has attained his goal, he has arrived in a situation which to him is an end-situation (Koffka, 1959, p. 108).

The emphasis is not on obtaining a reward for a behavioral item, but rather on achieving a completed state in which all the parts of the situation (physically or in the abstract) are brought into a 'good' relation to one another (cf. Hill, 1963, p. 98). It is possible to interpret this law as the direct contraposition to the basic law of operant conditioning, since it does minimize the role of reward in learning or other goal-directed behavior. But the Law of Closure deals essentially with motivation, insofar as concerns learning rather than perception: clearly an organism can complete an activity solely in order to complete it, rather than for any expected reward. This is most obviously true of humans, but often verifiable in the case of other species as well (we believe it to be true of certain aquatic mammals, for instance). One might legitimately cite the Gestalt Law of Closure to those people who have an intense feeling of discomfort at leaving a crossword puzzle or a novel incomplete. Perhaps the linguist dealing with prosodic features could find this law most useful: it is frequently observed that, although most normal people do not talk in so-called 'complete sentences', they nevertheless employ complete-sentence intonation with decisive terminal junctures in most or all of their conversation, and if they do not do so, then their listeners are likely to anticipate further remarks, that is, view the conversation as incomplete.

2.3.5. The Law of Good Continuation is the last of the more well-known postulates developed by Wertheimer. It states

organization in perception tends to occur in such a manner that a straight line appears to continue as a straight line, a part circle as a circle, and so on, even though many other kinds of perceptual structuring would be possible (p. 229).

This indicates both that we tend to supply 'missing' portions of events and objects perceived, and that we tend to remember such events and objects as being complete, regular, or good Gestalten. The more difficult it is to fill in or supply missing portions, the more difficult it will be to remember or work with the event or object.

2.4. Although Gestalt theory is better suited to explanation of perception than of learning, there is nevertheless a Gestalt description of learning, or more accurately of the interplay between experience and memory and between experience and current perceptual processes. This theory, commonly called the trace hypothesis, postulates an entity called the memory trace. Somewhat in the manner of the older concept of the 'engram', the trace is described as the present representation in the brain of a past process or event. In addition to traces, which persist from past experience, there is also presumed to be a present process, which can scan and select, reactivate or otherwise communicate with traces, resulting in a new process of recall or recognition (Hilgard, 1956, pp. 230-31). Memory traces may be regarded as real, physiological events, although one can only speculate upon their exact neurological nature. The trace is probably best regarded as a theoretical construct, the Gestalt equivalent of the stimulus-response bond.

Since the trace system is a Gestalt organization, it is naturally subject to the laws of perception as outlined above. Memory traces change over time, in other words, in the direction of the good Gestalt. Thus a circle with a small break in it, seen in a memory experiment, may be remembered and reproduced as a complete circle, and so on. The validity of this assumption has been demonstrated frequently. A well-known demonstration is that performed by Carmichael, Hogan and Walter (1932), in which a series of drawings was presented to two groups of subjects, with each group being given a different set of labels or names for the drawings. When the observers were subsequently required to reproduce the drawings, which were in actuality non-representational shapes, it was found that the reproductions showed a strong tendency to be modified to look more like the objects named. In a recent replication of the same experiment (Herman, Lawless and Marshall, 1957), it was found that this effect was even more pronounced when the subjects were unaware beforehand that they would have to reproduce the drawings. Since one might assume that such foreknowledge would tend to influence the subjects toward accuracy, this is precisely the effect that should be expected.

2.5. The memory trace hypothesis sketched very briefly above (it is actually quite involved and complex) is the main Gestalt attempt at describing the interaction between past learning and present processes of handling information. It is most generally felt that the strength of Gestalt psychology lies in its interpretation of more molar processes, as we have noted, and that association theory explanations of the learning process contribute more toward answering basic questions about learning. Although S-R and cognitive psychologies deal with rather different aspects of behavior, most Gestaltists have nevertheless felt it incumbent upon them to develop explanations or descriptive analyses of the most basic processes of learning. The following are some Gestalt theory explanations of typical learning problems (Hilgard, 1956, pp. 252-53):

2.5.1. *Capacity for learning.* – Learning requires "differentiation and restructuring of perceptual organizations", and higher forms of learning depend on natural capacities for these reactions. But the Gestalt school also notes that poor methods of instruction or presentation may inhibit learning as much as may lack of natural capacity. Since it is *per se* impossible to develop a valid and reliable method of instruction without a valid and reliable learning-process description, this situation has enormous consequences for the educational psychologist. Perhaps the main Gestalt point here is that an organism's failure to learn or to solve a problem is frequently blamed on the organism's lack of learning capacity, whereas it is really due to a presentation method which does not give the organism an opportunity to achieve pattern overview.

2.5.2. *Practice.* – According to the Gestalt psychologists, changes occur within, rather than as a result of, repetition. Repetitions are "successive exposures, bringing to light relationships to enter into restructurization". The more familiar an organism becomes with a problem situation, the better the organism will be able to comprehend how the pieces of the situation fit together and how best to work within this perceived structure. If the perceived structure of a situation is different from the manifest structure, presumably practice of a trial-and-error sort will bring this fact to light.

2.5.3. *Motivation.* – "Goals represent end-situations, and as such modify learning through the principle of closure." Unless the goal which motivates an organism is achieved, the organism will feel dissatisfied or unfulfilled, and so will be motivated to continue or resume the behavior which brings it closer to the goal. Those oriented toward behaviorism might think of closure as corresponding to a form of secondary reinforcement; the Gestaltist, however, seems to regard the drive toward closure as primary rather than secondary.

2.5.4. *Understanding.* – Topics considered by Gestalt pyschologists as relevant to understanding are the perceiving of relationships, awareness of the relationship between parts and whole, and means to particular goals. The adherent of this school says, of course, that "problems are to be solved sensibly, structurally, organically, rather than mechanically, stupidly, or by the running off of prior habits." What has been called 'logical thinking' is relevant to understanding: in order to understand a present situation and its possible future consequences, it is necessary to be able to trace the logical consequences or results of various alternative operations upon the present situation. This is important in order for the organism to adjust its behavior to changes in the environment. Much of current cybernetic theory, especially that concerned with feedback, is akin to basic tenets of Gestalt psychology in its description of how the organism reacts to its environment (cf., for instance, Wiener, 1954, pp. 22-27, 58-59).

2.5.5. *Transfer.* – Transfer refers to the effects of previous learning on a new learning situation. It may be positive, or facilitation of learning by previous experience, or negative, that is, obstruction of learning from the same cause. The Gestalt concept corresponding to transfer – which is essentially an association-theory term – is transposition: "A pattern of dynamic relationships discovered or understood in one situation may be applicable to another." What exists in common between the situations is said to be not identical individual elements but rather common patterns or relationships between components. The usual functioning of analogy is easily explained in these terms: in solving a problem by analogy, the individual assumes that because the problem has one or more elements in common with a past situation, then the problem is structured similarly to the past situation and will exhibit the same relationships between its elements. The higher the degree of positive transfer, the less the need for trial-and-error solution, of course.

2.5.6. *Forgetting.* – Gestalt psychology explains forgetting as destructive change in the memory trace. Traces are said to disappear through gradual decay, destruction because of belonging to a chaotic and ill-structured perceptual field, or through assimilation to new traces or processes.

3

B. F. SKINNER'S *VERBAL BEHAVIOR*

3.1. The most comprehensive association-theory-based description of the language-acquisition process is that developed by B. F. Skinner. As has been noted, Skinner was among the first to formulate the principles of instrumental or operant conditioning, and it is upon these principles that his theory of verbal behavior is based. Skinner's work on language learning, titled *Verbal Behavior* (1957), may be looked upon as the first major contribution to psycholinguistics, much as Leonard Bloomfield's *Language* (1933) is often considered to have initiated modern American linguistics.

The parallel between Skinner and Bloomfield is apt, not only in that each was a pioneer in his respective field. Just as linguistics has branched out in directions not foreseen by Bloomfield, so psycholinguistics is generally felt to have progressed beyond Skinner's 1957 work. Virtually all of developmental psycholinguistics has arisen within the last decade, and of course as new evidence and new discoveries accumulate, the relevance and scope of prior works is diminished. But the status of these works as the cornerstone of their field does not change, and it is quite as important to study them now as at the time of their first appearance, although perhaps for different reasons.

Skinner's *Verbal Behavior* may be considered as prototypic of learning-theoretic explanations of language acquisition, in that it works entirely within the framework of behaviorist psychology. An abstract and perhaps philosophical value of S-R-conditioning theory is that it in effect presents an integrated theory of human behavior, the ultimate goal of all sociobehavioral science. Within such a schema, all forms of observable behavior are treated as structurally similar, in that they are all composed of the same learning units, S-R bonds. At the time his work was published, Skinner believed that language too can be represented as a composite of stimulus-response associations and therefore can be fitted into a universally applicable description of human behavior. This has the advantage, according to the principle of economy sometimes known as *dicter simplicitas* or Occam's Razor,[1] of obviating the need for postulating a special language-learning mechanism, which would be species-specific and function in ways not describable through operant conditioning principles. Since behaviorism does not propose more than a few basic types of learning in animals, it seems empirically reasonable that human learning too should reduce to a small set of basic elements forming an underlay for the entire range of human behaviors.

Modern developmentalism, however, holds that such a theory of language is inadequate, and that it fails to take cognizance of such important aspects of language as its apparently constant age of onset. Few precepts of current developmental psycholinguistics stem directly from psychology; most come from, and reflect trends in, such other areas as neurology, genetics and linguistics itself. But linguistics today is a vastly different object from linguistics of the 1930's through the mid 1950's during which time *Verbal Behavior* was in preparation. Skinnerian language theory

[1] The principle of Occam's Razor was postulated by the Nominalist philosopher Willam of Occam (d. 1347); in its original form it states, "Entia praeter necessitatem non sunt multiplicanda", or, entities are not to be multiplied beyond necessity. It referred originally to the notion that universal concepts are subjective, real objects are individual or particular, and thus there is no need to postulate the existence of the former if one accepts the existence of the latter.

In its practical application, Occam's Razor (also known as *'dicter simplicitas'* or the simplicity metric) is taken as a principle of economy, implying that the simplest possible explanation consistent with observed facts is to be accepted, all other things being equal. It is simpler to postulate one Deity than to assume a rain god, a sun god, a war god and so on; it is simpler to postulate a single learning mechanism than to assume a language-learning device, a skill-learning device, a perception-acquisition device and so on – all other things being equal, which in the case of learning they appear not to be.

corresponds relatively well to the linguistics of the period; although there is no evidence to suggest that the author conducted any investigation of contemporaneous linguistics while preparing his book, the influence of linguistic theory on his hypotheses is clear. Structuralism is characterized by the same taxonomic approach to language that Skinner demonstrates, and displays the same concomitant failure to study language from the viewpoint of surface rather than deep structure (cf. Chomsky, 1967, p. 406 ff.). Both Skinner and the structuralists exclude the concept of meaning from their respective analyses, preferring to deal with objective quantities on which several observers can presumably agree. And too, both grant, either explicitly or implicitly, the existence of an unambiguous 'decision procedure' or set of algorithms[2] for dealing with a corpus of data:[2] for the structuralists, such a corpus consists in a series of utterances, analyzable through Immediate Constituent technique and taxonomic classification of the resulting units; for Skinner, a corpus consists in a series of 'speech events', analyzable through identification of the component verbal operants and likewise, classification of these operants according to their relationship to the eliciting stimulus conditions.

As we shall see presently, these similarities in procedure and underlying philosophy imply certain similar conclusions about the adequacy of each method. It is not accurate to state either that language is wholly linear or that it is wholly hierarchical; the internalized language-production machine, and its schematic counterpart, the model generative grammar, are two-dimensional structures, in whose functioning both linear association between units and hierarchical relationships play a part. Skinnerian psycholinguistics, like American structural linguistics, scans only one

[2] Algorithms are precise instructions or formulas for constructing a process; in contrast to algorithms are heuristics, empirical guidelines insusceptible to precise formulation. Tic-tac-toe is a game for which there are algorithms, or a series of formulated rules such that the player observing them will invariably either win or draw. There are algorithms for chess, but their number and complexity is such that they are not used; rather chess is played heuristically. Taube (1961) has estimated that in a forty-move chess game there are 10^{120} separate algorithmic instructions necessary to a formalized game.

dimension of linguistic operation, in much the same manner as a hypothetical two-dimensional being sees only a cross-section of three-dimensional objects passing through his space (as in Abbott, 1952). The great advances in modern psycholinguistics and technical linguistics, and the explanatory power of new theories in each, are due in large measure to the realization that in fact language is essentially two-dimensional – that is, linear and hierarchical – in structure, and that the narrower viewpoint of previous theories excluded much essential data.

A discussion of psycholinguistic thought cannot be considered complete without examination of the role learning theory has played in the discipline, despite current views of its lacks. We have already indicated one reason why this is so: insofar as language behavior is linear, S-R descriptions of language learning and production are still valuable. One should note that it is quite conceivable to make use of association theory in describing language, without subscribing specifically to any extant language theory, such as that of Skinner or of Mowrer. But the young psycholinguist interested in verbal conditioning and intraverbal associations cannot innovate intelligently without thorough knowledge of these works, else he may find himself having rediscovered long-known and perhaps -discarded principles. Skinner's work has enormous historical interest within the field, just as does Bloomfield's, although these works are perhaps better regarded as both exponents of the classical views of their respective fields, and launching-pads for new ideas relevant to the portions of language to which they apply. In the following treatments of the works of Skinner, Mowrer and Osgood – three of the major learning-theory psycholinguists – this viewpoint is to be borne in mind. It is necessary to maintain a panchronic perspective, remembering during these discussions not only the modern extensions and modifications of the hypotheses set forth, but also the state of the art at the time they were proposed and their consequent significance to psycholinguistic development at that time.

3.2. One of Skinner's most important concepts is the lack of a distinctive language-learning mechanism; it is his belief that verbal behavior is merely an exemplification of general, universally employed learning processes. Although he recognizes that language does have some special characteristics, he states:

The basic processes and relations which give verbal behavior its special characteristics are now fairly well understood. Much of the experimental work responsible for this advance has been carried out on other species, but the results have proved to be surprisingly free of species restrictions. Recent work has shown that the methods can be extended to human behavior without serious modifications (Skinner, 1957, p. 3);

(all further citations in this chapter are from this work unless otherwise noted). Since Skinner feels no need to postulate a difference between language behavior and other forms of human behavior, it is consistent that he also not consider language to be necessarily species-specific. To him verbal behavior is merely a complicated instance of stimulus-response conditioning, an analysis which permits language to be explained by operant conditioning laws.

In Skinner's system, the operant is the basic unit of verbal response, the quantum of which utterances or total speech situations are composed. He states that words, phrases, clauses, sentences or even smaller units than these may all have 'functional unity' as verbal operants, since any utterance which forms a unitary response to some stimulus is an operant. He notes too that "for most purposes 'operant' is interchangeable with the traditional 'response' " (p. 20). Skinner states that the verbal response is the dependent variable in his functional analysis, since "the probability that a verbal response of given form will occur at a given time is the basic datum to be predicted and controlled" (p. 28).

3.2.1. That the unit of speech is the verbal operant implies that language responses, in order to acquire strength, must be followed by reinforcement. This in turn indicates that, rather than studying how the child learns language, one should study how the child is conditioned or trained to language behavior and concomitantly what are the motives of the trainer. The beginnings of language in the child are conditioned by the parent, as one might expect: "The parent sets up a repertoire of responses in the child by reinforcing many instances of a response" (p. 29), so that each time the child utters an approximation to a correct utterance, the parent rewards him. Of course, a response must appear at least once before it can be reinforced, but since operant conditioning is a process of shaping behavior, it is not necessary that complex adult-language forms appear in the child's unconditioned verbal repertoire. Instead the parent reinforces any bit of verbal behavior which can usefully be developed into a complete form.

To explain this shaping process, Skinner says,

In teaching the young child to talk, the formal specifications upon which reinforcement is contingent are at first greatly relaxed. Any response which vaguely resembles the standard behavior of the community is reinforced. When these begin to appear frequently, a closer approximation is insisted upon. In this manner very complex verbal forms may be reached (pp. 29-30).

After the desired behavior is attained, continued reinforcement maintains the verbal responses at the desired strength. Skinner states that operant conditioning is

simply a way of controlling the probability of occurrence of a certain class of verbal responses. . . . A child acquires verbal behavior when relatively unpatterned vocalizations, selectively reinforced, gradually assume forms which produce appropriate consequences in a given verbal community (pp. 30-31).

Of course in order to control the probability of occurrence of an operant, it must become associated with a specific stimulus or set of stimuli. The type of stimulus control exerted over various categories of operant forms the basis for classification of verbal-behavior units, as we shall see.

3.2.2. Skinner divides the verbal operants into these main categories: mands; tacts; intraverbal behavior, chiefly exemplified by echoic responses; and autoclitics. These all may profitably be thought of as (S-R) psychological 'parts of speech', just as nouns and verbs are linguistic parts of speech. The MAND is a verbal operant in which the response is reinforced by a characteristic consequence and is therefore under the functional control of a relevant condition of deprivation or aversive stimulation (pp. 35-36). According to Skinner, the mand is "the type of verbal operant in which a response of given form is characteristically followed by a given consequence in a verbal community", and is "characterized by the unique relationship between the form of the response and the reinforcement characteristically received in a given verbal community." The unique relationship referred to is that the mand specifies its reinforcement. Mands may specify either a desired behavior on the part of the listener, or an ultimate reinforcement: the mands 'listen!', 'look!', 'say yes!' specify the former; 'bread!' and 'more soup!', the latter.

In regard to the function of the mand as a verbal operant, Skinner says,

A mand is a type of verbal operant singled out by its controlling variables. It is not a formal unit of analysis. No response can be said to be a mand from its form alone. As a general rule, in order to identify any type of verbal operant we need to know the kind of variables of which the response is a function. In a given verbal community, however, certain formal properties may be so closely associated with specific kinds of variables that the latter may often be safely inferred. In the present case, we may say that some responses, simply because of formal properties, are very probably mands.

Note that in order for classification systems to be valid, it is necessary that assignment of class membership be done on a constant basis: it is not proper to say that only some X's may be formally identified as Y's, since this implies lack of a uniform decision process and therefore insufficiently delimiting classes. However, in Skinner's system one need not seek to classify mands on the basis of form, but rather on the basis of the relationship either between the state of deprivation and the reinforcement, or between the response itself and the reinforcement. Neither of these alternatives is equivalent to identification of units based solely on their form or phonetic shape, for example.

3.2.2.1. Since the unit of verbal behavior is the operant, verbal behavior must need reinforcement in order to be acquired and maintained. Reinforcement for language behavior seems intuitively to come most often from a listener. Because this is so, Skinner emphasizes the importance of the listener-speaker relationship, and thus the necessity of describing an entire speech episode or situation rather than an utterance or monologue spoken by a single individual. A total speech episode is described by "listing all relevant events in the behavior of both speaker and listener in their proper temporal order" (p. 36). Description of the total episode is especially important in the case of the mand, since the mand is perhaps more closely linked to its reinforcement than any other class of verbal operant.

For instance, if one wishes to study the mand uttered by a speaker requesting some bread (i.e., 'bread, please!'), one must describe the total speech event in order to isolate the discriminative stimulus under whose functional control the mand occurs (p. 37). In this context, presuming a hungry speaker and a receptive listener, Skinner states that the mere presence of the listener provides the occasion or the S^D (cf. Chapter 1 of this work) for the speaker's mand, since "the speaker does not ordinarily emit the response when no one is present, but when a listener appears, the probability of response is increased." The occasion having been set, the speaker utters his mand, 'Bread, please!' The mand in turn provides a stimulus for the listener—an S^D for the listener's response of giving the speaker the bread. The mand is reinforced when the speaker receives the bread he requested, whereupon the speech episode may be said to have been concluded.

3.2.2.2. Although all mands are characterized by approximately the same relationship between deprivation state, utterance and reinforcement, it is possible to subcategorize mands according to the speaker-listener relationship created by each (pp. 38 ff.). A mand in which the listener is independently motivated to reinforce the speaker, Skinner calls a request. When the speaker's response, "in addition to specifying a reinforcement, may need to establish an aversive situation from which the listener can escape only by providing the appropriate mediation", or in other words when the listener's (not the speaker's) behavior is reinforced by reduction of a threat, then the mand is called a command. As examples the author cites 'Hands up!' and 'Your money or your life!'; he adds that in the latter example, "the first two words specify the reinforcement and the last two the aversive consequences with which the listener is threatened." Further subtypes of mand are prayers or entreaties, or mands which promote reinforcement by generating an emotional disposition of some sort; and questions, or mands which specify verbal action, and in which "the behavior of the listener permits us to classify it as a request, a command, or a prayer, as the case may be." 'What's your name?' is an example of a question mand, "a verbal stimulus for the listener who replies either because of a standing tendency to respond to the speaker or an implied threat in the speaker's response, or because the speaker has emotionally predisposed him to reply." Presumably the listener may also have been conditioned simply to respond to this particular question independent of its source.

Finally, although in general "a mand assumes a given form because of contingencies of reinforcement maintained by the listener or by the verbal community as a whole" (p. 46), nevertheless there are mands which cannot be explained by arguing that responses of the same form have been reinforced under similar circumstances in the past. This sort of mand, termed by Skinner the MAGICAL MAND, is explained either by accidental reinforcement of the response, or else by creation by analogy with previously heard mands. Sometimes the magical mand may be associated with wishing (e.g., 'My kingdom for a horse!'); sometimes with a vocative of various sorts (e.g., 'Milton, thou shouldst be living at this hour!'); sometimes with allusion ('Go and catch a falling star') or with the expression of conditions contrary to fact ('Would that I were king!'). When the magical mand is a literary device, the author is said to be reinforced by the expectation of the effect the mand will have on readers. On the subject of the magical mand in literature, Skinner states this:

Literature is the product of a special verbal practice which brings out behavior which would otherwise remain latent in the repertiores of most speakers. Among other things the tradition and practice of lyric poetry encourage the emission of behavior under the control of strong deprivations – in other words, responses in the form of mands. Evidently the lyric poet needs many things and needs them badly. He needs a reader and a reader's attention and participation. After that he needs to have someone or something brought to him or taken away. Verbal behavior strengthened as the result of these various deprivations is emitted, in spite of its manifest ineffectiveness or weakness, because of the poetic practice.

This same motivation might be said to influence writers of prose as well as poetry; it might be illuminating to view some modern works of fiction from this particular angle.

3.3. In reference to the causation of verbal responses, Skinner says that it is convenient to distinguish between instances in which the controlling stimuli are themselves verbal and those in which they are not. The simplest form of verbal behavior controlled by verbal stimuli is that in which "the response generates a sound-pattern similar to that of the stimulus", or in other words, echoic behavior. Echoic behavior, which may be considered a subcategory of general intraverbal behavior, can be produced by mands of the type, 'Say X', although this form of response commonly appears in the absence of explicit mands (p. 55). Reduplicative forms in language, such as 'helter-skelter' or 'willy-nilly', are said to exemplify fragmentary self-echoic behavior, in which both stimulus and response issue from the same speaker; reduplication, however, is a special case of echoic behavior, which is most often interpersonal.

In Skinner's opinion the echoic response is significant in child language because it aids the parent or teacher in eliciting and controlling the child's verbal behavior (but cf. Brown and Bellugi, 1964). He states that

an echoic repertoire is established in the child through 'educational' reinforcement because it is useful to parents, teachers and others. . . . The procedure continues to be used in formal education to permit the teacher to set up new forms of behavior or to bring a response under new forms of stimulus control, as, for example, in naming objects. In all these cases we explain the behavior of the reinforcing listener by pointing to an improvement in the possibility of controlling the speaker when he reinforces (p. 56).

Echoic behavior is said to be reinforced when it continues to reinstate the stimulus and to permit the speaker to react to it in other ways.

There is a distinction to be made between echoic behavior and superficially similar intraverbal responses: although other forms of intraverbal behavior may also be self-reinforcing, no such behavior may properly be called echoic if its main characteristic is merely that it appears to "resemble the speech of others heard at some other time". A verbal stimulus of corresponding form must immediately precede the true echoic response. Skinner comments too that echoic behavior

does not depend upon or demonstrate any instinct or faculty of imitation. The formal similarity of stimulus and response need not make the response more likely to occur or supply any help in its execution. The fact is, there *is* no similarity between a pattern of sounds and the muscular responses which produce a similar pattern. At best we can say that the self-stimulation resulting from an echoic response resembles the stimulus. The resemblance may play a role in reinforcing the response, even in the echoic relation, but it has no effect in evoking the response. A parrot does not echo a verbal stimulus because the stimulus sets up a train of events which naturally lead to a set of muscular activities producing the same sounds; the parrot's distinguishing capacity is to be reinforced when it makes sounds which resemble those it has heard. What is 'instinctive' in the parrot, if anything, is the capacity for being thus reinforced (p. 59).

In order to comprehend this explanation fully, it is necessary to understand that, for Skinner, the speech episode consisting of the utterance of a word by speaker$_1$ and its repetition by speaker$_2$ is in reality composed of four main factors – the speaker's muscular activity in producing the word, the actual pronunciation as heard by the second speaker, the latter's muscular activity in repeating the word, and the actual pronunciation of the echoic response. These may be symbolized respectively as articulation$_1$, utterance$_1$, articulation$_2$, and utterance$_2$. Of these, utterance$_1$ is the stimulus, and articulation$_2$ the response. Thus it is possible to state that the echoic response does not resemble the stimulus; rather it resembles the articulation of the stimulus. It is convenient to regard the situation in this process- rather than goal-oriented fashion, because in fact utterance$_2$ does not coincide exactly with utterance$_1$ at all: echoic behavior is significantly different from mimicking or parroting, although it is very difficult to take this into account in the present explanation. Note that, although one may say that the stimulus, utterance$_1$, elicits the response of muscular movement designed to produce the best possible imitation of the stimulus (i.e., articulation$_2$), there is given no explanation of the decision mechanism permitting the second speaker to be satisfied with his utterance. This difficulty may be avoided by saying that any echoic-type response for which speaker$_2$ is reinforced, automatically becomes satisfying; however, then one has the problem of finding the decision mechanism which prompts speaker$_1$ to reinforce speaker$_2$. An alternative way of putting this is, since the repetition is not equivalent to mimicking or parroting the original stimulus – i.e., it is not identical with utterance$_1$ but rather reproduces only certain features of utterance$_1$ – by what criteria does speaker$_1$ judge the echoic to be exact or 'good' enough to warrant reinforcement? This problem becomes particularly troublesome in the case of socalled talking birds, since these creatures do not in reality sound anything like humans, any more than whistling sounds like piano music; in both cases similar parameters are being employed, which give the illusion of identical results. But, presumably, a baby can recognize its repetitive efforts as alike to (if not identical with) its parent's utterances, despite the vast difference in acoustic properties between the two utterances. Considering articulation$_2$ to be the response rather than utterance$_2$ obviates the necessity for postulating a faculty of imitation, but it also avoids one of the main issues in echoic behavior theory, namely why repetitions are generally not exact (even between adult speakers) and why on the other hand both parties are satisfied with the inexact results.

As we have noted, there are other forms of intraverbal behavior besides the elusive echoic. Intraverbal behavior of other varieties shows no direct correspondence with the evoking verbal stimuli. Examples of this type of behavior are the response 'four' to the stimulus 'two plus two', or the response 'Paris' to the stimulus 'the capital of France' (pp. 71 ff.). Social formulas such as greetings are also intraverbal behavior, as are the results of free association of words (a process in which the subject responds verbally in automatic fashion to series of single-word stimuli).

In reference to this class of operant, Skinner says that

the intraverbal relations in any adult repertoire are the result of hundreds of thousands of reinforcements under a great variety of inconsistent and often conflicting contingencies. Many different responses are brought under the control of a given stimulus word, and many different stimulus words are placed in control of a single response (p. 74).

When a passage is memorized or a fact is learned, many different stimulus-response connections are established leading to intraverbal behavior (cf. McNeill, 1968, pp. 408-12). Thus intraverbal behavior may be any unit of memorized verbal material, anything which can be stored and retrieved intact as a unit instead of regenerated repeatedly. Skinner does not feel that the types of association in intraverbal responses demonstrate unique thought processes; he says that on the contrary, aside from intraverbal sequences specifically acquired, a verbal stimulus will be an occasion for the reinforcement of a verbal response of different form when for any reason the two forms frequently co-occur. Thus, in any given circumstances, it is presumably much more probable that a speaker will say something he has said before rather than issuing a novel utterance. As a matter of fact, it is somewhat problematic, given this explanation, how novel utterances might occur at all (and cf. Katz and Fodor, 1964, pp. 481-82; and for a contradictory view, Hockett, 1968, pp. 8 ff.).

3.4. That category of verbal operant considered by Skinner as most important is the TACT, defined as "a verbal operant in which a response of given form is evoked (or at least strengthened) by a particular object or property of an object or event" (pp. 81-82). Tacts are often considered as referring to, or naming, or denoting their stimulus, although the stimulus-response relationship is much like that obtaining in echoic or intraverbal behavior.

Skinner places the tact in an important position because of what he calls the unique control exerted by the prior stimulus in the formation of the tact. It will be recalled that, in the case of the mand, "the most efficient results are obtained by breaking down any connection with prior stimuli, thus leaving deprivation or aversive stimuli in control of the response", so that a response is reinforced in a single way under many different S^D's. Contrariwise, in reference to the tact, the relation to specific deprivation or aversive stimuli is weakened and a unique relation to a single S^D is set up. This relation is created by reinforcing the tact as consistently as possible in the presence of one stimulus, either with many different reinforcers or with a generalized reinforcer (cf. Chapter 1 of this work). Thus a given response comes to specify a given stimulus or stimulus property, this being the 'reference' of semantic theory (p. 83).

It is important to note that,

roughly speaking, the mand permits the listener to infer something about the condition of the speaker regardless of external circumstances, while the tact permits him to infer something about the circumstances regardless of the condition of the speaker.

This is because the mand allows a listener to make an inference about some aversive stimulus or deprivation condition impinging upon the speaker (i.e., an endogenous condition), whereas the tact allows the listener to make an inference about some object in the environment to which the speaker refers (i.e., an exogenous condition). Of course, one might point out with some justification that the tact too is essentially endogenous, in that it refers to the speaker's perception of, or reactions toward, an external object rather than directly to the object itself, but since there is agreement about references among speakers, this point is perhaps irrelevant in the present context.

Tacts are learned by the child in this manner:

A child is taught the names of objects, colors and so on when some generalized reinforcement (for example, the approval carried by the verbal stimulus *Right!*) is made contingent upon a response which bears an appropriate relation to a current stimulus (p. 84).

If a child sees a red object and says 'red', he is emitting a tact; if he receives the reinforcement 'Right!', he will most likely say 'red' again when encountering the same kind of stimulus situation.

A well-known and enlightening example of tact behavior and associated responses is contained in Skinner's description of the man who hears the word 'Fox!' shouted at him (pp. 86-88). J. B. Watson, Bertrand Russell and other early behaviorist-oriented writers asserted that one behaves toward the word 'fox' much as one behaves toward foxes themselves; as we shall see, this viewpoint is similar in some regards to Charles Osgood's theory of language behavior in more modern times. Such psychological theories claim that if a man is afraid of foxes, he will feel fear upon hearing the word 'fox' just as though the animal were present, and so will react by fleeing or by similar responses. But Skinner feels that, on the contrary, ". . . the verbal stimulus *fox* does not, because of simple conditioning, lead to any practical behavior appropriate to foxes." Although it may make the hearer look around, as would a cry of 'wolf!' or 'apteryx!', this is not how one behaves upon being approached by a fox. It is Skinner's contention that if upon hearing the cry 'fox!' in the past, the listener turned around and was reinforced for doing so by seeing a fox, then he will in all probability turn around upon hearing the word a second time. Such behavior becomes even more probable if the hearer has some "current interest in seeing foxes". Thus, in reference to the listener's behavior upon hearing a tact, Skinner says, "The relative frequency with which the listener engages in effective action in responding to behavior in the form of the tact will depend upon the extent and accuracy of the stimulus control in the behavior of the speaker."

A subcategory of tact is the EXTENDED TACT, a class created to explain phenomena such as 'generic extension' or calling a new type of chair 'a chair', metaphor, metonymy, nomination or giving new objects new names, and similar processes. In metaphor, the like appearance of the tact and its extension are the significant factors; Juliet is said to be 'the sun' because Juliet and the sun have some common properties in their effect upon the speaker and can thus be equated (pp. 91 ff.). This is a form of stimulus generalization, or the Gestalt principle of transposition, that is, treating two situations alike because of elements in common between the two. In metonymy, an extension of a tact occurs when a stimulus acquires control over the response because it frequently accompanies the stimulus upon which reinforcement is normally contingent.

3.5. The final class of operant defined in this work is the AUTO-CLITIC, an item of either self-descriptive behavior or behavior descriptive of verbal behavior (pp. 311 ff.). Autoclitics are frequently expressions used in assertion, negation, concession, doubt and the like; included are items such as 'I guess', 'I recall', 'I can't say', 'I confess', 'I regret to inform you'. They may function as mands upon the listener, as for instance 'I announce' or 'Lo!', both of which mean something like 'listen' or 'pay attention'. Such mands may require specialized behavior of the listener, e.g. the reconstruction of previous remarks as autoclitics of the form 'ditto' or 'that goes double for me' or 'and vice versa'. According to Skinner, autoclitics are effective in the formation of grammar, especially that category known as relational autoclitics, examples of which are the '-s' in 'the boys run' and in 'the boy's gun'. Predication is created by "a relational autoclitic to which has been added an autoclitic of assertion". In grammar, autoclitics function much in the manner of Pike's tagmemic frames (cf. Cook, 1969): Skinner notes that if a speaker has

acquired a series of responses such as *the boy's gun, the boy's shoe,* and *the boy's hat,* we may suppose that the partial frame *the boy's* —— is available for recombination with other responses. The first time the boy acquires a bicycle, the speaker can compose a new unit *the boy's bicycle* (p. 336).

Skinner adds that this is not simply the emission of two responses separately acquired: "The relational aspects of the situation strengthen a frame, and specific features of the situation strengthen the responses fitted into it." Further, the primary response must be made to an aspect of the situation or environment; subsequent responses are made, not to the environment, but rather to the first response, thus creating a relevant grammatical utterance. In other words, a sentence for Skinner is approximately a series of grammatical frames, into which verbal items are fit by a process of stimulus-response association, connected to the environment at the front end only.

4

B. F. SKINNER: EVALUATION AND APPLICATIONS

4.1. Analysis and evaluation of Skinner's work on verbal behavior may be approached from a number of viewpoints. A modern psycholinguist, rather than confining himself to consideration of the validity and internal consistency of Skinner's descriptive system itself, would tend to examine the larger question of whether any stimulus-response-oriented theory of language acquisition and operation can succeed. This perspective is not unreasonable, since the faults of Skinnerian language-theory are in large part the faults of all S-R descriptions of verbal behavior. But other psychologists as well as Skinner have set forth behaviorist explanations of language, some of them differing rather widely from that contained in *Verbal Behavior* and embodying essentially non-Skinnerian concepts such as mediated stimulus-response conditioning and latent learning. Thus, the relevance of stimulus-response psychology to problems of language learning should not stand or fall on the basis of the acceptability of this one work. Since Skinner set himself certain goals in construction of his verbal behavior system, a just evaluation could well be limited to analyzing his success in meeting these goals and in constructing a consistent and powerful explanatory technique.

However, as well as having pioneered in the field of learning-theory psycholinguistics, Skinner is distinguished by having produced the work most widely known and influential in this area. Since his is the most comprehensive description of language operations, it has been considered as the only significant attempt at an S-R language-learning theory and thus as the sole representative of early psycholinguistics. Moreover, Skinner's book provided the source for an important document of developmental psycholinguistics, which appeared in the form of a review of *Verbal Behavior* some two years after the latter's publication (Chomsky, 1964). Noam Chomsky's review of *Verbal Behavior* not only contains a strong and thorough criticism of the book, but it is also felt to have dealt a death-blow to learning-theory-based psycholinguistics in general by pointing out areas of language acquisition and operation insusceptible to stimulus-response treatment. Since Chomsky's remarks in this review are of immeasurable aid in evaluating Skinner's book, and since the review is further significant as a motivating force in the new psycholinguistics, it will be valuable for us to employ it as a guideline for the subsequent discussion.

4.2.   Chomsky's criticism of the Skinner verbal-behavior system is approached from both of the standpoints indicated above: according to the reviewer, Skinner's work represents a minimal contribution to psycholinguistics, both because it lacks internal consistency and genuine explanatory power, and additionally because, in Chomsky's opinion, any S-R description of language is incapable of giving much insight into the language-learning process. Although it is impossible to deal meaningfully with any individual behaviorist work without considering the latter opinion, we shall for the present concentrate chiefly upon the merits of *Verbal Behavior* in itself.

   4.2.1.   Perhaps no factor in Skinner's work has been taken to task so much as his use of the technical terminology of stimulus-response psychology. Since Skinner attempts in this work to create an explanation of language learning consonant with his generalized operant-conditioning descriptions, it is to be presumed – and the author gives no reason for thinking otherwise – that the terminology employed in *Verbal Behavior* has the same set of meanings or referents here as in his other works on learning and indeed as in standard association-theory writings by other psychologists. But it proves most difficult to obtain a consistent interpretation of the Skinnerian verbal-behavior terminology on this basis.

For example, it is generally taken for granted that consecutive events are to be labeled respectively 'stimulus' and 'response' only if some demonstrably lawful relationship exists between them; that is, if the first can properly be called an independent variable and the second, a dependent variable, such that the relationship between the two is predictable, controllable and susceptible of expression by some sort of correlation measure, for instance a learning curve. Thus, when of two events, one is called a stimulus and the other a response, it is expected that the occurrence of the latter be unambiguously predictable from the occurrence of the former. However, in Skinner's system of verbal-behavior analysis, it is generally impossible to identify stimuli until their putatively corresponding responses have occurred. This leads the observer to suspect that, no matter what sort of behavior has occurred, some 'stimulus' can be found on an *ex post facto* basis to form a causal explanation satisfactory to Skinner.

Chomsky notes, for instance, that Skinner mentions the response 'Dutch' to a painting as an example of a tact under the functional control of certain stimulus properties of the painting (Chomsky, 1964, p. 552; further page citations in this chapter are taken from this work unless otherwise noted). But as Chomsky comments, any number of other possible responses might have occurred in the same context; he gives the responses 'Clashes with the wallpaper', 'Hanging too low', 'Beautiful', 'Hideous' as examples, among others. Presumably Skinner would say that "each of these responses is under the control of some other stimulus property of the physical object". But this would be a trivial explanation: since any given object has an open-ended number of properties, practically any response may be said to be under the control of some property of the object unidentifiable until the response has been emitted. Moreover, there is no way of controlling the particular property of the object to which the speaker will react. Since Skinner nominated as his main goal the determination of "the probability that a verbal response of given form will occur at a given time" (Skinner, 1957, p. 28), clearly the situation in regard to stimulus-response relationships represents no progress toward his postulated terminal result.

The lack of a proper decision procedure for identifying stimuli leads in turn to inconsistencies in the concept of 'response'. Chomsky describes Skinner's difficulties in this area as follows:

The unit of verbal behavior – the verbal operant – is defined as a class of responses of identifiable form functionally related to one or more controlling variables. No method is suggested for determining in a particular instance what are the controlling variables, how many such units have occurred, or where their boundaries are in the total response. Nor is any attempt made to specify how much or what kind of similarity in form or *control* is required for two physical events to be considered instances of the same operant (p. 554).

In the labeling of a behavioral unit as a response is implied the recognition of a lawful relationship between that unit and some other specifically identifiable unit which is a stimulus. Now, in the sense that all behavior is caused by some event or series of events, all behavior may be termed a response to some (known or unknown) stimuli; but in such an instance, the term 'response' becomes merely a direct substitute for terms such as 'behavioral unit' or 'activity' or, in the case of language, 'utterance'.

The main fault to be found with such a terminological system is its conflict with standard association-theory usage. Part of the 'lawful relationship' presumed to exist between a stimulus and a response is manifested in certain basic ways permitting of quantitative measurement. For instance, it is proper to talk of 'response strength', defined by operant-conditioning theorists as the probability of emission of the given response within a given time period. The frequency of a response is presumably related to the frequency of occurrence of controlling variables, where the response is under functional control of some S^D or set of S^D's; or it may be related to drive strength, measurable in terms of the length of time that deprivation or aversive stimulation has been in effect. There are also other measures of response strength; in relation to the verbal operant, Skinner mentions, among other such measures, energy level, approximately equivalent to pitch and loudness; appearance of the response in "inappropriate, difficult or ambiguous circumstances"; speed of response; repetition of response. Most of these measures are irrelevant to standard concepts of a behavioral response, thus suggesting that for Skinner the 'verbal response' is, at least implicitly, defined differently from the ordinary 'behavioral response'.

Further, in order for these measures of response strength to be meaningful, they must be clearly shown to be measuring the same thing. But, as Chomsky points out (p. 555), these measures do not co-vary. Quick verbal responses do not at all tend consistently to be loud; responses uttered in difficult or ambiguous circumstances most probably tend to be slow and hesitant. There is no clear notion of what 'probability of occurrence' might signify in regard to verbal responses, especially since speakers frequently produce loud, quick, etc. novel utterances (cf. e.g., Chomsky, 1964a., p. 37).

As a final note on Skinner's use of 'stimulus' and 'response' one might consider what appears to be an essential difference between an utterance and a unit of behavioral response such as bar-pressing by a conditioned rat; there is, relatively speaking, quite a bit going on at the same time in an utterance of any given length. This is especially true at the socalled molecular level, which in verbal behavior can be observed through various sorts of acoustic analysis, spectrography for example. Although this causes no difficulty whatever for the normal speaker or hearer, it does greatly complicate quantization of speech into units of psychophysical 'verbal behavior'. There is no particular reason to isolate a portion of an utterance as 'the response', and consider the remainder as indicators of response strength, as Skinner does by considering intonation, stress and juncture as separate entities from his 'verbal response' proper. Probability of occurrence of a response must mean probability of occurrence of the entire response as a unit; presumably when someone has seen a painting twice, and said 'Dutch' quietly the first time and exclaimed the same word loudly the second time (perhaps in the face of a companion's disbelief), the speaker has emitted two different responses. Now, no speaker of English would accept this analysis, but this is because of something other than the mere physical shape of the two remarks. There is no readily apparent way of resolving the problem within the bounds of Skinnerian analysis, especially in view of the rather trite descriptive-linguistic dictum that 'no two utterances are ever exactly alike'. Both systematic-phonological and morphosyntactic criteria of a very complicated sort must be taken into account merely to make the decision as to whether two responses are equivalent, and such factors have no place at all in Skinnerian S-R theory.

4.2.2. A question which must be considered separately from Skinner's use of 'stimulus' and 'response' is his concept of 'reinforcement' in verbal behavior. In general, a reinforcement is defined as any stimulus capable of increasing the strength of an operant. If a change in response strength occurs following presentation of some kind of stimulus, then the stimulus is said to be reinforcing. Skinner indicates that in verbal behavior, as in other forms of behavior, reinforcement is necessary to acquisition and maintenance of operant strength (Skinner, 1957, pp. 29-30). This being the case, one would expect the concept of reinforcement to be central to a theory of verbal behavior, and thus to be most carefully delineated.

It is Chomsky's opinion, however, that Skinner fails to define reinforcement meaningfully, a failure which he considers manifested by the wide variety of conditions cited by Skinner as possible reinforcements. Chomsky notes that among the circumstances listed by Skinner as reinforcements are these: self-stimulation, emitted verbal behavior of others, lack of verbal behavior of others (i.e., listening or attentive behavior), appropriate actions of others, and such idiosyncratic reinforcers as injuring someone by bringing bad news, avoiding repetition, describing circumstances which would be reinforcing should they occur, and the like. In Chomsky's opinion, Skinner uses the phrase, 'X is reinforced by Y', as a cover term for 'X wants Y', 'X likes Y', 'X wishes that Y were the case', and similar circumstances (p. 558), a substitution which the reviewer feels may obscure essential differences among the various exemplifications of reinforcement mentioned here: "Invoking the term *reinforcement* has no explanatory force, and any idea that this paraphrase introduces any new clarity or objectivity into the description of wishing, liking, etc., is a serious delusion." Chomsky comments further that

Skinner's claim that all verbal behavior is acquired and maintained in 'strength' through reinforcement is quite empty, because his notion of reinforcement has no clear content, functioning only as a cover term for any factor, detectable or not, related to acquisition or maintenance of verbal behavior (p. 559).

Understanding Skinner's use of the term 'reinforcement' is contingent upon understanding his basic description of the learning process. It is in essence his notion that any factor which strengthens a response can be called reinforcing, with respect to that response. A reinforcement is thus recognizable only through its effects on the associated response. Whereas one can generally state that an organism will be reinforced by certain processes such as removal of deprivation or aversive stimulation and satisfaction of drives, nevertheless what will be reinforcing to a particular organism does depend to an extent on the nature of the organism. It is not feasible to discuss reinforcement only in terms of drive reduction, for instance, both because of the widespread efficacy of secondary and generalized reinforcers and because even experimental animals frequently are reinforced (in the sense of having a particular response strengthened) by factors apparently unrelated to drives in the usual meaning of the term.

In order to predict what will serve as a reinforcement to a particular organism, one must have various sorts of detailed information about the organism, in regard to its neurophysiology, its previous learning, the nature of its environment and its standard reactions thereto, and so forth. Although it is not really possible to make a categorical statement on the matter, one might be justified in stating that the learning of more complex organisms generally involves more factors than that of simpler organisms, for most definitions of 'complex'. This is approximately the reason why Skinner specifies that reinforcing stimuli are to be identified retroactively, in the case of human learning at least. Since the total learning background of an individual is never available to the experimenter, let alone neurological or genetic descriptions approaching comprehensive accuracy, one cannot tell in any given case what will be a secondary reinforcer to the individual. The psychologist who recognizes that an enormous, apparently openended variety of events carry reinforcing properties in human learning, even if certain of these events co-occur only with certain classes of response, is extraordinarily perceptive. Except in classical conditioning, naming the particular reinforcement which has been effective in a given case is probably as precise as one can be under the circumstances. Skinner's realization of the extremely varied nature of reinforcements in verbal or other learning is a strength of his system rather than a weakness, contrary to Chomsky's assessment (cf. also Jensen, 1967, p. 110).

4.2.3. The discussion so far is in many ways applicable to S-R language theory in general as well as to Skinner's own work, since the difficulties in quantizing a language corpus for stimulus-response analysis and in demonstrating lawful relationships between verbal responses and external stimuli obtain in all such association-theory descriptions. But there are also a number of questions which one can raise about properties peculiar to the Skinnerian system alone. The most pressing of these is in regard to the consistency and efficiency of Skinner's classificatory system.

It does not appear that Skinner employed a uniform basis for determining his classes of verbal operants. Although he says, for instance, that "some responses, simply because of normal properties, are very probably mands" (1957, p. 36), he nevertheless does not use formal criteria in creating this or any of his classes. This is primarily because it does not seem possible to classify verbal responses by form alone, particularly in a system in which the verbal operant may be anything from a syllable or word to an extended utterance. Skinner gives the impression of realizing that a formal description of a linguistic system is not only far beyond the scope of his work in complexity but also irrelevant to his main task, the more so since *Verbal Behavior* purports to describe the process of acquiring and maintaining any language rather than one language (e.g., English) in particular.

Since Skinner cannot work with formal descriptive criteria, he has instead utilized a variety of other means to isolate response types. For instance, although he says that a mand is defined as "a verbal operant in which the response is reinforced by a characteristic consequence and is therefore under the functional control of relevant conditions of deprivation or aversive stimulation" (Skinner, 1957, pp. 35-36), mands are in fact chiefly identifiable through the behavior of the listener rather than the deprivation state of the speaker. As Chomsky points out (p. 566), deprivation is defined in terms of the length of time that the experimental animal has been prevented from eating or drinking, and thus it is impossible to relate the concept of deprivation to Skinner's mand, especially when the mands take such forms as 'Give me the book', 'Take me for a ride', or 'Let me fix it'. Since one expects deprivation to be related to primary drives in some sense, there is no deprivation involved in examples such as these; nor is it possible to identify any aversive stimuli which might have motivated the mands. It is therefore clear that Skinner is in reality working with criteria other than the internal state of the speaker, even in the case of the mand, the only verbal operant (outside of the echoic, of course) which seems to have some formal identifying features.

Mands, then, are actually differentiated according to the behavior which is expected to follow them. Chomsky describes the situation thus:

". . . a question is a mand which 'specifies verbal action, and the behavior of the listener permits us to classify it as a request, a command, or a prayer'. It is a request if 'the listener is independently motivated to reinforce the speaker'; a command if 'the listener's behavior is . . . reinforced by reducing a threat'; a prayer if the mand 'promotes reinforcement by generating an emotional disposition'. The mand is advice if the listener is positively reinforced by the consequences of mediating the reinforcement of the speaker; it is a warning if 'by carrying out the behavior specified by the speaker, the listener escapes from aversive stimulation'; and so on. All this is obviously wrong if Skinner is using the words *request, command*, etc., in anything like the sense of the corresponding English words. The word *question* does not cover commands. *Please pass the salt* is a request (but not a question) whether or not the listener happens to be motivated to fulfill it; not everyone to whom a request is addressed is favorably disposed. A response does not cease to be a command if it is not followed; nor does a question become a command if the speaker answers it because of an implied or imagined threat. Not all advice is good advice, and a response does not cease to be advice if it is not followed. Similarly, a warning may be misguided; heeding it may cause aversive stimulation, and ignoring it may be positively reinforcing. In short, the entire classification is beside the point (p. 567).

It is of course necessary to realize that a classification or taxonomy is not the same as a set of names for classes; one must consider the basis for the taxonomy apart from the class names themselves. Since an utterance is not a single unitary stimulus presented to a listener in a 'clear' or experimentally isolated environment, it is not possible to predict what the response to a mand will be, as the reviewer indicates. A listener may be positively reinforced by mediating the reinforcement of the speaker at one time but, given the same mand and different circumstances, may feel quite different about it a second time. If the mand was really the same on both occasions (e.g., 'I suggest you shut the window'), one should nevertheless have to classify it as advice on the first occasion and something (unspecified) other than a mand on the second, despite the speaker's identical intent on both occasions. It is of course possible to identify types of mands by the effect that they have had on the listener, rather than the effect they are expected or predicted to have. The way to do this would be by observing the various sorts of responses possible to mands and creating a classification accordingly; the procedure would be valid, however, only if behavioral responses alone were used, rather than estimates of the listener's motivation to respond or reactions to, e.g., implied hostility on the part of the speaker. But it must be noted that, once such categories were set up, it would not be particularly important what they were called; that is, formally defined categories of mand might be called 'advice', 'commands', 'threats', and so on, or 'class A', 'class B', 'class C', and so on, without affecting the validity of the system. That Skinner's naming system for mands appears to be in conflict with normal English usage would be no problem whatever, given consistent and usable definitions for each class.

4.2.3. We have seen, then, that the mand is purportedly controlled by deprivation or aversive stimulation, although in practice this is rarely the case. The second main category of operant, the tact, is identified by completely different criteria: "A tact may be defined as a verbal operant in which a response of given form is evoked (or at least strengthened) by a particular object or event or property of an object or event" (Skinner, 1957, pp. 81-82). One difficulty with this, namely the impossibility of identifying the stimulus prior to emission of the response, has already been discussed. But there are also further limitations on the utility of the tact as an operational category.

Tacts are learned, according to Skinner, by frequent reinforcement of the speaker's association of the tact with the object or property being named. Were one attempting to be completely formal and to treat language as any other form of behavior (i.e., ignoring meaning and similar hidden processes), one would be compelled to wonder how the child learns to connect the tact with the relevant object in the first instance (cf. Brown, 1958). Rarely does the average child hear a noun in isolation, for instance, while seeing its parent pointing at the object being named. Nouns and other tacts more generally occur in sentences, even if the sentences may be of the type, 'That is a chair'. If this sentence consisted of 'Bex wug tib rad', for example, one might find somewhat more difficulty in explaining how the child is able to identify the word in the sentence which in fact refers to the object (stress is only one possible answer). Since an utterance does not typically consist of discrete words but rather of a continuum, the problem becomes even more acute: in what way can the child's ability to quantize the speech stream and isolate relevant portions of it be analyzed? Any word in the sentence might refer to any property of the object, assuming quantization of each. Tact learning is a process in concept identification, but the latter is far more complex than mere learning of naming behavior through associating a word with an object.

Tacts are one of the few facets of language behavior for which Skinner offers a tentative description of child learning. The process of shaping and reinforcing of the child's verbal behavior is indeed most relevant to tact learning. But one naturally raises the question of so-called 'abstract nouns' in this connection, and how their learning may be effected. It is more or less reasonable that children learn to name objects by pointing at them; but they do not learn nouns such as 'angel' or 'charity' or 'Republican' in this fashion, all of which do seem to denote an object or event or property thereof. Generally a child either hears these words and deduces their meaning from the context, or else receives a definition of them from a parent or teacher. This is not equivalent to associating the word with the physical object. When the child has learned the word, he can thereafter use it properly and be reinforced for so doing. Most nouns and adjectives could be considered as tacts, with this added proviso, namely that some words are associated with objects and some with other words; but Skinner failed to state so.

Perhaps a more serious problem with the tact occurs in reference to the process of reinforcement. Chomsky notes the lack of scientific rigor in stating that parents and teachers condition verbal behavior in children in order to increase their control over the children; indeed this does not intuitively seem to be the most prevalent reason for teaching children language. However, the essential question is, To what extent are children actually taught language at all? It is very likely that parents of academic or other professional background might seek deliberately to teach their young children various facets of language behavior, concomitant to valuing such behavior in their children rather highly and thus rewarding it. But this is not the typical situation at all. Frequently in this country, and very frequently elsewhere in the world, the exigencies of life are such that children largely have to fend for themselves and are neither talked to nor reinforced by reward for any particular behavior save perhaps remaining silent. Skinner emphasizes the role of reinforcement in the maintenance of verbal behavior to such an extent that one must wonder how children manage to learn their language in indifferent or actively hostile environments, as they demonstrably do. Now, a child not reinforced for using tacts may not use many tacts; another way of putting this is that children in such negative or non-telic environments often have limited productive vocabularies (and note that differential reinforcement affects language behavior or performance, but not language learning or competence except in abnormal instances). But since these children understand the language of those around them, the solution does not lie with saying that they have not learned language, but only that they have not learned, or do not use, some words. Again there is no answer to this problem through the Skinnerian system nor, since it hinges upon the nature of comprehension versus production, through other stimulus-response systems of language acquisition and production either.

4.2.4. The mand and the tact differ significantly in that the former is defined behaviorally, whereas the latter is at least implicitly defined by its meaning. Definitions based on meaning are less than objective, because they rely on criteria outside the logical precepts of the learning schema itself: there is no way of knowing that a tact or other word 'means' an object (or an event or property thereof, even less so) without knowing the language in which the tact occurs. This fact is perhaps obscured somewhat by Skinner's use of English as the main object for his description. But if a child points at a chair and says 'Isu!', for instance, there is no way of discerning which property of the object the word is meant to indicate or even whether the word is a tact at all rather than a remark such as, 'Give me!' or perhaps 'Billy!', unless one knows in advance that the word does mean 'chair'. If someone responds to the child's remark by manipulating the chair, then the word may be classed as a mand; but in any case there is no way of identifying the word as 'meaning' the object, or some property of the object, unless one is acquainted with, in the present instance, Japanese. It is Chomsky's opinion that Skinner has included a number of mentalistic premises in his theory; this is surely so in the case of the tact.

The lack of behavioral identification procedure is equally as evident in the category of 'autoclitics', which are defined as either self-descriptive verbal behavior or verbal behavior descriptive of other verbal behavior. Whereas in the example cited above, it is possible to tell that a child pointing at a chair and speaking is probably commenting in some way about the chair, no such decision is possibly where one simply hears a remark such as, 'őszintén bevallva', without accompanying gestures on the part of the speaker. It does not suffice to say that, since no object is clearly being referred to, then the speaker must be referring to verbal behavior; he could as easily be referring to an absent object, or in fact demanding something or repeating a previously heard remark, instead of merely saying, "I must say", which is what the remark means. The autoclitic can be identified neither by external stimuli, nor by deprivation state, nor by observed or predicted behavior of a listener. There is nothing in the autoclitic to indicate directly that it refers to itself or to other verbal behavior. This is even more strikingly the case for those autoclitics classed as 'relational', such as the plural suffix in 'the boys speak'. In order to know that this is an autoclitic one must have recourse to the grammar of the language, especially since in English there happens to be a homophonous morpheme to this one, rendering the spoken sentence "It's the Smiths (or 'Smith's')" ambiguous. Relational autoclitics do not even refer to verbal behavior in any apparent way.

In regard to the function of autoclitics in sentence production, Chomsky notes (pp. 573-74) that Skinner considers a sentence to be a set of key responses on a skeletal frame, which is a traditional concept both of psychology and of structural linguistics. The reviewer adds that to this concept Skinner contributes "only the very implausible speculation that in the internal process of composition, the nouns, verbs, and adjectives are chosen first and then are arranged, qualified, etc., by autoclitic responses to these internal activities".

Modern linguistics has progressed beyond the concept of sentences as frames into which words are placed in linear arrangement. Chomsky states,

> This view of sentence structure, whether phrased in terms of autoclitics, syncategorematic expressions, or grammatical and lexical morphemes, is inadequate. *Sheep provide wool* has no (physical) frame at all, but no other arrangement of these words is an English sentence. The sequences *furiously sleep ideas green colorless* and *friendly young dogs seem harmless* have the same frames, but only one is a sentence of English (similarly, only one of the sequences formed by reading these from back to front). *Struggling artists can be a nuisance* has the same frame as *marking papers can be a nuisance*, but is quite different in sentence structure, as can be seen by replacing *can be* by *is* or *are* in both cases. There are many other similar and equally simple examples. It is evident that more is involved in sentence structure that insertion of lexical items in grammatical frames; no approach to language that fails to take these deeper processes into account can possibly achieve much success in accounting for actual linguistic behavior (p. 574).

The main point here is of course that sentence structure cannot be deduced directly from the form of the sentence, since sentences are more than linear arrangements of words. Skinner's sentence frames are probably tagmemic in nature, rather than being created solely by autoclitics; if this is the case, then 'Sheep provide wool' has the frame 'noun slot – verb slot – object slot' (omitting items of number, tense etc. for simplicity), and the second pair of sentences quoted above have different frames, since the first one is something like 'adverb-verb-noun-adjective-adjective', probably listed as a non-permissible sequence, and the second, 'adjective-adjective-noun-verb-adjective'. The only difficulty with such an analysis is that, again, one must know the grammar of the language in order to engage in even this traditionally taxonomic form of slot-labeling, and more obviously so in order to determine what is or is not a permissible sequence.

Skinner's linear concept of language makes no provisions for relations among sentences, nor for the fact that native speakers of
a language can theoretically produce an infinite number of (in-
finitely long) novel sentences and understand those produced by
others (cf. Garrett and Fodor, 1968, p. 454 ff.). And, as will be
discussed in a subsequent section, this view of syntax is not consonant with the observed facts of child language learning either.

4.2.5. Viewing Skinner's system of verbal behavior analysis in
perspective, one might well say simply that the present state of
psycholinguistic technology does not yet permit construction of a
comprehensive language-acquisition and -production system. Observations of child language do not indicate the prevalence of
direct conditioning as an important factor in language learning;
the work of generative linguists indicates that linear sentence-
construction based upon chains of stimuli and responses is inadequate as a theory of language operation (cf. Miller, Galanter
and Pribram, 1960, pp. 139-48). Of course, Skinner's system was
created before these conclusions came to light; nevertheless, they
do invalidate much of the theory on which his description is
based.

It is further clear that even within the bounds of his system,
Skinner does not attain the comprehensiveness for which he
strives. The majority of utterances – even the majority of words –
do not fall into any of his main categories of verbal operant. The
class of autoclitics especially is far too loosely defined, seemingly
able to include in an epicyclic manner most responses not subsumed elsewhere.[1] It is probably not impossible to create an

---

[1] Epicycles: The term is used to indicate the condition of a system in which
explanatory techniques are not rigorously controlled, but rather are structured loosely enough to permit the system to be opened and to add new
elements whenever a new fact must be explained or accounted for. This is
typically characteristic of a system organized to explain a limited amount
or organized physical data, but unable to cope with the discovery or series
of discoveries that the data is far more complex than originally imagined.
The prototypic example of such a system, created to explain what at first
seemed to be a fairly simple and straightforward collocation of data, is
pre-Copernican astronomy, especially that portion often credited to Ptolemy
(although actually developed by Eudoxus and Appolonius of Perga, among

adequate stimulus-response theory of linguistic interaction (although not of language learning or production *per se*); in order to do this, however, one would need to construct a completely formal system, in which, for example, responses could be classified according to the actual (not predicted) behavior which followed them. Considerations of meaning would have no place in such a system, nor would it be permissible to include categories based upon knowledge of the specific language concerned, either in relation to lexicon or to syntactic structure. But only in an interaction-based system can the criterion of the listener's behavior be sensibly used to classify responses, since one intuitively feels that an utterance is of the same type regardless of what behavior follows it, if any.[2] With a narrower scope, and focus upon

---

others, some three to five hundred years antecedent to him). This astronomy attempts to deal with the apparent retrograde motion of Mars, Jupiter and Saturn. Observations of planetary paths before the discovery of retrograde motion had given rise to a relatively simple system of circular orbits. However, with this discovery originated the theory of epicycles, or small circles of planetary rotation tangential to their regular orbits. But retrograde motion was gradually seen to be far more complicated than the astronomers had anticipated, and their system could not handle it without extensive revision. Therefore, every time a new fact of planetary motion was discovered, a new epicycle was introduced, until astronomical charts began to take on the aspect of moiré patterns.

[2] One reason why it is unsatisfactory to classify utterances according to the listener's behavior is that sometimes there is no listener; a speaker may talk to himself or may write material not intended for others, as in a diary. It is conceivable under such circumstances to assume the hypothetical listener to be the speaker himself, and thus to assert that a speaker can issue mands to himself and respond to these mands; it is, however, somewhat more sensible to postulate that both the command and the response, in such an instance, are motivated by the same factor, rather than the former providing a stimulus for the latter.

Skinner does not entirely omit this point; he does discuss the speaker as his own audience. His explanation is basically on the order of the following: "People frequently talk to themselves. This can be observed when vocal behavior is overt – either because it has not yet been 'repressed' to the covert level or has returned to the overt level under conditions of limited feed-back. In such cases, and probably when talking to others, the speaker reacts as a listener to his own behavior. Insofar as he automatically reinforces himself, he must be regarded as an audience affecting the strength of relevant parts of his behavior" (Skinner, 1957, pp. 179-80). Skinner also

interaction instead of learning and producing sentences, portions of *Verbal Behavior* might still find applications. But it is essential for any such effort to take cognizance of the widespread and deeply significant differences between language and other forms of behavior (especially skill-learning or habit conditioning), and between language and forms of animal behavior – to be rather obvious, either such a system must explain why only human young can be conditioned to learn language (or in fact learn it when not conditioned at all) and why the process of language learning is congruent for all normal members of the species, or else the system must entirely omit considerations of learning in favor of studying the completed behavioral system itself.

---

notes that, in the case of the diary-writer, the verbal behavior controlled by the self may show progressive changes over time, but is of interest even when it does not.

5

O. H. MOWRER'S THEORIES OF VERBAL BEHAVIOR

5.1. Although all analyses of verbal behavior derived from stimulus-response theory are similar in that they share many assumptions about the relationship of language to other forms of learned behavior, nevertheless the more recent theories show trends not evidenced in earlier works. In the field of learning-theory psycholinguistics, Skinner's *Verbal Behavior* may be considered not only a vanguard but also a dividing line: works postdating Skinner's tend to be narrower in scope, frequently focussing on the processes whereby words acquire meaning; such works are less taxonomically oriented than that of Skinner, preferring to deal with general explanatory hypotheses rather than classification of response types; and they often are based on kinds of learning not subsumed under standard associative conditioning description. The work of O. Hobart Mowrer on language learning exemplifies all these trends: rather than seeking to explain a wide variety of lexical types and syntactic structures, Mowrer concentrates in his language material on several specific problems, such as the establishment of word-referent connections and the learning of predication; far from being taxonomically inclined, he asserts that there are major components of meaning common to all words, and thus does not set up response subtypes corresponding to, e.g., the mand and the tact; and finally, Mowrer's verbal-behavior work is significant in its treatment of latent learning, secondary reinforcement and the mediated response as basic to language acquisition.

5.1.1. Mowrer, like Skinner, derived the precepts of his language-learning theory from a general learning model which he developed. This learning model, which Mowrer called the two-factor theory, postulates the basic importance of secondary re-inforcement in both habit conditioning and socalled avoidance learning. Mowrer set forth two versions of the two-factor theory, differing chiefly in the relative importance placed by each version on classical and instrumental conditioning, a distinction labeled by Mowrer as 'sign learning' and 'solution learning' respectively. Mowrer's first learning theory appeared in the late 1940's; his work at this time was an attempt to reconcile Pavlov's work on conditioning with that of Thorndike and others on trial-and-error behavior. Although this attempt was Mowrer's first formally pos-tulated theory, he called it "a *second* version of two-factor theory" since he considered the hypotheses of C. L. Hull some five years earlier to be the first two-factored system.

Mowrer's first theory was two-factored in two ways: first, in that it differentiated between sign learning and solution learning; and second, in that it considered habit conditioning and avoidance learning to be effected through two distinct processes. Mowrer explains the difference between sign learning and solution learn-ing, as embodied in his early 'second version of two-factor learn-ing', thus:

When a buzzer sounds in the presence of a laboratory animal and the animal then receives a brief but moderately painful electric shock, we can be sure that the reaction of *fear*, originally aroused by the shock, will, after a few pairings of buzzer and shock, start occurring to the buzzer alone. Here the buzzer becomes a *sign* that shock is imminent, but no 'solution' is yet in sight. Only when the subject, now motivated by the secondary (acquired, conditioned) drive of fear, starts *behaving* (as opposed to merely feeling) is he likely to hit upon some response which will 'turn off' the danger signal and enable the subject to avert the shock. This, however, is no longer conditioning, or stimulus sub-stitution, but habit formation. Here it seems that the subject first learns to be *afraid* and then what to *do* about the fear. These stages or steps were assumed to involve two separate and distinct *kinds* of learning: sign learning, i.e., the process whereby the fear gets shifted from the unconditioned to the conditioned stimulus; *and* solution learning, i.e., the process whereby an organism acquires the correct, effective instrumental response needed to lessen or eliminate the fear" (Mowrer, 1960, pp. 4-5; further citations in this chapter refer to this work unless otherwise stated).

Mowrer, in other words, at this time viewed punishment as something other than an effect which weakens the pathway or connection between a previously-associated stimulus and response. He noted that just as the buzzer in the above experiment takes on the property of arousing fear after having been paired with electric shock, so fear conditioning also occurs when the shock is paired with some specific action on the part of the subject rather than with an external stimulus. The main effect of punishment, especially punishment correlated with a behavioral response, is thus said to be that of causing fear to become associated with the behavior, or, more precisely, with the stimuli or sensations co-occurrent with the behavior.

Mowrer summarizes the contributions of his first two-factor theory as follows:

Pavlov had completely by-passed the problem of motivation and had tried to derive a wholly objective science of behavior from the concept of stimulus-substitution; in the second two-factor theory, it was assumed that what conditioning does, pre-eminently, is to attach *fears* to formerly neutral (independent or response-dependent) stimuli and that these fears then instigate trial-and-error behavior along lines very similar to those suggested by Thorndike. However, trial-and-error theory was also modified in two important ways: (1) whereas Thorndike had been interested almost exclusively in primary drives, such as hunger and thirst, the new two-factor position stressed the possibility of trial-and-error learning in response to secondary, as well as primary, drives; and (2), on the assumption that fears (once conditioned) may act as motivators and their reduction as reinforcers, a new conception of punishment (as well as active avoidance) emerged which was very different from the one advocated by Thorndike (p. 6).

5.1.2. This first two-factor theory was significant in that it appeared to subsume within one system two types of learning previously considered irreconcilable. However, further study revealed to Mowrer several weaknesses in his postulated learning theory, chief among these being the explanation of habit learning and avoidance learning by quite different processes, since only the latter type was theoretically due to second-order conditioning. A major impetus in Mowrer's revision of his theory was his reconsideration of Pavlov's findings on second-order conditioning in his well-known experiments on conditioning the salivary response in dogs (cf. Pavlov, 1960, p. 33 f.). Essentially, Pavlov found that once the salivary response had been paired to a blinking light, this response could thereafter be 'transferred' to a new stimulus, in this case the ticking of a metronome, through pairing of the light with the ticking noise. Thus the original CS could serve as an unconditioned stimulus, as it were, in second-order conditioning. Mowrer notes that first-order CS's can apparently become secondary reinforcers in other ways as well; he states, for example, that a hungry dog conditioned to salivate upon presentation of a blinking light will thereafter, upon being given the opportunity, turn on the light itself,

thus indicating that a first-order conditioned stimulus can serve as a secondary reinforcer, not only in the sense of establishing higher-order salivary conditioning, but also in the sense of setting up *new habits* (p. 8).

From this Mowrer deduces that the conditioned stimulus not only makes the subject salivate, it also makes him feel hope, in exactly the same manner as a pain-associated stimulus makes the subject feel fear. Further, in the postulation of his first theory, Mowrer stated that fear can become conditioned either to an independent stimulus or situation from which the subject can flee or which he can avoid, or else to a response-correlated stimulus which occurs concurrently with a form of behavior and ceases when the behavior ceases. Likewise, in the new version of his theory Mowrer postulated that there be two forms of approach behavior, just as there are two forms of avoidance behavior; these forms of approach behavior are exemplified by literal approach, that is, moving toward a hope-associated stimulus, and by the emission of a response in conjunction with which hope-associated stimuli have occurred.

In the second two-factor theory postulated by Mowrer, then, approach behavior and avoidance behavior are both explained in the same terms, namely by the mediation of hope or fear as secondary reinforcers. In this theory, all learning is said to be sign learning, solution learning being considered a special case thereof. The theory remains two-factored in that it assumes two different forms of reinforcement, namely drive decrement and drive increment, or reward and punishment respectively. Mowrer says,

stated most concisely, the thesis is that much of the adjustive, self-regulatory behavior of living organisms can be subsumed under four rubrics: the *avoidance* of places and the *inhibition* of responses which have been negatively (incrementally) reinforced and the *approach* to places and the *facilitation* of responses which have been positively (decrementally) reinforced (p. 11).

It is upon this second version of his two-factor theory, with its postulation of hope and fear as the basic second-order conditioned stimuli in all learning, that Mowrer bases his explanations of language acquisition.

5.2. Rather than attempting so broad a scope as Skinner, Mowrer in his language theory concentrates on those aspects of verbal behavior which he feels can be explained as direct consequences of his learning model. He inquires into these main topics of interest to the psycholinguist: the learning of words, specifically the process whereby words acquire meaning; the production of words by the child; the phylogenetic origins of language; and the extent and significance of predication in human language and of corresponding processes in animal communication.

5.2.1. In regard to the learning of words, Mowrer feels that understanding and production may best be treated as separate processes or phases. He notes the traditional explanation, which he credits to Bertrand Russell, stating in effect that the understanding of words is due to sign learning and their production, to solution learning. Since a basic tenet of Mowrer's final two-factor theory is that all learning is sign learning, he does not accept this explanation. Mowrer views understanding of words as taking place through second-order conditioning:

If a word, as heard, is temporally contiguous with a thing, person, or event which is itself 'meaningful', a part of that meaning will become attached to the word. Things and events are meaningful mainly in the sense of being good or bad, helpful or harmful; and it is precisely these two effects that have, as we have seen, the capacity to act as reinforcing agents and to cause stimuli which are contiguous therewith to take on the surrogate properties of secondary reinforcement and secondary motivation, respectively (p. 71).

Although Mowrer does not believe that evaluation is the sole component of meaning, he considers it the most prominent and that having most influence on the acquisition of understanding.

5.2.2. Mowrer's concept of language acquisition as a two-phase operation, divisible into understanding and reproduction, does not lead him to formulate separate explanations for each phase; on the contrary, he is opposed to the view that understanding is effected through conditioning and production, through selective reinforcement of trial-and-error-produced responses. As other psychologists and psycholinguists also have observed, Mowrer cites the apparent lack of true trial-and-error behavior in the child's acquisition of language. The problem, as he sees it, is not that the child's behavior is something other than random; rather it is that much of the child's verbal behavior seems to be elicited rather than emitted. Mowrer notes that mothers commonly talk to their children, instead of waiting passively for the children to emit some behavior worthy of reinforcement, and that the mothers thereafter rely on their children's capacity for imitation (cf. also Brown & Bellugi, 1964, 140 ff.).

As the author observes, it does not appear possible to explain word learning, much less any other phase of language learning, through classical-conditioning techniques. This is primarily because, as he puts it, "there *are* no 'unconditioned' stimuli which can be relied upon to elicit words, on an unlearned, reflexive, nativistic basis", since words can scarcely be considered reflexive in any sense. For this reason, it occurred to Mowrer that he might profitably search for analogous, and unequivocably conditioned, behavior among animals as a starting-point in his study of human language. He states,

In view of the many divergent hypotheses which had been advanced concerning the nature and course of language learning by human infants, it seemed that something more specific and definite might be learned if a systematic study was made of the circumstances under which parrots and other species of birds learn to make human, word-like sounds (pp. 72-73).

Mowrer's observation that such birds commonly learn to 'speak' only if given love and attention by their trainers indicated to him that this learning might be due to the type of second-order conditioning, based upon hope, which forms the basis for habit learning according to the two-factor theory. He notes that,

as a result of being repeatedly uttered by the trainer in conjunction with some dependable, 'primary' form of decremental reinforcement, a given word or phrase, as heard, takes on secondary-reinforcement properties. When, subsequently, in its verbal play or 'babbling', the bird makes – and itself *hears* – a sound somewhat like the word, there will be ready-made, or 'built-in', reinforcement of the response; and the more nearly the sound made by the bird approximates (or 'imitates') the sound made by the trainer, the more it will be, in this way, reinforced and repeated. Imitation, as thus interpreted, becomes a sort of automatic trial-and-error process, one which is dependent upon reward from another organism, or 'parent person', only in an indirect, derived sense. The response has become 'baited' so that whenever the bird makes it, satisfaction and reinforcement will be powerful and prompt – and self-administered! – provided appropriate motivation is present (p. 73).

In other words, since the trainer provides love and sustenance for the bird, at the same time as he utters a particular word, the bird's pleasant feelings (and especially the feeling of hope engendered by the presence of the trainer) become associated with the sound of the word. Then, as is stated by Mowrer, "the secondary reinforcement which has become conditioned to the word stimulus as made by the trainer *generalizes* to the word stimulus as made *by the bird itself*". Further, the bird acquires the habit of uttering this word not by practicing the word, but rather by hearing it uttered, a significant point since it constitutes an explicit recognition of the role of latent learning in speech acquisition.

5.2.3. This process of secondary reinforcement, by which so-called talking birds learn to utter words, is postulated by Mowrer as being the same process by which the young child learns words, and in fact as the process by which any organism learns to repli-cate the behavior of another (but cf. Chomsky, 1966a, p. 4 f.; Lenneberg, 1967, p. 231, pp. 329-30 [the latter commentary is on Lorenz, 1952, p. 96 f.]). He notes that

the mechanics of 'habit formation' are most transparently seen when a given pattern of stimulation can be produced *by others* and thus brought into repeated contiguity, for the subject, with reinforcement. Then, whenever the subject (properly motivated) himself behaves so as to reproduce this pattern of stimulation, such behavior will im-mediately have the properties of a 'habit' (p. 76).

According to the author, a dog might be trained to bark by em-ploying this principle: in order to do this, one would obtain some recordings of the dog's barking; then, when the dog is hungry, one would periodically allow it to hear some of this recorded barking at the same time as one gave it food. Thus the barking would presumably become a stimulus indicating imminent re-ward, and so produce the reaction of hope, resulting in the dog's "wishing to *hear himself* make the response".[1]

---

[1] Mowrer adds the following footnote to this section: "Since this chapter was written, Zimmerman (1958), under the author's direction, has per-formed an experiment with dogs of the kind indicated. The results were *completely negative!* Despite intensive training, over a period of several weeks, not one of five kennel-bred Brittinary Spaniels and four assorted house-pet dogs learned to bark when hungry as a result of hearing their own recorded barks and then being fed. In light of the varied evidence already cited and more to be cited, this finding is most remarkable. Whether it discredits the theory which the experiment was designed to test or tells us something special about the psychology (and neurology) of dogs will be left for the reader to decide. But this much is clear: if human words were tape recorded and the experiment repeated with properly motivated parrots, myna birds, or children, imitative learning would be a foregone conclusion. The writer's best guess is that in the dog experiment we were working against a neurological defect or powerful instinctive mechanism of some sort. Incidentally, the situation is made all the more puzzling by the fact that some house dogs are apparently able to bark ('speak') on command ... yet, as a supplement to the experiment in question, a professional dog trainer was unable to establish such behavior in any of our subjects" (p. 78 n.).

This type of conditioning forms the basis for what Mowrer calls "the autism theory of word learning". Again analogizing from the training of talking birds, he states that by far the most important factor in inducing these birds to begin speaking is the connection or association of the given words with pleasant situations. In particular, the sounds must apparently be associated with the trainer and his care-taking activities, because then, as Mowrer hypothesizes, when the bird comes to love the trainer, it will seek to be like him insofar as is possible, and this 'being like' the trainer will result in the bird's imitation of the trainer's speech. The sounds the bird imitates become 'good sounds' when they are associated with basic satisfaction for the bird, and thus the bird is motivated to reproduce them.

In just this way, human speech presumably develops:

So far as can be determined at present, essentially the same account holds, at least up to a point, for acquisition of speech by human infants. Words or other human sounds are first made by infants, it seems, because the words have been associated with relief and other satisfactions and as a result, have themselves come to sound good. Human infants, like birds, are vocally versatile creatures and in the course of random activities in this area will eventually make sounds somewhat similar to those which have already acquired pleasant connotations and will, for reasons indicated, have a special incentive for trying to repeat and refine these sounds (p. 80).

In order that they may be motivated to talk, words for the baby must become associated with pleasant events, just as for birds or dogs being trained to produce utterances. If the child is talked to while being given love and attention by its mother, it will associate the sounds of language with pleasant feelings and will react with equal pleasure when it utters the same sounds itself (cf. also Fry, 1966, p. 188).

Suppose, for example, that the infant is put into a pleasant situation: it is given love and attention by its mother, then sees its bottle and receives milk, to which it reacts with pleasure. While this is taking place the child may hear the word 'milk'. Should the situation re-occur frequently enough, when the word 'milk' is heard the child will anticipate its pleasant reaction to the situation in which it occurs and will have a feeling of hope engendered by the word. It hears the word 'milk', feels hope, then receives the milk and feels pleasure. The association with the word of the hope and other pleasant feelings connected to the milk is instrumental in the child's understanding of the word. And eventually the child will find that repeating the word brings the same pleasant feelings as merely hearing it, so that production as well as understanding is effected.

5.2.4. Mowrer found the autism theory of word learning useful on a practical as well as a theoretical level, and employed its principles in clinical situations, especially in dealing with speech-delayed children. He cites, for example, the case of a mother whose child would neither talk nor respond to speech. The child proved to be partially deaf, but this alone was not sufficient to account for her apparent complete lack of motivation to learn language. It developed that the only language which the little girl was able to hear was that shouted at her by her mother, and this consisted mainly of scoldings, prohibitions and other 'bad' sounds. Mowrer advised the mother to speak pleasantly to the child in loud enough sounds that she might hear them; when this advice was accepted, the child's language development progressed rapidly.

The outcome of cases such as the above might lead one to wonder how children come to learn negative words, those with unpleasant connotation. In this regard Mowrer explains that the infant has "relatively enormous experience with human sounds (especially those uttered by the mother) in all kinds of positively reinforcing contexts, long before there is any negative use of voice", by which time the child has discovered that language is useful in many situations and in all its facets, and so has become willing to learn both positive and negative words. But Mowrer notes that in the earliest phases of language learning especially, motivation to speak must be instilled by the association of words with pleasant or hope-connected stimuli, in order that the child's own utterance of these words may come to bring about these good feelings. Where such association cannot take place, for one reason or another, language learning is likely to be severely impaired. Mowrer feels that this is well illustrated by the language behavior of deaf children:

It is an interesting and instructive circumstance that infants who are born totally deaf do not *babble*, or do so very little. In terms of our present thinking, there are two reasons for this, the first being that since such children are unable to hear the sounds which *others* make in rewarding contexts, there is no secondary reinforcement to generalize to their own vocalizations (p. 84).

The second reason, namely that control of vocal responses depends to a great extent on sensory feedback, is that more generally cited by those in this area.

5.3. From his theories of linguistic ontogeny or individual language development, Mowrer derived a theory of linguistic phylogeny or the origins of language in the species. This theory is of interest not merely in regard to its own credibility, but also in its very existence; although the topic of linguistic phylogeny enjoyed periods of avid investigation, it has in latter years been generally regarded as indeterminable and thus of dubious scientific merit (but cf. Diamond, 1965, for more on this). Nevertheless, any theory of the origins of language which proceeds from a well-founded and fairly comprehensive theory of contemporary human learning and behavior must per se have some claim to possible validity, and thus attempts to solve the problem will doubtless continue to be made.

5.3.1. Mowrer believes that the first language system arose from imitation of natural sounds and association of these sounds with the objects which made them. He says,

We conjecture that man, or protoman, was indeed first drawn into play with 'words' because, by means of them, he could reproduce sounds which he *liked* to hear and that, in the beginning, he was very careful *not* to reproduce bad sounds. But later, when man had begun to discover the marvels of language, he became more venturesome and found that even 'bad' sounds can have a good effect when properly used. . . . We thus see that there is a good deal of support for the view that those *natural* sounds which, in the course of ordinary daily experience, had taken on secondary-reinforcement value for members of some prehistoric human group probably provided the models, or prototypes, for those *social* sounds which we now call words (pp. 96-97).

5.3.2. The author remarks that "at least one superficial objection to this theory" has been raised, an objection which he phrases as

the fact that different groups developed *different* languages, different vocabularies and sentence structures. Assuming Nature to be uniform and her sounds and their significances to be relatively constant throughout the world, would we not expect, on the basis of the foregoing analysis, the emergence of a *universal* language, rather than the innumerable languages which actually exist?

To this objection, Mowrer presents two rejoinders. He notes first that it is

highly arbitrary to assume that human experiences, in widely separated and diverse parts of the world, *are* the same. Pretty clearly, both the environment and man's activities therein vary considerably with geography; hence, language variability, rather than uniformity, would be the expectation.

In the second place, Mowrer emphasizes that he has been speaking

only about the *most primitive* origins of words. Once a human, or protohuman, group had discovered the magic of language from the use of a handful of words modeled upon natural sounds, it would almost invariably come about, human ingenuity being what it is, that new words would then begin to be created, more or less *ad hoc*; and in the course of time, these 'artificial', though no less useful or effective, words numerically overshadow the onomatopoetic words and thus create a quite misleading impression about 'word origins'. The fact that a good many clearly onomatopoetic words are still found in various languages and that new ones continue to come into contemporary use every now and then certainly leaves considerable basis for supposing that onomatopoeia may, indeed, have provided the 'start' for human language development, historically speaking (p. 97).

5.4. The last of Mowrer's major inquiries into verbal processes concerns itself with why language developed – with the question,

"Why did the race, or why does the individual, *want* language? What *good*, what practical *use* is it?" – and with those features which distinguish human language from the communication of animals.

Although Mowrer mentions that "from our study of learning in lower animals we obtain a sound conceptual underpinning for our study of language in human beings, which is just an intricate system of sign functions", nevertheless he agrees that the study of animals is limited in its applications to human speech, and that, as Thorndike put it, "language is man's greatest invention" and his property alone. He notes some major differences between the speech of humans and the vocal behavior of animals; an example of such difference is that, although rats will vocalize when subjected to pain, they will not do so in order to avoid pain. He says this is because, for a captured or domesticated animal, it does not matter whether vocalization is prompted by pain or by its threat; but if the animal is free, vocalizing from fear of being captured might serve to attract the predator. Mowrer says, "Thus we see the reasonableness of the assumption that nature (evolution) has taken pains to control, and indeed, *suppress* vocalization in animals, except in special circumstances". The only state in which animals are presumably inclined to vocalize, with the exception of captivity, is upon feeling pain or where reproduction of the species is at stake. Animals in captivity vocalize more freely because their domestication provides sufficient protection that they need not fear to utter sounds.

The limited vocalization of animals is accompanied by equally limited function of this vocalization. Animal communication appears to concern only physically present objects, never absent objects, wherein lies its most significant divergence from human language according to Mowrer. He feels that the basic feature of human language is predication, use of a topic and a comment related to the topic symbolically rather than signally. In animal utterances there is purported to be only quasi-predication, in which the subject of the 'sentence' is physically present with only the predicate symbolized or verbalized. The warning cry of an animal to others in a herd, signalling the presence of danger, is an example of quasi-predication: the subject of the sentence, namely the danger, is physically present, whereas the predicate is the warning cry. Animal utterances thus have two immediate constituents, as it were, namely a topic extant in the real world as an object or event and a comment, equivalent to the vocalization in its entirety. Even the utterances of talking birds are examples of quasi-predication, despite their superficial resemblance to human speech, since there is no understanding or attempt at symbolic behavior involved.

Predication is of course characteristic of human language, although it does not appear, according to the author, until the age of about eight to twelve months. Previous to this time, and indeed often for some time thereafter, the child employs one-word utterances or 'holophrases'. Mowrer notes that adults too may employ this speech device, as in the utterance of mands. But these one-word sentences presumably always imply or refer to something, and thus he considers them to function in a restricted way as two-sign complexes or true sentences. Thus, when a baby says 'bottle', this implies 'I want bottle'; when an adult says 'stop!' he implies 'discontinue what you are now doing'; if a speaker cries 'Ouch!' upon picking up a bee this implies, according to Mowrer, 'Take care; the object is dangerous and will cause pain'. Although one-word sentences can thus be considered as two-sign complexes, they are characterized by an inability to refer to absent objects or events, or to past or future events, and thus they are not truly predicative in Mowrer's sense of the word.

The nature of a true sentence, according to Mowrer, is its predication. This is separate from the function of the sentence, which is presumably to convey information in some way. It has been postulated that sentences function by transferring meanings from one person's mind to another's. But Mowrer disagrees, and states instead that

in communication we are not transferring meanings from person to person as much as we are transferring meanings *from sign to sign* within a given person, within a single mind. Said a little differently, the suggestion is that in order for us to communicate effectively with another person, he must already *have* the meanings with which we shall be dealing and that in the communicative act we are, for the most part, merely changing the signs to which particular meanings are attached, merely shifting or transferring meanings from one sign to another (p. 139).

When we say, for instance, 'Tom is a thief', we have merely transferred some of the reaction evoked by the second sign, namely 'thief', to the first sign, 'Tom'. If the communication has been effective, the listener will thereafter respond to the word 'Tom' somewhat as he had responded to the word 'thief'. The sentence may therefore be looked upon as a conditioning device, of which the chief effect is "to produce new associations, new learning, just as any other paired presentation of stimuli may do". The mediating response is the key to this conditioning, in that communication consists in the transfer of some of the reactions toward one sign to another sign. And thus, finally,

if, as a result of hearing or reading a sentence, an individual's behavior, on some future occasion, with respect to some person, thing, or event not present when the sentence occurred, is different from what it would otherwise have been, then that sentence may be said to have been 'understood' and to have functioned effectively (p. 143).

6

O. H. MOWRER: EVALUATION AND APPLICATIONS

6.1. Because Mowrer's work as well as Skinner's is based on an associative-conditioning view of learning, some of the same issues will necessarily occur in the evaluation of each. Clearly the two share the concept of language as an array of linear associations wherein novel utterances are represented as new combinations of properly classified units already stored by the speaker. Although it is conceivable that the S-R approach to language may be treated in other, possibly more valid ways by adherents of newer schools of psychology (cf. Osgood, 1968), nevertheless the entire question of whether it is relevant to regard language as being composed of response chains is crucial to evaluation of these works. Somewhat less explicit is the companion notion to this outlook – a notion rather more manifest in Mowrer's work than in Skinner's – which states in essence that language must be specifically taught to children rather than being learned through processes in some sense intrinsic to the learner.

Although there is relatively little data on the role of the conditioning agent in language acquisition, it might be valuable to examine this position in light of the relatively small observed variation in type and sequence of language learning stages in a generally large variety of environmental conditions. The further suggestion that portions of language must be taught while other portions are merely learned without need of instruction does not represent, as it may at first appear to, an intermediate position. This is because, among other reasons, the existence of language behavior must be considered apart from the morphemic and lexical units typically cited as the objects of such instruction: without the capacity for interrelating and systematizing such material, there is obviously no language but rather a group of memorized nonsense syllables. The point may appear self-evident, but it is intended only to illustrate the proposition that either the variety of systematizing and other capabilities that we call language behavior are taught (apart from the teaching of, e.g., words) or else they are not; if taught, one must inquire into the method of instruction and look for evidence of the teaching or conditioning process; if not, then an alternative explanation must be sought. Now, since most speakers do not seem able to verbalize to any extent the rules by which they form sentences, let alone consistently identify novel ones as well-formed or grammatical, the way in which this information could be transmitted through formal training is highly problematic. Nor does it appear obvious that, bearing in mind the wide difference in individual teaching methods, such uniformity as we may find in stages of child language could be the result. It is undoubtedly true that portions of language, or better, of speech, are learned through associative methods, but this fact holds no particular implications for the acquisition of the linguistic competence itself. It will be seen presently how this notion may be applied to the hypotheses of O. H. Mowrer.

6.2.   Although Mowrer notes his intent to treat language learning as being composed of two phases, namely understanding and production, he describes both as due to essentially the same second-order conditioning process. One will recall his statement that "if a word, as heard, is temporally contiguous with a thing, person, or event which is itself 'meaningful', a part of that meaning will become attached to the word" (p. 71). To this Mowrer adds that the good-bad dimension is most significant in determining meaning.

   This statement, taken literally, becomes somewhat difficult to interpret. Presumably the author intended to convey the notion that a word acquires connotation from the context in which it is first heard; this is especially the deduction one would make considering his further statement that "the reaction of fear, or of hope, aroused by a word is a good place to start in studying meaning". Setting aside the question of whether it is in fact the context in which a word is first heard, rather than some later context, which determines the final connotations of the word, one is still left with what appears to be a fairly limited conception of meaning. Insofar as an organism reacts with hope or fear to a stimulus, this stimulus may indeed be said to have the 'meaning' of hope or of fear to the organism, although this is a somewhat metaphoric use of the word 'meaning'. Further, even this is a matter of behavioral reaction rather than of connotation, since the 'meaning' of a stimulus to an organism is properly defined by the organism's response to the stimulus.

Even on the surface, however, this simple definition seems to depart from those processes involved in understanding of words. It is possible, if somewhat artificial, to speak of connotative versus denotative meaning of lexical items – but neither the former nor the latter can be consistently defined in terms of overt behavioral response on the part of speaker or listener. In the former case, the concept of semantic field or *Wortfeld* is probably more relevant to the study of meaning than is connotation, which probably should be treated as a different process altogether. Thus it is not correct to state, as does Mowrer, that "a study of the meanings of words, made possible by an objective method described by Osgood and Suci (1955), shows that the good-bad dimension accounts for about 70% of all the meaning which words have" (p. 71), any more than it would be correct to propose that because the words 'white', 'woman' and 'song' are similarly rated by this method they may be considered to have the same meaning. Whereas it is possible to call forth the fact that many speakers have similar connotative reactions to these three words, the fact has only marginal relevance to the speaker's ability to use and understand the words in normal context, for which the concept of associative meaning might be more useful. This is in part because such connotative reactions are almost entirely covert and vary widely with context, a situation most difficult to describe formally through the type of simple second-order conditioning postulated by Mowrer as basic to word learning. In the case of referential or denotative meaning the explanatory problem becomes even more acute. It does not seem especially convincing to postulate that the primary meaning component of words such as 'tree' or 'buggy' or 'door', or other common items in the child's lexicon, is one of affective reaction, nor is it possible to correlate the degree of affective reaction to such words with the degree to which they are 'understood'. Mowrer, although aware of the existence of referential meaning (cf. p. 71, p. 167), does not indicate how it develops – since his explanation of language learning in essence describes the transfer of an increment of hope or fear from context to a given word, and does not even take into account the transfer of a similar increment of meaning from referent to sign, one may see that only a very small portion of what is usually understood by 'meaning' is herewith explained.

A further difficulty with Mowrer's theory of word learning is that there are types of words to which it does not apply. Whereas most items in the child's early lexicon do have a clear good-bad connotation, at a later stage further items appear which do not have such connotation, or indeed any connotation or denotation at all. These are sometimes referred to as functors, or form words, or words with grammatical rather than lexical meaning; in English they are prepositions, determiners and the like. Since these relational markers do not ordinarily have an evaluate component (i.e., a rating on the good-bad scale), they cannot properly be spoken of as meaningful at all within the Mowrer schema, particularly in light of their lack of denotative meaning. Since they further do not typically occur in early child language, it does not seem that they are learned through direct imitation of the parent, even secondarily reinforced imitation such as is postulated by the autism theory of word learning.

There are a number of alternative ways of dealing with this difficulty. It is not precisely accurate to state that relational markers do not exist in child language; it appears that relations within child language are merely indicated in other ways, as for instance by word order (rather than being entirely absent, in which case e.g., the child's two-word sentences would be not so much ungrammatical as agrammatical). With this in mind, one can postulate that children learn sentence frames by word order alone, in which the markers already exist and are merely chained to the proper positions (as, 'The X is a Y'); this in fact approaches the standard modern associative-conditioning explanation. Or, one might wish to propose that relational units are present in the child's grammar right from the start, first rewritten or represented by order and later expanded and filled in with real phonological sequences as language acquisition progresses – this would be similar to suggesting that in the child's two-word-sentence grammar, the pattern described as P + O (pivot class plus open class) consists of three units rather than two, namely 'P', '+' and 'O'. Finally, it is possible to suggest that functors or relational markers are learned in conjunction with words, not by a separate process at all, so that the child finds it reinforcing to say not 'chair' but 'a chair' or 'the chair', and so on. Other solutions can undoubtedly be found. It does not appear, however, that functors can be treated in the same way as words with lexical meaning, in a system in which second-order conditioning mediated by hope or fear is considered basic to learning. (For more on this topic, cf. Menyuk, 1969, e.g. pp. 58 ff.) It is a grave shortcoming of Mowrer's language-learning system that he simply chose to omit the point.

6.3.   Since the same essential processes purportedly underlie both comprehension and production of words, according to Mowrer, one may view his discussion of them as subparts of one explanatory system. This being the case, it is not immediately apparent why the author found the necessity to elaborate upon his schema for word understanding with analogies from the study of so-called talking birds. One might consider it opportune to point out once more the search by social and behavioral scientists for an integrated theory of behavior – human at least, but including as much of the behavior of other organisms as possible. It is commendable in principle that Mowrer, like Skinner, is enough in sympathy with this effort to seek out parallels between aspects of human and animal behavior. Wide numbers of such parallels do indeed exist, many in areas of learning. Unfortunately, however, language is an aspect of human behavior which seems to represent almost a complete break with many other forms of human behavior and with nearly all behaviors of other species.

The ways in which the imitative behavior of talking birds differs from the language-acquisition behavior of human children are virtually open-ended, so that one cannot perforce list them exhaustively. Unless one is concerned with voluntary control of the articulatory mechanism, significant similarities in behavior between the two species do not exist, although there may be such similarities in learning methods. Specifically, it may be worthwhile to note that both birds (talking varieties and otherwise) and human children can be conditioned to various sorts of behavior, in particular imitative behavior, and further that secondary reinforcement may play a role in this conditioning. This is however not a statement related especially to language behavior, since one is discussing the conditioning process rather than the product of the conditioning, in much the same manner as the psychologist is interested in Skinner's operant-conditioning techniques rather than in the fact that they may result in behavior in pigeons analogous to human ping-pong playing.

In considering Mowrer's autism theory, one must question analogies between bird and child learning in regard to both the learning process and the product of the learning. It is not at all certain that either birds or children learn in the manner in which this psychologist says that they do; at any rate, it is surely not the case that children are taught words by the same techniques used with 'talking birds'. Birds being trained to utter a word commonly hear that word repeated at them a great many times – perhaps indeed while being fed and petted, although not necessarily so – and further, although they may hear other conversation in their environment, only the specific word to which they are being trained is thus repeated and emphasized in their immediate presence. A trainer wishing to teach a bird to say the word 'hello', for instance, generally says this word in isolation to the bird over and over, rewarding the bird for successful imitation. Clearly no such situation occurs with any frequency in normal mother-child interchange; despite Mowrer's assertion to the contrary, parents tend to talk to their children naturally rather than to elicit imitation from them, and children very rarely hear any word except in some (however brief) context.

There are other differences between child and bird learning situations which lead one to posit a concomitant difference in learning processes. A brief sampling of such differences might note that birds do not have the problem of picking words or other units out of complex and noisy contexts, as do children; bird imitations are usually either totally successful or totally unsuccessful (typically represented by silence), rarely a series of successive approximations to human speech; and, as has been mentioned several times, children learn words even in indifferent or hostile environments, in which they are not reinforced, either primarily or secondarily, for verbal behavior. It is admittedly very difficult for any S-R theory to deal with the problem of context or the 'noisy channel'; the first utterances of children are invariably single words, despite their having generally heard these words only in context, and Mowrer suggests no method by which this might come to be. There is no single-word stimulus repeatedly presented to the child, either accompanied by a US or otherwise, so that the basic elements of any linguistic conditioning process are nearly impossible to isolate.

It is significant too that children's imitations are not exact at first, but rather aberrant; and further, they are aberrant in specific ways. Another way of saying this is that child language has some phonological regularity ('phonemic' would not be quite accurate; cf. Olmsted, 1969). The inexactness of children's imitations is more noticeable, and more important to language acquisition theory, on the syntactic level. As Brown and Bellugi have noted (1964), children hear normal adult sentences but imitate them in reduced fashion, in non-random or patterned ways (cf. Fraser,

Bellugi and Brown, 1963). Neither repeated attempts at elicitation
nor reward is guaranteed to be successful in eliciting the entire,
correct adult utterance from a young child of two or three years
of age. This is not a question of 'response strength': if a mother
says, for example, 'See the car, Johnny', and the child repeats
'See car', the response has properly speaking not been made at
all, since in order to judge that the child's remark is in fact a
version of the mother's one needs to bring in a variety of non-
formal criteria, especially in view of what is likely to be the
child's idiosyncratic phonology and prosody. Again this is not an
easy concept to grasp, speaking of one's own language; but if the
child had said, for example, *[iyðəka:], one could not justifiably
call this a less successful response than the former except in
light of specific linguistic criteria. And children do not do this.
Children's 'bad' imitations of adult speech are regularly bad,
despite gross attempts at alteration of their speech (cf. McNeill,
1966, p. 69), a fact which leads one to believe that something
other than conditioning is taking place. With birds, of course, the
situation is quite different; there is no sign of any progressive
development of either phonological or morphosyntactic capability
in birds' imitations of human speech, and birds learn utterances
in the same way in which they learn any other unitary response.

Finally the whole question of teaching method must be examined. The differential language ability of children in affectionate
or in stimulus-rich environments as against those in more negative or deprived environments has been noted, but the difference,
if there is one, appears to be one of degree rather than of kind.
There are many problems with supposing that child language
learning proceeds according to primary or secondary reinforcement. This proposition can be defended only on the most general
level: one might hold that any utterances made by the mother are
hope-arousing to the child, since the mother on occasion behaves
in ways reinforcing to the child; this of course is not equivalent
to maintaining that any particular utterance is learned through
association with a specific rewarding situation. In other words,
the child might be motivated to repeat any language behavior in

general, because language has been commonly associated with a pleasant object for him. Since the verbal behavior of the mother varies so widely that no particular utterance can be guaranteed to have accompanied, e.g., feeding or cuddling over a period of time, such a position might be more reasonable. It is not, however, especially informative, because one is still left with the problems of how the child picks out single words to repeat, how the phonological system is acquired and why imitations are not exact from the start, why children do not in fact imitate their mothers' speech far more than they observably do if it is a source of derived pleasure. With birds the problem does not arise, since one specific utterance does indeed accompany presentation of unconditioned stimuli during bird training and thus the conditioning process is clear-cut and evident. And presumably birds would learn no language at all in hostile or indifferent surroundings, as children so frequently do.

The discussion so far has centered around the process of learning; but one must devote some brief attention to the product as well. It cannot conceivably be seriously maintained, of course, that birds learn language in any way; even crediting them with 'verbal behavior' might justifiably be regarded as an exaggeration. This point need hardly be belabored; somehow child language acquisition results in the development of a language system, among the most complex known behavioral systems and based upon various sorts of hierarchization so far known to exist only among human behaviors. Although birds may learn surprisingly long segments of language (we have heard of one that could purportedly recite a two- or three-stanza verse), their behavior exhibits none of the more complicated characteristics of language, such as the rather low-level ability to recombine known linguistic elements to form new sentences. Birds cannot do this even to the extent of forming novel ungrammatical utterances. Even were one completely ignorant of the conditions under which birds and children learn utterances, the unrelatedness of the products of the respective processes would suffice to indicate a different learning process in each case. However children learn language, they do not seem to be conditioned to it as Mowrer suggests that they are.

6.4. Since Mowrer's explanation of language learning concerns itself only with acquisition of lexicon, and does not raise the matter of syntactic acquisition in any detail, one may turn now to consideration of his hypotheses on the origins of language. His hypothesis that language originated from imitation of natural sounds is no less plausible than any other so far advanced, although it must be borne in mind that Mowrer is extrapolating from his concepts of how modern man can be expected to behave. Whether or not the theory is plausible is not the main issue, however, since nearly all the theories on this subject have been plausible. Perhaps of more interest is the method by which he derives this theory from his model of language learning.

The explanation that protoman initiated language behavior by his imitation of sounds which he 'liked to hear' is not in the least convincing. One may speculate that there must have been few enough sounds which protoman, in an exceedingly dangerous and hostile environment, could find reinforcing enough to imitate; most animals and other entities (e.g. thunderstorms) which made definite noises were probably inimical or threatening to him. Although protoman was a hunter, he frequently stood a rather good chance of being injured or killed by his prey, so that some animals – and thus some animal noises – must have been ambivalent in their affect. It is possible that early man might have imitated animal noises in the hope of attracting the animals themselves; or perhaps to describe an incident he had experienced; or again, perhaps in order to frighten away other animals or hostile humans. However, none of these speculations is equivalent to Mowrer's hypothesis. It is difficult to conceive of circumstances under which a sound could have been accompanied frequently enough by conditions pleasant enough to early man that he might have been inclined to imitate the sound merely in order to feel the hope associated with the learning context.

Mowrer notes that his theory of language origin has been objected to on the grounds that different groups manifest different languages; to this objection he offers the rejoinders that human experiences vary widely around the world as do languages, and that in any case only the most primitive words were derived from natural sounds since, "human ingenuity being what it is", other more efficient means of coining words were soon found.

Neither of these rebuttals serves to answer the basic objection. It is not clear that human experience varies to the extent that languages do, or even how one would go about determining this. Environmental conditions may have been subject to far less geographical variation during the period in which language originated. Even today, no correlation can be found between linguistic structure and geography or fauna peculiar to the area (admittedly this is partially because few modern languages are spoken in the areas in which they originated). Because of the uniformity of human genetic and neurological equipment, it may be maintained that human experiences do not in fact vary to any great extent, so that the search for origins of the differences among languages must proceed in other directions. The incidental point might be mentioned that one respect in which languages differ quite widely is their formalized imitations of natural sounds (Spanish roosters are considered to make a sound resembling 'kikiriki' instead of 'cock-a-doodle-doo'; Mandarin Chinese dogs, to bark 'wang-wang' instead of 'bow-wow', etc.). Mowrer's further remark to the effect that only the most primitive words developed from imitation is not so much implausible as indeterminable. There is evidence neither to support this proposition nor to deny it. The concept of human ingenuity, however, is irrelevant here since human ingenuity might as well have managed with a language composed entirely of onomatopoeia or other analog-type communications, or found other more efficient means of referring to animals and natural events in the first place. Nor does the continuing presence of onomatopoetic words in language testify to their role in early language development, any more than the presence of pronouns in all or most languages can be considered evidence that these were the first words.

The theory of onomatopoeia as the basis for language did not originate with Mowrer. This speculation has been advanced many times, since of course it cannot be refuted by normal scientific means. Mowrer's main contribution to the topic is his explanation of this onomatopoeia as due to essentially the same secondary-reinforcement processes held responsible for linguistic ontogeny. If for some reason it should become necessary to reach an accepted decision on the origins of language, the most reasonable base for any position on the matter would be a comprehensive theory of linguistic ontogeny – thus Mowrer has proceeded logically in deriving his notions of language origins from his model of child language acquisition. There are, however, some inescapable differences between linguistic phylogeny and modern child language learning. The most striking of these is of course precisely the difference between acquiring a system already present in the sum of human knowledge or ability, and creating such a system from whole cloth, as it were. It is difficult for the modern psychologist or psycholinguist to conceptualize early stages of human language; one might presume that they were the result of early stages of human neurological development as well, and thus may have been quite different, qualitatively as well as quantitatively, from present languages (cf. Lenneberg, 1964, 1967). A well organized theory of what sorts of systematization and hierarchization abilities are prerequisite to language is necessary in order to speculate profitably on this topic. Although Mowrer is surely not alone in his lack of such a theory, the inadequacy of his child language acquisition theory is reflected in this area of his hypothesizing as well.

6.5. The final relevant section of Mowrer's work concerns itself with some general features of language behavior as contrasted with characteristics of animal communication. His discussion of predication seems designed to make the point that animal communication is signal whereas human communication is symbolic. While such a statement is accurate, Mowrer appears to feel that sentences of human language which do not function symbolically, or in his terms, which do not refer to absent objects, are in some sense not true sentences. This notion is further complicated by Mowrer's apparent tendency to confuse symbolic communication with predication. Clearly all sentences which exhibit predication, or topic-comment immediate constituency, need not refer to absent objects; it is significant merely that human language admits of this possibility, not that language must be symbolic at all times. Mowrer's speaker who, upon picking up a bee, cries 'Ouch!', is not implying 'Take care; the object is dangerous and will cause pain' at all. In fact he is communicating in exactly the same way that an animal stung by a bee would do. It happens that this utterance is neither symbolic (except in some philosophical sense) nor predicative; but there are utterances which are only one or the other but not both (e.g., 'I'm eating'; 'Help!'). Although Mowrer's basic point about symbolic versus signal communication is essentially correct, there are other and equally important distinctions between human and animal communication which might well have been included in the discussion (cf. Hockett, 1960).

The argument that a sentence functions effectively only if it works in transferring reactions from one sign to another, is not easily justified. It is clear that not all sentences are of a type to which this criterion is relevant; an example might be 'John saw the dog', a case in which presumably portions of the response to the term 'John' do not become transferred to the term 'dog' nor vice versa. Such transferance of reaction is rather an abstract concept in any case; apparently Mowrer wishes to indicate that if a response (e.g., a GSR) is conditioned to the word 'thief', then upon presentation of the sentence 'Tom is a thief' some of the response will transfer to the word 'Tom'. It is not idle speculation to wonder how the results of such an experiment might vary with sentences such as 'Tom was a thief', 'Tom will be a thief', 'Tom might have been a thief', and so on. Although the concept of transfer of response may not be irrelevant to simple present-tense sentences with the verb 'be' or some variant thereof, the applications of the concept to such divergent sentence types as the above is a bit strained. Not all sentences produce "new associations, new learning", as Mowrer proposes; some sentences contribute no new information whatever to the listener, and do not change the future behavior of the listener at all; yet such sentences are quite well understood and cannot be considered as other than true sentences (examples: 'The earth revolves around the sun', 'water is wet'). As we have noted when discussing Skinner's work, the well-formedness of an utterance cannot be judged on the basis of observed or especially predicted behavior of the listener. This is simply another area in which linguistic criteria must supplant those of stimulus-response description in order to make the requisite judgment.

7

CHARLES E. OSGOOD'S THEORIES OF
MEANING ACQUISITION

7.1. Although the descriptions of language acquisition so far considered differ in approach and scope, it has been shown that various characteristics are shared by both. It is significant that both Skinner and Mowrer developed their theories of language from general learning models applicable to much other behavior as well, rather than taking language as a central concern. Consequently both theories treat language as a rather complicated but not unique form of learned behavior, subject to those laws of associative conditioning considered basic by each psychologist. The view that language can be thus analyzed also implies that individual aspects of language need not be credited to unique processes, so that phonology, syntax and lexicon are all held to be acquired through the same essential S-R-derived processes. Since these general postulates about learning can be applied to a wide range of specific instances, it is not surprising that Skinner and Mowrer attempted to explain a relatively large and divergent selection of factors in the language acquisition process.

Since the principles of association theory, derived as they are from molecular analysis of many instances of learning processes, are presumed to obtain throughout human behavior, it is perforce implicit in S-R-type systems that language and other forms of putatively learned behavior be treated in a unified manner. However, those psychologists in whose work language is a central rather than peripheral issue have tended to find relatively more evidence of processes unique to language, as well as the concomitant need to apply the principles of associative conditioning in somewhat different ways to each of these processes. As a result, psychologists who concentrate on language learning often tend to study fairly narrow aspects of the language-acquisition process. For example, the psychologist Charles Osgood has in his psycholinguistic work dealt for the most part specifically with those processes whereby words acquire connotative meaning and with the development of techniques for measuring such connotation. Although the explanation set forth by Osgood to explain meaning acquisition is based upon associative conditioning principles, it differs from these, as will be seen, in its emphasis on the mediational response as basic to the establishment of connotative reaction. The Osgood theory is broad enough to cover denotational as well as connotational meaning to some extent, although its explanatory success is definitely superior in regard to the latter; but the theory was devised for the lexical domain of language only and pertains specifically thereto. Extensions of Osgood's theories of meaning acquisition to syntactic development have principally been made by other psychologists, for example A. W. and C. K. Staats, some of whose work will be examined conjointly with that of Osgood himself.

7.2.   The main focus of Osgood's psycholinguistic work is evidenced by the title of his co-authored book, *The Measurement of Meaning* (1957), in which the main principles of his meaning acquisition and measurement theory are presented (an expanded but essentially little changed version of his theory appears in Osgood [1963a]). The problem to which the 1957 work is devoted is how words acquire meanings for the child, or otherwise stated, how a sign – an arbitrary non-meaningful event for the child – becomes connected to a significate or referent. As Osgood notes, the connection between word and referent is not self-evident. On the contrary, "*the pattern of stimulation which is a sign is never identical with the pattern of stimulation which is the significate*" (Osgood, Suci and Tannenbaum, 1957, p. 3. Further citations in this section refer to this work unless otherwise noted.) A word is a pattern of sound waves; an object, a complex of visual, tactile and other stimulations. Despite this, as he states, the sign elicits behaviors which are in some way relevant to the significate, and thus can be distinguished from stimuli which are not signs of this significate. It is Osgood's intent to investigate the conditions under which a stimulus not similar to the significate becomes a sign of that significate.

The problem is not a new one, and a variety of explanations have been posed to solve it. The most widely accepted is probably that derived from classical conditioning theory, which states in effect that the pairing of the sign with the significate is a result of conditioning, wherein an object evokes a given response in an organism, a particular sign is frequently associated with this object, and thus the sign becomes able to evoke the same response as the object. In other words, as Osgood puts it, this theory proposes that *"whenever something which is not the significate evokes in an organism the same reactions evoked by the significate, it is a sign of that significate"* (p. 5).

To Osgood, this explanation contains a fallacy, namely the assumption that signs are seen by the reacting organism as identical to their significates. However, reactions to signs are clearly not the same as the reactions to the relevant significates, although the two are connected in some less obvious way. His solution is to propose that the response to a word contains only a small portion of the response to the referent rather than the two being equivalent. He states that *"whenever some stimulus other than the significate is contiguous with the significate, it will acquire an increment of association with some portion of the total behavior elicited by the significate as a representational mediation process"* (p. 6). When a sign is heard it produces a response which represents some small fraction of the response normally elicited by the significate. This in turn produces internal stimuli which can become associated with a variety of responses in some sense 'appropriate to' the significate in question. As Osgood states, this process is representational because it is part of the same total behavior produced by the significate itself; it is mediational because this fractional response and the associated stimuli (frequently abbreviated together as $r_m \rightarrow s_m$) intervene between the stimulus of the sign and the instrumental acts or responses finally associated therewith. Osgood's formal statement of this concept is as follows:

A pattern of stimulation which is not the significate is a sign of that significate if it evokes in the organism a mediating process, this process being (a) some fractional part of the total behavior elicited by the significate and (b) producing responses which would not occur without the previous contiguity of non-significate and significate patterns of stimulation (p. 7).

It will be noted that this theory of the mediating process, although defined as uniquely that process whereby a sign, whether a word or otherwise, comes to acquire the 'meaning' of a significate, nevertheless is basically an extension of standard stimulus-response models. Osgood notes that he is essentially dividing this stimulus-response paradigm into two stages, which he terms respectively 'decoding' and 'encoding'. The decoding stage is the association of the sign with representational mediators, or 'interpretation'; the encoding stage is "the association of mediated self-stimulation with overt instrumental sequences", or "expression of ideas". The author notes further that because each stage of this process is itself a stimulus-response association, all the laws of single-stage S-R psychology may be transferred *mutatis mutandis* to the present model.

In language there are two ways in which words may acquire meaning: either they may be associated directly with objects or events, or else they must acquire meaning through some process other than ostensive definition or direct association. It is clear, in other words, that children learn words through association of the word with the referent; but they also learn the meaning of many words for which they have never seen a corresponding referent. For this reason Osgood recognizes two subcategories of linguistic sign, namely the ordinary sign and the assign. Signs are those units the meaning of which has been acquired through direct association with a significate. Assigns, on the other hand, have their meanings 'assigned' to them through other signs rather than through this direct association. A typical sign might be the word 'table', learned in most instances by direct connection with the object in question. As a typical assign Osgood gives the word 'zebra', understood by most young children even though they have never seen the animal but rather have had the concept defined for them: "They have seen pictures of them, been told that they have stripes, run like horses, and are usually found wild", as a result of which "this new stimulus pattern, *zebra* . . . acquires portions of the mediating reactions already associated with the primary signs" (p. 8). Osgood notes too that reading is a process of assign learning, since the marks on the page are associated typically with auditory signs rather than with the objects signified. The majority of words are in fact assigns, although few if any nonlinguistic signs are assigns.

7.3. The mediated response theory is applicable not only to initial word-learning but also to various processes of interrelationship among words. One of these is the complex of processes often known as semantic generalization, in which essentially two conditioned stimuli may elicit the same or similar responses in proportion as they are perceived as more or less similar. The stimuli in semantic generalization may be either signs or a sign and a significate; the generalization may thus be from word to object, from object to word, and from one word to another. It might be noted that the process of word-object generalization is basic to the field of General Semantics, which includes the study of how the speaker's response to words is generalized or transferred to the corresponding objects and events (cf. e.g. Hayakawa, 1964).

An example of an experiment in word-object generalization, and an explanation of the results in terms of mediated-response theory, is set forth in Staats and Staats (1964, pp. 147 f.). In this experiment, the word 'blue' was used as a conditioned stimulus, to which the response of a GSR was conditioned through presentation of the word accompanied by a mild electric shock. The object of the experiment was to ascertain to what degree this CR to the word 'blue' would generalize to a blue object without the response having been specifically conditioned to the latter. Accordingly the experimenters, after having effected the initial conditioning, presented the subject with a blue light, and found that the GSR was elicited by the light. This is presumably because the word 'blue', often having been paired with something of that color, would tend to elicit a portion of the sensory response normally made to the color, a response which may be symbolized as $rm_{bl} \rightarrow s$. In the first part of the experiment, the $rm_{bl} \rightarrow s$ elicited by the word 'blue' became associated with the GSR. Since this mediating response is shared by the blue light (a significate of the word 'blue'), the latter will also elicit the GSR associated with the mediating response. The experiment would have shown the same results if conducted in reverse, or in other words if the GSR had been conditioned to the blue light and the subject had subsequently been presented with the word 'blue' instead of vice versa.

Staats and Staats also cite an experiment in word-word semantic generalization, performed by L. W. Phillips (1958), in which degrees of generalization among five related words were studied. Phillips presented his subjects with five shades of gray, ranging from light to dark, and gave each shade a 'name' consisting of a different Turkish word (since this language was unknown to his subjects). Thus each shade was associated with one word. Subsequently the word associated with the darkest shade of gray was paired with a loud noise, so that it came to elicit a GSR. The hypothesis of the experimenter was that the other four words would also elicit the GSR, to the extent that their meanings were perceived as similar to that of the word representing the shade of gray to which the GSR occurred. It was found, as predicted, that the word associated with the second darkest shade of gray elicited a fairly strong GSR; the word associated with the third darkest shade, somewhat less of a response, and so forth. The ratio of the original GSR to those elicited by the other four words would presumably represent a measure of the degree to which the words were perceived as synonymous.

The concept of the mediating response has additionally been applied to two further processes observable in experimental studies of verbal conditioning, namely serial and paired-associate learning. In typical studies of serial learning, a list of nonsense syllables, words or digits is presented to the subject by means of a displaying device called a memory drum. During the first presentation the subject is instructed to read the list, either aloud or silently. In subsequent trials the subject, upon seeing each item, must predict what the next item will be; generally this procedure is repeated until the subject can do this without error for the entire list (cf. Staats and Staats, 1964, pp. 158 ff.).

During the first trial in such experiments, the printed words act as stimuli for the response of reading the words aloud. This verbal behavior in turn produces stimuli, such as those caused by the subject's hearing himself say each word (and corresponding kinesthetic stimuli, etc.). Since after he has read each word, the next appears, the stimuli associated with the reading of each item become associated with the response made to the following item, thus establishing a chain. After a time, the stimuli of the printed words may be eliminated and the subject will be able to recite the entire list without prompting.

In paired-associate learning, stimulus items are presented in pairs; the subject is expected to give one member of a pair as a response when presented with the corresponding stimulus word. The procedure in establishing this sort of association schema is similar to that used in serial learning:

On the first presentation of the paired-associate learning task the two syllables are presented, and the subject responds to each of them. . . . Later, however, the subject is instructed to read the first syllable and respond with the second syllable. The stimulus properties of the 'reading' response to the first syllable (the reading response may also be implicit) come to elicit the second response. . . . After a number of such trials, the subject gives the second response when only the first word is presented . . . (Staats and Staats, p. 160).

7.4. As has been noted, Osgood designed his theory of the mediating response as specifically applicable to acquisition of lexical (as distinct from grammatical) meaning. There have, however, been a number of attempts at application of this theory to formation of syntax and similar processes.[1] A. W. and C. K. Staats, for example, have investigated extensively the range of linguistic processes to which Osgood's explanatory device may have relevance. These psychologists feel that the relationship between units in an utterance is essentially one of stimulus and response – that, in other words, language is a system of habits formed by serial processes. It might be mentioned that such a viewpoint greatly simplifies any general explanation of language acquisition, since it implies that overt, observable verbal behavior is the entirety of human language, thus obviating the necessity to search for any hidden processes such as linguistic competence or inbuilt language acquisition mechanisms.

Staats and Staats, much in the manner of B. F. Skinner, describe the formation of novel utterances as based on recombination of previously learned units and patterns with new units which fit these patterns. For example, they set themselves the task of explaining how it is that a child who has learned the utterance, 'See the car', can then emit the response 'car' in such diverse other contexts as 'I own a car', 'The car is new', and 'This car is mine' (Staats and Staats, pp. 171-72).

In their description of this event, the authors note that such words as 'a', 'the', 'this' have already come to have

extensive association with many words. For example, the child has heard, read, and been reinforced for saying THE HORSE, THE HOUSE, THE DOG, THE TABLE, and so on. The stimuli provided by the vocal response THE should come as a consequence (according to the principles of conditioning) to tend to elicit many word responses.

This has presumably taken place as follows: if the child has learned to say 'the horse', for example, his utterance of the word 'the' produces, as will any behavioral response, self-stimulation which in turn can become associated with another response, in this case the next word, namely 'horse'. The mediating stimulation

---

[1]   In the form presented in his 1963(a) article, Osgood's theory has formed the basis of the most widely-used test of language ability, the Illinois Test of Psycholinguistic Abilities or ITPA.

produced by the verbal response of uttering 'the' is associated with a wide variety of responses, namely all those which have been observed by the child to occur in conjunction with the word 'the'. This procedure is identical, according to this explanation, with that described in the discussion of serial learning, above. Thus, any word which the child has heard and repeated following the word 'the' may be elicited as a response to the s_m associated with the word 'the'.

It is further added that

in turn, however, one could expect THE to be elicited by the stimuli produced by many other word responses. SEE, OWN, WHAT, for example, should all come to elicit THE through being in contiguity with THE in sentences such as SEE THE BLANK, I OWN THE BLANK, DO YOU KNOW WHAT THE BLANK IS?, and so on.

When a new word is heard following the previously learned word 'the' this new word comes to be associated therewith and thus can also be elicited by the word 'the':

The sentence SEE THE CAR, for example, would establish the sequence THE CAR. As a consequence, the response CAR would tend to occur in all situations that elicited THE – for example, I OWN THE CAR. The key to the syntactically appropriate emission of CAR would depend upon the association R——s——R . Any time THE
    the   car
would be elicited, one of the words it would tend to elicit would now be CAR: (p. 172).

The pattern is enlarged even further, since other words can occur in the same position as the definite article, for example, 'this', 'that', 'a'. These words are all functionally synonymous, or able to elicit the same responses, so that when e.g. 'car' is associated with the word 'the' it can thereafter be elicited as well by 'a', 'this' and so on. In this way new sentences are formed.

Staats and Staats note the efficacy of this conditioning model in explaining many facets of the child's language development. They describe, for example, the studies conducted by R. Brown and C. Fraser on the language of two- and three-year-olds, particularly in regard to the telegraphic speech observed by the experimenters, and state that "an analysis of children's speech development in terms of behavior principles suggests the determinants of the 'telegraphic English', as well as the development of the increased ability to repeat sentences ('memory span')".

Staats and Staats present this explanation of telegraphic speech:

As an example, let us say that a young child has just been conditioned to say the single word BALL as a tact, a mand, or an echoic response. The child, of course, will not be able to repeat the sentence GIVE ME THE RED BALL solely on the basis of this training. In time, however, the child should, by the same type of training, be able to tact, mand, or echo the response sequence RED BALL. Each time he does this the tendency for the first response to elicit the second would be strengthened. In time the child will also, through conditioning, come to make the response GIVE and thus to be able to emit the sequence GIVE RED BALL. In further training the child will be prompted to repeat *THE* RED BALL instead of the simpler phrase, and when he makes the complete response he is more heavily reinforced. Finally, articles and pronouns would be expected to be habitually included in such verbal response sequences, and the child comes to say GIVE ME THE RED BALL (pp. 174-75).

This is set forth as the process by which language gradually develops; it results in groups or classes of words which operate on the basis of word order; items which can elicit the same response are classed together. Staats and Staats give this example of such an order-based classification, by means of which sentences are produced; each response in the sequence produced stimuli which in turn elicit the subsequent response (p. 175):

R–s	R–s	R–s	R–s	R–s
GIVE	HIM	THE	RED	BALL
THROW	HER	A	BLUE	CAR
PUSH	ME	THIS	SMALL	SHIRT

Thus it is seen that the word 'give', for instance, can elicit 'me', but so would such other responses as 'throw', 'push', and so on. All these can elicit not only 'me' but also 'him', 'her', 'it', and so on. The number of words and word groups in each category, in the final adult grammar, is extremely large, but the number of combinations possible is even larger. And

after such hierarchies of responses had been formed the child would find no difficulty in echoing a sentence that was composed of any of these alternatives; the associations would already be there. This would be true even though the new sequence of responses (the new sentence) had never occurred before in that particular combination. As long as GIVE tended to elicit HER and HER elicited THIS and THIS elicited SMALL and SMALL elicited SHIRT, the sentence GIVE HER THIS SMALL SHIRT could be readily emitted, controlled either by environmental or verbal stimuli, even though the child had never heard or repeated such a sentence before (p. 176).

The authors add the suggestion that the sources of the child's memory span are "the skilled vocal responses and the various associations between (sequences of) these responses".

The same process presumably accounts for the addition of new items to the lexicon. For example, the word response 'is' should, as Staats and Staats remark, in part come to be elicited by the response 'the', but only when 'the' is followed by another sequence as in 'the horse', 'the toy' and so forth. The response 'is' would be reinforced when it occurs in the sequence 'the X is' but not when it occurs directly following 'the' (e.g., 'the is'), for instance. When the child hears a new word preceded by 'the', for instance 'the gex', he would be reinforced for the sequence 'the gex is'. In this way new words are automatically added to the correct categories. Word endings and other such items are also considered to be learned by this process; for example, in forming the English plural for regularly pluralized nouns, the child is reinforced for producing the voiceless sibilant /-s/ following a plural stimulus object ending in a voiceless consonant.

Finally, these psychologists discuss the factors involved in determining why a particular utterance is produced on a given occasion; this is needed because there is, for example, some qualitative difference between 'he is here' and 'he was here' such that one should not like to describe 'is' and 'was' as mere alternative responses drawn randomly from a basket of possible responses.

They state:

Some 'grammatical' differences in verbal behavior may result from processes involved in the learning of meaning. In the child's training the verbal response IS tends to occur in contiguity with an ongoing stimulus event or a present stimulus object, as when the response HE IS HERE occurs in the presence of some stimulus object. On the other hand, WAS tends to occur after the stimulus object was present or the event has taken place – HE WAS HERE, THE DOG WAS PLAYING, and so on. As a consequence, the unconditioned stimuli with which these verbal stimuli of different tense are systematically paired are different and should elicit different responses in the individual. Thus, it would be expected that the meaning responses conditioned to these two different verbal stimuli would be different in certain features. Since the unconditioned stimuli, although different, would nevertheless be similar in certain respects, the meaning responses of the different verb forms would also share common features (p. 178).

8

CHARLES OSGOOD: THE SEMANTIC DIFFERENTIAL, EVALUATION AND APPLICATIONS

8.1. The word-learning model developed by Charles Osgood is significant in that it provides not only a powerful device for explaining the meaning acquisition process but also a technique for inventorying the results of this process. Osgood's measuring technique, known as the Semantic Differential (frequently abbreviated as SD), is an outgrowth of his mediating-response theory and provides a consistent and widely applicable method for studying variations in connotative meaning.

It will be remembered that, in his description of the two-stage word learning process, Osgood spoke of a decoding and an encoding phase. The final or encoding phase consists of what he terms "the selective evocation of overt instrumental acts by the representational mediation process", such acts being responses to the sign which have been learned through prior association of sign and significate. If the meaning of a sign is defined in terms of responses made to the sign, then clearly a sample of the verbal responses made to a given stimulus word, elicited under circumstances controlled in certain specific ways, will represent at least some portion of the meaning of that stimulus word to the subject (but cf. Fodor, 1965).

Working from this basis, Osgood notes that one way of eliciting verbal responses to a word is to ask a subject what the word means to him. The answer is likely to be in terms of synonyms to the given word (or perhaps antonyms, where relevant), contextual illustration of its function, and so forth. If, on the other hand, a subject is asked for associations to the word, a different set of responses will be forthcoming.[1] In either case, one may say that

---

[1] The type of response depends also on the age of the subject (cf. Ervin-Tripp, 1961).

the meaning of the word to that particular subject has been sampled. However, this method of investigating meaning presents certain problems. Some people are naturally less verbally fluent than others and so find it difficult to produce associations to a word without being given any guidelines; additionally, since subjects may not all think of the same associated words or definitions to a stimulus word, even presupposing that there is a common core of such associations, statistical comparison of the results of tests would be difficult or impossible. Osgood states,

It is apparent that if we are to use linguistic encoding as an index of meaning we need (a) a carefully devised *sample of alternative verbal responses* which can be standardized across subjects, (b) these alternatives to be *elicited from* subjects rather than emitted so that encoding fluency is eliminated as a variable, and (c) these alternatives to be *representative* of the major ways in which meanings vary (Osgood, p. 19).

The way in which Osgood chose to elicit meaning responses is by what he describes as "a game of 'Twenty Questions' ", a series of binary-choice questions, standardized for all subjects, from which connotative reactions to a stimulus word could be determined. As an example, he cites the stimulus word 'sophisticated', and poses as sample questions, 'is it *hard* or *soft*? Is it *pleasant* or *unpleasant*? Is it *fast* or *slow*?' Osgood adds that

just as in 'Twenty Questions' the selection of successive alternatives gradually eliminates uncertainty as to the object being thought about, so selection among successive pairs of common verbal opposites should gradually isolate the 'meaning' of the stimulus sign. To increase the sensitivity of our instrument, we may insert a scale between each pair of terms, so that the subject can indicate both the *direction* and the *intensity* of each judgment (pp. 14-20).

Thus the semantic differential consists essentially of a set of bipolar adjectival scales, to be applied to a given concept. Verbal fluency is not at issue, since the subject is required only to indicate, for each pairing of a concept with a scale, the direction of the association and its intensity on this scale. After experimentation, a seven-step scale was adopted as standard. Osgood notes that the crux of the method, of course, lies in selecting the sample of descriptive polar terms. Ideally, the sample should be as representative as possible of all the ways in which meaningful judgments can vary, and yet be small enough in size to be efficient in practice.

This sample must in other words be culled from the great number of pairs of polarly-opposed adjectives in the language, but must still contain enough terms so that the subject's responses can be considered a good approximation of his total meaning response to the given term.

The concept of the SD did not arise solely from extrapolation from more common ways to elicit meaning responses. It was in part suggested by Osgood's research, in conjunction with Karwoski and Odbert of Dartmouth (cf. Odbert, Karwoski and Eckerson, 1942), on the phenomenon known as synesthesia. Synesthesia, or transfer across sensory modalities such that a stimulus in one modality elicits a response in another, had previously been studied mainly in its pathological aspects (e.g., Blum, 1961, Chapter 14); but these researchers found that synesthesia, especially in regard to color responses to music, is apparently a common occurrence. It was discovered that cross-modality stimulus equivalence shows continuity along dimensions of experience, so that a crescendo-diminuendo tone heard by subject might be impressionistically represented in a drawing by a solid form which grows thicker and then thinner, or darker and then lighter. Similarly, terms such as 'dark', 'heavy', 'slow', 'dull', 'low' tend to be grouped together by a vast preponderance of subjects, and likewise terms such as 'bright', 'light', 'quick', 'sharp', 'high'. Osgood remarks, "It seems clear from these studies that the imagery found in synesthesia is intimately tied up with language metaphor, and that both represent *semantic* relations" (p. 23). This is presumably due to a complex form of mediated generalization, in which, for example, the visual stimulus of large objects is frequently paired with the auditory stimulus of low-pitched tones, and so on for the other relevant stimulus dimensions. This process, the result of which is association of a "hierarchy of equivalent signs . . . with a common mediation process", can be considered the cause of correlations among semantic evaluations in general, and in addition led Osgood to the notion of presenting subjects with large numbers of polar adjectives for semantic rating purposes and then searching for such correlations among the scales.

8.2. The graphic portrayal of meaning reactions according to this technique is accomplished in what Osgood terms the semantic space, defined as

a region of some unknown dimensionality and Euclidean in character. Each semantic scale, defined by a pair of polar (opposite-in-meaning) adjectives, is assumed to represent a straight line function that passes through the origin of this space, and a sample of such scales then represents a multidimensional space. The larger or more representative the sample, the better defined is the space as a whole.

But from the synesthesia and similar studies, Osgood determined that ratings on many of the SD scales should correlate well enough that the total number of scales used could be greatly reduced, so that a minimum number of necessary orthogonal dimensions might be ascertained.

Osgood's explanation of how the semantic space functions as a backdrop against which to differentiate the meaning of concepts is as follows:

When a subject judges a concept against a series of scales . . . each judgment represents a selection among a set of given alternatives and serves to localize the concept as a point in the semantic space. The larger the number of scales and the more representative the selection of these scales, the more validly does this point in the space represent the operational meaning of the concept. And conversely, of course: Given the location of such a point in the space, the original judgments are reproducible in that each point has an orthogonal projection onto any line that passes through the origin of the space. By semantic differentiation, then, we mean successive allocation of a concept to a point in the multidimensional semantic space by selection from among a set of given scaled semantic alternatives. Difference in the meaning between two concepts is then merely a function of the differences in their respective allocations within the same space, i.e., it is a function of the multidimensional distance between the two points (p. 26).

By such semantic differentiation is obtained a representative picture of the meaning of the term being rated. This picture in semantic space serves to define one aspect of meaning, the other definition being in terms of the representational mediation process which forms the theoretical basis for the SD.

Although meaning as defined by the mediating process on the one hand and by the semantic differential technique on the other may at first appear only tenuously related, the connection between these two definitions is a substantive one: When the scales on which words are rated are placed orthogonally, they form graphs of as many dimensions as there are scales. Since the graphs are Cartesian, each point on them has two distinguishing attributes, namely direction from the origin and distance from the origin. Osgood identifies direction from the origin with the quality of meaning, since it indicates whether a subject tends toward a response or the negative of the response (r_m or $\bar{r}_m$), and distance from the origin with the intensity of the meaning reaction: it is assumed that there is some "finite number of representational mediation reactions available to the organism", and further that the number of these alternative reactions corresponds to the number of dimensions or scales in the semantic space, so that "direction of a point in the semantic space will then correspond to what reactions are elicited by the sign, and distance from the origin will correspond to the *intensity* of the reactions".

Osgood performed a number of experiments to determine the minimum number of scales necessary to define the meaning of a concept. The first of these consisted in instructing a group of subjects to read a list of 40 stimulus nouns and to write down after each the first descriptive adjective that occurred to them. From the adjectives thus elicited a set of 50 was selected, each adjective paired with its polar opposite. Then Osgood chose 20 concepts and paired them with the 50 scales, giving these to 100 subjects with the instructions to rate each concept on each scale (a 7-step scale was set up between each pair of polar adjectives).

A standard factor analysis technique was applied to the resulting matrix of correlations, and a number of further samples were also taken as a check on the first.[2]

From analysis of these data, three main factors were isolated as representative of most of the relevant meaning dimensions. The first factor is identified as evaluative; scales with high loadings on this factor are e.g. good-bad, beautiful-ugly, happy-sad, fair-unfair. The second factor is considered as a potency variable; scales with the highest loadings here are large-small, strong-weak, heavy-light and thick-thin. The final factor, which may be labeled as representing activity, has as the most distinctively loaded scales active-passive, fast-slow and hot-cold. Although there are also a number of other factors around which scales tend to cluster and which are not contained in these three categories (e.g., stability, represented by the scale stable-changeable; novelty, by new-old; receptivity, by savory-tasteless), the evaluative, potency and activity scales may be considered as the stable core of meaning reactions. Thus the display of a subject's ratings of a concept on these three dimensions portrays a concise definition of that subject's notions of the meaning of that concept, insofar as connotation is concerned.

The rating of a particular concept on the semantic differential scales becomes meaningful chiefly when compared to the ratings of other related concepts (or to other subjects' ratings of the same concept), since in order to evaluate SD ratings one must have some relational criteria against which to measure them. Osgood has set forth a number of criteria, based on the geometry of the semantic space, by which the similarity of two concepts may be determined according to their rating on the SD scales. His assumptions regarding the general rationale of the SD model, and the relationship of concepts within it, are as follows:

1. *Semantic judgments can be completely represented in a space defined by a set of elemental semantic factors.* Thus far, three such

---

[2] The twenty concepts to be rated in this study were: lady, boulder, sin, father, lake, symphony, Russian, feather, me, fire, baby, fraud, God, patriot, tornado, sword, mother, statue, cop, America.

elemental types have been identified with some confidence (evaluation, potency, and activity) and have been found to account for a large number and variety of discriminations; later these may be modified and certainly must be extended.

2. *Any axis or dimensional placed through the origin of the semantic space represents a potential semantic scale or attribute of judgment.* This dimension may or may not have discrete and unitary verbal labels available in the language code.

3. *The semantic nature of any such attribute is given by its relations with the elemental factors.* These relations are determined from the projections of a unit portion of the attribute on the elementary factors, i.e., the relation is given by the cosines of the angles the attribute makes with the original dimensions.

4. *Every concept in semantic space may be said to be 'contained' by its characteristic attribute.* The characteristic attribute of a concept is represented by the axis passing through the concept and the origin. All concepts located on this same axis share the same characteristic attribute which serves to differentiate a concept from the other concepts in two ways:

a. Another concept is different from this concept by having a characteristic which is independent of (not co-linear with) the characteristic attribute of this concept;

b. another concept is different by virtue of having more or less of the same characteristic attribute.

5. *Two concepts may interact to the extent that they are contained by the same attribute.* This is assumed to include all conceivable kinds of interaction among concepts whereby the meaning of one is influenced by the meaning of the other. For example, when two concepts share the same characteristic attribute, they may be directly *compared*; if their characteristic attributes are orthogonal to each other, they are simply not comparable (pp. 116-17).

The following diagrams illustrate the relationships described above:

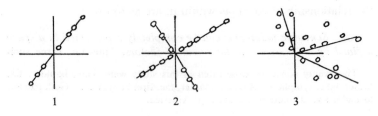

1   2   3

In case (1), the concepts all form a single line and therefore they all share in different degrees of the same attribute, enabling them to be readily compared. In (2), the concepts fall into two sets, each with its own characteristic attribute. The attributes here happen to be orthogonal, but they need not be so. In this instance the concepts are not readily comparable, although some attribute characteristic of neither set but partially containing both, such as the main axes, might be used to compare them. The situation in graph (3), with concepts scattered about somewhat randomly, is more likely to occur. Here the dominant characteristic attributes, that is, the ones with which these concepts have most in common, are represented by those lines closest to as many points as possible, as shown (pp. 117-19).

As an example of the application of these principles, one might select an experiment carried out by Osgood and his associates on the politically-oriented reactions of one group each of Eisenhower Republicans, Taft Republicans and Stevenson Democrats during the 1952 Presidential election. The subjects were asked to rate twenty concepts of current political interest – 10 'person' concepts and 10 'issue' concepts chosen in part to detect party bias – on a 10-scale differential.[3] From the results, three factors emerged, represented by the scales 'fair-unfair' (evaluation), 'strong-weak' (potency) and 'active-passive' (activity). As would be expected, the concepts rated did not cluster around these three main axes but rather around some major intermediate characteristic attributes. The main dimensions of ratings identified were labeled as 'fair-strong-active' vs. 'unfair-weak-passive' (with connotations respectively of admiration, benevolent strength, respect vs. cowardice, disgust, repugnance); 'unfair-strong-active' vs. 'fair-weak-passive' (e.g., fear, anger, powerful effective evil,

---

[3] The twenty concepts to be rated in this study were: Robert Taft, Adlai Stevenson, Winston Churchill, General MacArthur, Estes Kefauver, Josef Stalin, Harry S. Truman, General Eisenhower, Franklin D. Roosevelt, Senator McCarthy, Universal Military Training, U.S. Policy in China, Federal Spending, Socialism, Government Employees, Government Price Controls, European Aid, Labor Unionism, Use of Atomic Bomb, United Nations.

vs. well-wishing but ineffective, milk-toast-like); and 'weak-active' vs. 'strong-passive', neither containing an evaluative component. The experimenters were able to determine, for example, that

Roosevelt, highly and unambiguously respected by the Stevenson voters, is perceived with both respect and fear by the Republicans. On the other hand, Stevenson voters perceive Taft with ambivalence, in contrast to the Republican groups. . . . Whereas McCarthy is unambiguously *bad* to the Stevenson voters and tends to be unambiguously *good* to the Taft Republicans Eisenhower Republicans are more ambivalent toward him–which seems somehow prognostic of events which were to follow (p. 122).

From this briefly described example, the extreme sensitivity of the semantic differential as a social psychological measuring device may be seen.

8.3. It is perhaps most equitable to evaluate the semantic differential apart from the language acquisition model which in part gave rise to it. One reason for such a decision is that, as has been noted, the broader applications of mediated response models to language learning have largely been made by psychologists other than Osgood. The semantic differential itself remains unrivalled as a technique for measuring attitude and specific aspects of meaning both in breadth and in depth. Although it might perhaps have been more fortuitously labeled a measure of connotation rather than of meaning, since it provides no method of considering referential or denotative meaning, one must remember that the SD was not designed for these purposes and that the tool is both reliable and valid in sampling those areas of meaning on which it concentrates (cf. e.g., Osgood, 1964).

8.3.1. Insofar as simple word-learning is concerned, the theory of mediating responses provides a more reasonable interpretation than the position, cited by Osgood, which holds that responses to words are identical with the responses to the associated referents. This latter position, it should be noted, has seldom been seriously maintained in recent times. Osgood has said in effect that, to the extent that a speaker behaves toward a sign as though it were the significate of that sign, the response elicited by the sign is the same as that elicited by the significate – but never are the two identical, since the r_m elicited by the sign is by definition a fraction of the total behavior produced by the significate itself.

It should be clear, however, that this theory is an explanation of sign-referent association rather than of word learning per se, since in fact only a fraction of the response elicited by the *sign* is similar to responses elicited by the significate; part of the r_m produced by the sign is other than referential. Another way of stating this is that one does not behave *in toto* toward words as one does toward things, not only because the total significate-produced R is not involved in sign learning, but also because the r_m produced by the sign is made up of a portion of this significate-produced R plus certain other responses as well. A contrastive set of diagrams might make this somewhat easier to conceptualize. Osgood's 1957 illustration of the development of sign processes is as follows:

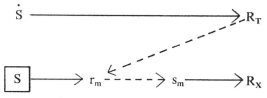

In this diagram, 'Ṡ' represents the significate, and 'R_T' the total behavior produced by the significate. The stimulus-producing process '$r_m {\rightarrow} s_m$' is a part of the same behavior produced by the significate, which is why the sign is said to represent or refer to that particular significate (pp. 6-7). On the other hand, however, only a portion of one's behavior toward a sign resembles a portion of one's behavior toward the significate; in part, behavior toward words is completely different from behavior toward objects, and this other behavior toward words must be acquired somehow as well. This is best understood by regarding both the significate-produced R_T and the total mediating process instrumental in producing the R_X associated with the sign as being made up of component processes, as follows:

Here, '$r_{m_t} \to s_{m_t}$' is the total representational (and other associative) mediational process which elicits the final R_X or total response to the signs. This r_{m_t} is composed of a number of mediating processes, of which one is that described by Osgood, wherein the sign acquires an increment of the total behavior displayed toward the significate. This process is indicated by 'r_{m_1}', although the sequence is not significant; r_{m_1} is shown as being composed of some, not all, of the component Rs displayed toward the significate, in the manner outlined by Osgood.

It is reasonable to state that all signs in language are in part assigns, inasmuch as all words have meaning components not acquired through association with significates. These meaning components, here represented as '$r_{m_2} \to s_{m_2}$', '$r_{m_3} \to s_{m_3}$', and so forth, comprise the non-referential – that is, neither connotative nor denotative – components of the total response commonly conceptualized as 'understanding' a word in such a way that one is able to use it in normal language. The fractional responses which we have termed non-referential are of interest because they, rather than the representational mediating responses of reference, function in integrating lexicon into the total language system.

For example, if the sign in question is the word 'table' (in English or some other language), '$r_{m_1} \to s_{m_1}$' is the representational mediation process, described by Osgood, which is composed of a fraction of the total response toward the object *table* and through which the word 'table' acquires its referential, that is denotative and presumably connotative, meaning. There are additionally a very large number of other (internalized) responses made to this word: 'noun' as contrasted with other grammatical categories; 'count noun' as contrasted with 'mass noun'; 'inanimate'; gender or noun class and case, in languages expressing them (e.g., 'der Tisch' rather than 'die Tisch' or 'das Tisch'); possible position within the noun phrase and within the sentence as a whole; phonemic (not phonetic) structure of the word; associated rhyming words; the orthographic representation of the word, for written languages; and undoubtedly many other such items. These responses, all of which are learned, are indicated here by '$r_{m_2} \rightarrow s_{m_2}$', and so forth.

One might with justification inquire in greater detail into the learning process relevant to these non-referential meaning components. To take a relatively simple case, it is clear that the sign 'table' is conceptualized as belonging to a particular grammatical category, probably 'pivot class' in the young child's grammar and 'noun' in other grammars. Of course, there is no reason to expect speakers to know the names of these categories; this conceptualization is evidenced through positional and co-occurrence restrictions within the grammar, rather than by a class label – although this too may be present – but the grammar exists in one form or another long before the child is made aware that 'table' is a noun. Put another way, the statement " 'table' is a noun" is not a direction or prescription but rather a comment about the way the word is used. Grammatical category, which is a functional rather than structural concept, is abstracted or induced from input data, so that the child presumably learns what may occur in environments such as Det + X + Gen + No + Case, all dominated by NP. A specific sign, in the present case the word 'table', is associated with these and various other grammatical and contextual markers, and acquires an increment of meaning therefrom, so that one might say that 'table' becomes a sign of the various characteristics of the category 'noun' in much the same manner as it becomes a sign of the object *table*. The obvious difference is that this cannot take place through ostension. Instead, one must presume that it takes place through association of the sign in question with characteristics of an internalized concept of the relevant grammatical category. That the learning does take place is shown by production of grammatical utterances, and shown also by the twin facts that grammatical category or 'part-of-speech-ness' is seen as inhering in a word, thus enabling children to be taught to pick the nouns from a list of words; and that no child has any difficulty in identifying the unknown term in e.g., 'The four groplings were playing in the mud' as an animate noun.

One advantage of viewing the learning of lexicon in this manner is that the present explanation can also serve *mutatis mutandis* for grammatical categories other than nouns and verbs. In the case of determiners or prepositions in English, for example, the diagram above again illustrates the correct word-learning paradigm, with the exception that the first mediational process – that which we have termed 'referential' – is omitted. One supposes that learning the meaning of such words consists solely in learning the grammatical-category characteristics, the phonology, positional variations, orthography and so on, with neither denotation nor connotation involved. It is of course prerequisite to this theory to presume that there is an internalized grammar at each stage of the speaker's linguistic development, at least from the occurrence of two-word sentences and very probably priorly as well.[4]

8.3.2. Although the mediating-response learning model can thus be amended to explain the learning of lexicon, it does not meet with equal success in the area of syntax. The difficulties of regarding a sentence as an ordered chain of form-class slots have already been discussed (cf. Chapter 4 of this work). Despite ex-

---

[4] This model is by no means incompatible with a generative framework (cf. Houston, forthcoming). However, transformational grammar may not accommodate this or any other current theory of lexicon acquisition as well as other generative models. The lexicon-oriented language theory known as Categorial Grammar, probably in some extended form not yet developed, may offer a solution to the incompatibility of syntactic theory with learning processes (cf. Bar-Hillel, 1964; Miller, 1962).

panded versions of such a learning paradigm (cf., for example, Jenkins and Palermo, 1964), the non-linear nature of language is manifest in such cases as Chomsky's well-known pair of sentences, 'Marking papers can be a nuisance' and 'Struggling artists can be a nuisance', in which surface similarities do not reflect the obvious underlying structural differences. One cannot but be uncomfortable with a theory which does not take such common phenomena into account, or for that matter which does not include any way of describing any relationship between 'John is here' and 'Is John here?'.

In addition to the inadequacy of the S-R model in explaining the broader aspects of language acquisition, some specific shortcomings of the work of Staats and Staats must be noted. It is true only in the most general sense that the reason that the child can form sentences such as, 'See the car', is that in his grammar 'see' has come to elicit 'the' and 'the' has come to elicit 'car'. What is wrong with this is precisely expressed by the additional explanation by these authors that 'the' can also elicit many other words, such as 'horse', 'cow', 'truck' and so forth as well as such words as 'large', 'small', 'pretty'.

It has been pointed out in a previous section that in order for two events to be properly labeled 'stimulus' and 'response', a lawful relationship must exist between them. It is difficult under any circumstances to deal adequately with response equivalence paradigms; in the present instance, it is not sufficient explanation to state that a given stimulus may elicit a variety of totally dissimilar responses, without also noting the circumstances under which one or another of these responses is predicted to occur. It is far from clear, for instance, why 'the' should elicit 'car' on one occasion and 'small' on another. If these responses occur in random variation, then one cannot immediately see in what sense they may be considered as directly associated with the given stimulus, since their physical shape is so different as to preclude normal types of response generalization on a continuum basis. If, alternatively, different circumstances elicit these different responses, then they are responses not to the stimulus 'the' but rather to the contextual circumstances under which they occur, or at the very least to a combination of the two. But since a child can say both 'see the car' and 'see the big truck', without either a car or a truck being present (e.g., when telling a story), the contingencies of occurrence, if they are other than linguistic, cannot be specifically isolated. It is clear that event$_2$ cannot invariably be considered a response to event$_1$ merely because event$_2$ occurs after event$_1$, if one is to employ the terms 'stimulus' and 'response' in a manner similar to their commonly accepted use.

The difficulties of the S-R model in explaining the young child's simple demonstrative sentences are compounded in the consideration of other types of syntactic construct. One will recall the remarks of Staats and Staats to the effect that 'is' and 'was' occur in different nonlinguistic contexts because the former "tends to occur in contiguity with an ongoing stimulus event or a present stimulus object" whereas the latter "tends to occur after the stimulus object was present or the event has taken place", so that the unconditioned stimuli with which these words are paired are different and so should elicit different responses (p. 178). It is difficult to conceive of how a past event can serve as an unconditioned stimulus to the use of the past tense, especially if the event did not occur in the presence of the speaker (e.g., 'George Washington slept here', 'Primitive man painted on his cave walls'). It is possible, and in some languages essential, to speak of a present tense and a non-present tense; but it should be noted that the absence of an object is not a real stimulus condition as is the presence of an object, unless specific training has occurred in this connection; but in any case the absence of an object or event does not necessitate its having been present or occurred in the past, so that one cannot predict what the response to such a condition will be. There are likewise many uses of the present tense besides the indication of an ongoing stimulus event or a present object, as for instance 'Charity begins at home', or 'He is late again' (said before 'he' has arrived). It should be clear by now, however, that the general inadequacy of stimulus-response models to explain the more important aspects of language acquisition is more significant than any particular flaws in one or another representative of this model. It is sufficient, rather than enumerating difficulties with the learning theory presently under discussion, to point out that no conditioning model yet developed has proved capable of dealing with the ability of speakers to recognize and deal with complicated relationships among sentences, to form and understand novel utterances, to construct sentences of any given length and complexity, to repeat the utterance of another, and so forth. The overwhelming complexity of the language system and the enormous amount of inherent ability brought to the task of learning it seem to preclude associative-conditioning explanations of the process, even though such explanations are admirably suited to certain aspects of language learning rather than to the broader process as a whole.

JEAN PIAGET AND MODERN CORRELATES

9.1. The material presented so far may be considered representative of those language acquisition models developed in America from about 1930 to the mid 1950's. Since such models tended to stem from the traditions of association-theory psychology, it is not surprising that they show concern with those portions of language explicable as resulting from conditioning processes. There are, however, also language acquisition theories developed during the same period but derived from other traditions within psychology – for example, from European psychology and psychoanalytic thinking – and these theories frequently view language from an entirely different perspective than that of the American behaviorist. Among the most significant work of this latter sort is that of the Swiss psychologist Jean Piaget, whose hypotheses on the development of language and cognition, although formulated in large part during the 1930's are highly relevant to modern psycholinguistics.

Piaget's work is basically developmentally oriented, and so displays a broader scope and more molar viewpoint than that of the behaviorists. He has devoted most of his effort to determining the way in which the child's logic, reasoning and other conceptual processes develop, and how these processes are mirrored in the child's changing use of language. Most of Piaget's later work consists in experimental investigations of the child's concepts of cause and effect and similar notions (cf. Piaget, 1952, 1954, 1958); it is largely in his earlier work that the theories are presented on which this experimentation is based and which are most significant from the standpoint of the modern field.

The data on which Piaget bases his conclusions was assembled through a number of intensive studies of children's conversation. Rather than using an interview technique exclusively, Piaget and his associates commenced by observing children talking among themselves, following the children for months and recording virtually all of their remarks in context. Because these studies were so tedious and time-consuming, they were necessarily limited in size. Thus Piaget's general hypotheses about child development tend to be based on studies of only a few children, a point on which he has been criticized and which modern replications of some of his experiments have attempted to remedy (cf. Elkind, 1965).

In one rather well-known study (Piaget, 1955, pp. 28 ff. All subsequent citations in this chapter are from this work unless otherwise noted), Piaget and his assistant observed the utterances of two six-year-old boys at a French progressive school for about one month, noting in detail and in its context everything that the boys said. The experimenters discovered some apparent anomalies in the language behavior of these children. For example, the boys talked extensively, irrespective of whether or not anyone appeared to be attending to them; further, often what seemed to be a genuine conversation between the children, with statements and replies, upon closer examination turned out to be something else entirely. Frequently each of the children would be commenting on his own train of thought without reference to what the other was saying. Piaget found this self-centered speech, as he described it, to be so common and ordinary that he felt it could be justifiably regarded as a normal characteristic of children's speech. This led him to classify speech into two categories, the first of which is primarily found among children, namely ego-centric and socialized speech. As the terms indicate, these refer respectively to inner-oriented and outward-oriented linguistic behavior.

The distinction between ego-centric and socialized speech is proposed as corresponding to the most important distinction between childish and adult reasoning processes, and is an overriding distinction characteristic of all the utterances and concept formations of the child until about the age of seven or seven-and-a-half.

In ego-centric speech, it may be observed that the child talks without bothering to ascertain whom he is addressing or even whether anyone is listening; he talks either for himself or for the pleasure of associating anyone present with the activity of the moment. Not only does the child speak mainly about himself and matters of direct concern to him in this type of speech, but he does not make any attempt to attune his remarks to the listener's viewpoint or capabilities, presumably because all he desires is another person with some apparent interest in him even if this person neither understands nor consistently hears him. Piaget notes that a child engaging in ego-centric speech has no wish to influence his hearer or to change his views at all; to the extent that his behavior is communicative, it should probably be considered phatic.

Both ego-centric and socialized speech may be subdivided, as follows: ego-centric speech consists of repetition, monologue, and dual or collective monologue; socialized speech, of adapted information; criticism; commands, requests and threats; questions; and answers (pp. 32-34). In ego-centric speech, perhaps the more interesting of the two main categories, the behaviors involved in both simple repetition and solo monologue are familiar to observers of child language. They are individual language behavior, and generally do not resemble communicative behavior in the usual sense at all. Piaget describes imitation as caused by

a confusion between the I and the not-I, between the activity of one's own body and that of other people's bodies. At his most imitative stage, the child mimics with his whole being, identifying himself with his model. But this game, though it seems to imply an essentially social attitude, really indicates one that is essentially ego-centric. The copied movements and behaviour have nothing in them to interest the child, there is no adaptation of the I to anyone else; there is a confusion by which the child does not know that he is imitating, but plays his game as though it were his own creation. This is why children up to the age of 6 or 7, when they have had something explained to them and are asked to do it immediately afterwards, invariably imagine that they have discovered by themselves what in reality they are only repeating from a model (pp. 34-35).

The concept which Piaget is describing in this passage is frequently known as ego boundary, or roughly the concept of identity or of the self-other distinction. It is implicit in much of Piaget's writing that until the concept of ego boundary has developed, the child is largely incapable of normal interpersonal relations; and concomitantly, until the child becomes capable of such interpersonal contact and interchange, his thought processes show a lack of logical continuity and ability to comprehend cause-and-effect chains. This point has been made more recently by other psychologists and psycholinguists (cf. Bettelheim, 1967; Houston, 1967).

In regard to the monologue, both individual and collective, Piaget notes that "for the child words are much nearer to action and movement than for us" (p. 36). Thus children rather automatically accompany their actions with speech, even when alone, and contrariwise, they frequently feel that words can function in creating or changing reality in a magical manner, that once they have said that something is so, it will have become so. This is probably the reason for much of the child's observed prevarication, that is, not so much deliberate untruth as an attempt to change past realities. At any rate, Piaget feels that for the child words and actions are undifferentiated either as cause or as effect, and that the child talks constantly not because it is reinforcing to him but rather because it does not occur to him that he can keep silent. As Piaget states, the monologue marks the rhythm of the child's activities and is an integral portion of them, functioning not to produce and transmit information but instead solely for the child's own satisfaction. Both the monologue *solus* and the collective monologue precede the child's beginning social development, and precede therefore his understanding that the rest of the world is somehow separate from himself and that there are other people who do not know his thoughts, with whom he can communicate through language and related means.

Although it might appear on the surface that the collective monologue represents progress toward social growth since it is an event in which two or more children participate, Piaget emphasizes the ego-centric nature of his form of verbal activity. It is demonstrated by the child's lack of surprise when his putative questions to other children are neither answered nor otherwise acknowledged, which is usually the case. The two six-year-old boys studied by Piaget carried on collective monologues around 25 percent of the time. One should note that the collective mono-logue does not appear in the adult's linguistic repertoire, despite superficial resemblances between casual conversations and the collective monologue – this is presumably because the stage of mental development instrumental in producing the monologue has altered, probably structurally, by adulthood. In child lan-guage, the collective monologue gradually disappears in favor of more socialized forms of language: as soon as the child attempts to inform his listeners about something, or otherwise to colla-borate verbally with his listeners in a genuine dialogue, he has reached the stage of handling adaptive information. Adaptive information, which is a full communicative process, is present to some very slight extent even when the child is quite young, and of course becomes predominant with maturation. It is not pre-cisely accurate to state that the child 'learns' that he can or should communicate with others; the stage of adaptive information-pro-cessing comes about through what Hebb (1966, p. 157) has called "psychological maturation". That is, it is not learned, but requires that certain other learning has taken place (Hebb, 1958, p. 163) in order to develop.

In his conclusions about ego-centric speech and its functions, Piaget notes that this type of speech is not equivalent to secrecy or a deliberate attempt to be noncommunicative and keep infor-mation to oneself. On the contrary, as has been mentioned, the child is until a certain age (thought by Piaget to be around seven) literally incapable of keeping anything to himself, and so says everything which occurs to him. But this does not indicate either that children are social beings merely because they talk endlessly, since before speech is used for communication it is used as a mere accompaniment and reinforcement to thought. Piaget states that whereas the adult thinks socially, keeps his hearers constantly

in mind and attempts to be comprehensible to them, the child
has no listener in mind at all and says things regardless of their
effect, or lack of it, on his audience. Thus ego-centric children
are neither individualized (since they cannot keep anything secret
nor do they think of themselves as separate and discrete entities)
nor are they socialized (since their communality is not accompanied by any réal interchange of information or ideas). They
are instead another category, presocialized and ego-centric. It
should be mentioned that this theory is significant regardless of
one's opinion on the actual frequency of ego-centric behavior;
Piaget implies a qualitative as well as quantitative difference between children and adults, a difference of maturational stage
rather than of amount of prior learning (although the two are of
course connected). It is obvious that, for whatever reasons,
children process input data differently from the way in which
adults process it; the learning mechanisms are presumably similar,
insofar as they are associative, but the way that information is
organized prior to being learned seems quite different.

As children grow older, they become capable of conversation.
Conversation according to Piaget may properly be said to occur
among children whenever "three consecutive remarks about the
same subject are made by at least two interlocutors" (p. 71). In
other words, if child A makes a remark, B answers A, and then
A says something adapted to B's remark, then a conversation has
taken place. If after the first two remarks a child C makes a statement relevant to what A and B had said, this too would be classed
as a conversation. The increasing presence of conversations in
child language signals the child's growing concept of the distinctions between himself and others.

An important developmental milestone in the growth of social
behavior is the child's acquisition of the manner in which to construct a well-formed argument or quarrel (pp. 83 ff.). At first,
children's quarrels are primitive, as Piaget states; rather than
arguing by presenting their respective views and trying to support
them logically, very young children (age four or five) typically
conduct their quarrels solely by gesture rather than by word. Even

slightly older children frequently quarrel chiefly by exchange of verbal or nonverbal threat rather than by logical dispute. Any sort of dispute is termed a quarrel by Piaget; quarrels become arguments when the speakers set forth their respective points of view instead of trying principally to harass or threaten each other. In primitive arguments the points of view are stated and repeated without any reasoning process involved, in the 'yes it is, no it isn't' variety of dispute. This is a simple clash of opinions and not an attempt to win over the opponent. Between the ages of seven and eight, the child's mind begins to be more coherent and he becomes capable of unifying his thoughts and utilizing reasoned and logical processes in his debates. It is likely also that the subject matter of children's debates changes considerably over the years; one might propose that the topics of early debates do not necessarily lend themselves to logical persuasive methods, since they are generally expressions of belief systems rather than positions on real issues. However, that children do in fact choose such subjects to argue about is indicative of the general tenor of child thought processes.

From his hypotheses about the aberrant nature of child logic, Piaget developed the notion that children before the age of seven or so do not really communicate with each other more than a fraction of the time, even when it is necessary that they do so. In order to test this hypothesis, he conducted an experiment with 30 children of ages seven to eight, and twenty of ages six to seven (pp. 96 ff.). He worked with two children at a time. One would be sent out of the room and the other would be told either one of three simple stories or fables, or else a mechanical explanation of a simple device such as a water-faucet or syringe. The latter explanations were illustrated with diagrams to make them clearer to the children. After the first child had been told the story or shown how the mechanism operates, the second would be called in, and child A (to whom Piaget had talked) would tell the story or explain the device to child B, who subsequently was required to repeat it back to Piaget.

Piaget found that child A in each pair seemed to have understood the given material well enough. But as had been predicted, communication between the two children tended to be minimal. Although child A had understood, he rarely proved capable of explaining the tale or mechanism comprehensibly. In relating this material, he generally confused the order of portions of the story, reversed or ignored causal relationships, confused characters and temporal sequences, and so forth. Further, the child listening usually failed to pay complete attention, nor did he typically seem to understand well even when presented with relatively accurate data. Piaget's conclusions were that this disordering, lack of attention to detail and to characters, and other illogicalities are symptoms from which may be deduced significant information about the child's thought processes. One will not be surprised to learn that children maintain their characteristic ego-centrism even when compelled to carry on real conversations and supply information to others, that they do not consider their linguistic behavior from the view point of the listener nor do they take what others say at face value but rather distort it to fit their own interests and perceptions.

From the children's misunderstandings of the stories, Piaget deduced that children do not seem to have clear concepts of causality. In the stories and mechanical explanations, the children would indicate causal relationships by mere concatenation of elements, stressing events themselves rather than relations of time, order or cause which united them. Piaget felt that the child A in each pair knew what was the correct order of occurrence of events in the story, or how the different effects of a mechanism follow from one another, but the child assumed when retelling the material to child B that these matters can be taken for granted and so no narrative importance need be attached to them. Piaget concludes that adults relate stories, etc., in their logical order because they wish to be understood; the child, on the other hand, believes himself to be immediately understood by his hearer, insofar as he considers the matter at all, and thus does not explain events logically.

One might note that there is apparently justification for proposing a competence-performance distinction in logic or reasoning or conceptualization, just as in language itself: although the children in Piaget's experiments were categorically unable to retell his stories comprehensibly, despite their realization that this was required of them, nevertheless he is quite firm in stating that the children to whom he talked evidenced understanding of the stories as he told them. This is probably a maturational problem, not one of learning *per se*; it is not especially surprising that children tend to concatenate logical elements to indicate causality just as they tend to concatenate linguistic elements to show other types of hierarchical relationship. Nor is it anomalous that children's spontaneous storytelling shows the same general characteristics as their repetition of given stories. There may be an internalized mechanism for producing text of a certain degree of complexity, just as there is an internalized mechanism for producing utterances of a given structure at each stage of development. It is obvious that children's storytelling is not randomly structured, any more than are children's sentences. This is a problem that merits further study.

From his experiments on child thought and verbal behavior Piaget determined the major characteristic of child reasoning, which he termed syncretism. Syncretism is stated to be reasoning which proceeds from premiss to conclusion in one intuitive leap without overt intermediary steps, depends heavily on idiosyncratic schemas of imagery, and depends also to a great extent on a kind of proximate analogy. It is additionally characterized by a strong belief on the part of the child that he understands everything perfectly. This all constitutes the type of syncretism called by Piaget syncretism of thought. But he notes that

a child may cease between the ages of 7 and 11 to 12 to show any signs of syncretism in his perceptive intelligence, *i.e.*, in those of his thoughts that are connected with immediate observation (whether these are accompanied by language or not), and yet retain very obvious traces of syncretism in his verbal intelligence, *i.e.*, in those of his thoughts that are separate from immediate observation. This syncretism, which appears only after the age of 7-8, will be called *Verbal Syncretism* . . . (p. 141).

Thus verbal syncretism does not tend to appear until syncretism of thought has largely disappeared.

Verbal syncretism in general seems to consist of, or perhaps to accompany, the tendency to perceive and reason from the whole to the part rather than comprehending parts of a situation and deducing therefrom the nature of the whole. Piaget believes that children perceive by means of general schemas or Gestalten, and reason by immediate analogy in which any degree of resemblance between two units, or even their linear concatenation, is sufficient to relate or equate them.

To test the workings of this alogical reasoning process, Piaget devised the following experiment (pp. 148-170): to a group of children between eight and eleven years of age he gave a set of ten, twenty or thirty common proverbs (in French, the language in which most of his early work was carried out). Along with the proverbs were presented an equal number of sentences in ordinary language, each one explaining or rewording one of the proverbs, as well as a number of such sentences not corresponding to any of the proverbs. The two sets of sentences were given to the children, with instructions to match each proverb with the sentence giving its meaning and to defend their choices.

The results were most interesting. Although the children had no difficulty in matching each proverb with a sentence, they demonstrated a somewhat alarming tendency to match sentences incorrectly (the number of correct answers for nine-year-olds ranged from one, in two cases, to twenty-three, in one case). In regard to the justifications for the answers, Piaget notes that

the children on whom we worked were below the level required for most of the proverbs. In order, however, that the experiment should not be absurd, we analysed only the answers given by children who had been able to discover and defend the correct correspondence for at least one or two proverbs, and had thus proved their capacity for carrying out the instructions necessary for the experiment (p. 148).

However, the nature of some of these justifications indicates that perhaps the correct answers too occurred only by syncretistic chance. As an example, Piaget quotes the discussion of a girl aged eight years and eight months, who connected the proverb "When the cat's away the mice can play", with the sentence "some people get very excited but never do anything". Piaget says that the child,

who would understand the meaning of each of these sentences if they were separate, yet declares that they mean 'the same thing'. – 'Why do these sentences mean the same thing? – Because the words are about the same. – What is meant by "some people" . . . [etc.?] – It means that some people get very excited, but afterwards they do nothing, they are too tired. There are some people who get excited. It's like when cats run after hens or chicks. They come and rest in the shade and go to sleep. There are lots of people who run about a great deal, who get too excited. Then afterwards they are worn out, and go to bed (p. 149).

Piaget comments that to this child, the proverb apparently means 'the cat runs after the mice'. One might comment further that the child did not seem to understand either the proverb or the sentence which she chose as explaining it. This is described by Piaget as "a case of almost pure syncretistic reasoning". Further examples: from an eight-year-old, 'Drunken once will get drunk again' was equated with the sentence, 'By pleasing some we displease others'; the child said these mean the same thing because "when someone is drinking, you go and disturb him". From a nine-year-old, 'White dust will ne'er come out of sack of coal' was equated with, 'We work to live', because "Money is needed to buy coal"

Piaget concluded that children reduce the proverbs, as they do any (novel) situation, to the absolute minimum elements, and then analogize to these elements wherever they can. In syncretism, which is illustrated by this type of reasoning, any new perception can be connected in some way with that which immediately precedes it. According to Piaget, children have the conviction that everything is connected with everything else, so that any event can be verbally justified by connecting it with any other which has even the slightest resemblance of form or content. All 'why' questions can be answered, all pairs of sentences can be linked together and be said to mean the same. The child cannot conceive of the accidental or arbitrary, since the same network of analogy, imagery and interconnection forms the perceptual base for their entire universe. Syncretism is said to stem naturally from the child's ego-centric thought, since the ego-centric thought processes cause the child to be satisfied with individual and arbitrary explanations rather than seeking genuine and objective analogy.

The description of syncretism provides the key to how children's perceptions of the environment develop. Piaget says that when a child listens to someone else talking, his ego-centrism induces him to believe that he understands everything said to him. This effectively prevents him from understanding utterances word for word, or analyzing in detail that which he perceives; instead he reasons about it as a whole. The child's lack of adaptation to others causes him to think in general schemas. For example, many of the proverbs in the above experiment contained words not understood or previously seen by the children. A mind free from ego-centrism would in such circumstances be interested in the new word and try to obtain a definition of it, or make a logical guess of its meaning from context. But the self-centered child believes that he understands everything already, that no word is unknown to him, and thus continues with his thinking as though no difficulty were present.

This behavior points to Piaget's concept of the Gestalt nature of the child's thinking: the whole is understood before the parts are analyzed. Understanding of the details takes place, whether correctly or incorrectly, as a function of the general schema. The child ignores all the difficult words in an utterance he hears, and then connects the familiar words into a unified schema which subsequently enables him to interpret the words not originally understood. This process of course does eventually lead the child to correct understanding of new parts of the environment, since analogy and successive approximation are good processes by which to assimilate new information. But often there are mistakes. These seem more striking to the observer than the correct guesses, since they are often alien to the standard adult way of thinking. But it must be emphasized once more that mistakes in reasoning, as those in language, are generated by consistent and non-random rules (cf. Klima and Bellugi, 1966, pp. 183-84), and are integrated into the child's total conceptualization and information-processing system.

From his studies of syncretism in reasoning and in language, Piaget proposed a general model of thought development in the child. He said essentially that the child passes through four main stages of mental development, as follows: (1) under two years, the acquisition of perceptual invariants; (2) from about two to about seven, preoperational intuitive thinking, characterized by ego-centrism; (3) from about seven to about eleven, concrete operational thinking, characterized by verbal syncretism; and finally (4) after eleven, formal propositional thinking (cf. Carroll, 1964, pp. 78-79). In the first stage the child begins to discover objects and movements in the environment; initially he reacts to objects in the main by grasping or sucking, but soon acquires the capacity to handle objects more selectively. During the second stage the child attains elementary concepts of space, time and causality, although these concepts are purportedly based on his internal notions rather than on objective reality. By the third stage, that of concrete operational thinking, the child has learned the permanence of objects, that is, that an object remains the same no matter at what angle it is viewed, and that it does not abruptly cease to exist when the child has lost sight of it. During this stage the child becomes better able to recognize genuine equivalences between physical or logical units. Abstract conceptualization is not yet fully developed, but the child can work efficiently with real, present objects. Finally, the ability to reason logically and to handle abstract concepts develops during the fourth stage, after the age of eleven or so.

This general schema of mental growth is one of maturation, not apparently influenced to any great extent by the individual's experiences at least insofar as sequence of stages is concerned. Piaget believes, as do a number of other behavioral scientists (cf. for example Leach, 1964, pp. 34-35), that the child first sees the world as an undifferentiated continuum and then later comes to understand the unchanging nature of objects surrounding him, and the boundaries between himself and the rest of the world. The process is one of analysis rather than synthesis, presumably because this is the way the species is organized; that is, the child does not learn to operate in this fashion, but rather does so automatically.

Piaget shares the Gestalt conviction that humans structure the universe according to their innate perceptions, and that the functional activity of reason is obviously connected with the general heredity of the organism. What he calls the 'hereditary psychological reality' is of primary importance for the development of the mental processes, and he states that

if there truly in fact exists a functional nucleus of the intellectual organization which comes from the biological organization in its most general aspects, it is apparent that this invariant will orient the whole of the successive structures which the mind will then work out in its contact with reality.

One implication of this is that it is probably fruitful to search for behavioral or at least perceptual universals. The relevance to the modern linguistic position, *mutatis mutandis*, may easily be recognized.

9.2. Piaget's hypotheses of child development have proved applicable to many diverse situations. An especially interesting recent use of his work concerns a form of childhood psychosis known as autism, a schizophrenic condition marked by various sorts of withdrawal from a reality viewed by the child as threatening and hostile. Autistic children may be wild and uncontrollable or silent and unresponsive to environmental stimuli. Although not all such children are very young – the condition may effect even teenagers – all tend to manifest varying degrees of regression, or behavior characteristic of a chronological age younger than their own. Autism as a psychological condition has apparently been in existence for a long time, and has always been a source of alarm and confusion to observers. This is because the behavior of the autistic child is alien to that of normal children, and occasionally so animal-like that the autistic child has been described by bewildered doctors as a feral or wolf child, thought to have been reared by animals in the forest.

The hypothesis that most reported instances of wolf children deal in fact with cases of autism was proposed by the psychologist Bruno Bettelheim (1967, pp. 343 ff.). It is his further observation that the regression of the autistic child can be described most accurately through Piaget's model of development; many facets of child behavior, especially that of young normal children, are characteristic of older autistic children. For example, one may consider Piaget's concept of ego-centrism in the small child, which he says is due partly to lack of either self-perception or objectivity, and in which the child sees himself as blending with the universe as a whole and feels that the environment must of necessity center around him. Such notions are especially present in the child of three or younger. Bettelheim, on the other hand, notes the ego-centrism of the autistic child, who also must acquire perception both of self and of objects before he can relate to his environment. Since the autistic child does not believe that he can have any effect on his environment, he may cease all activity, and live within a self-made environment centered around himself although remaining unaware of the self-other distinction. Ego-centrism may characterize autistic children of eleven, twelve, or even older.

Again, the concept of permanence of objects is mentioned by Piaget as crucial to the organization of space, time and causality. The child of 18-36 months instantly loses interest in an object when he can no longer see it, since for him it does not exist once it is hidden from sight. Bettelheim notes that the autistic child too can only function in a static and unchanging environment. Objects are real to him only when present or readily available in their customary place. Since the autistic child is unconvinced of his own existence and is further unable to differentiate himself from the rest of the world, he is consequently also unable to believe in permanence of any sort. Change to him becomes catastrophe, exactly as Piaget says that it is to the normal baby. At the end of this chapter will be found a brief outline of some of Piaget's concepts of normal behavior related to Bettelheim's concepts of autistic behavior (from Bettelheim, 1967, pp. 443-59). One might notice that the Piaget system provides a most efficient means of describing the form of regression manifested by these children.

As has been indicated, one reason that Piaget's work is relevant to modern psycholinguistics is that Piaget tended to forecast the present emphasis on a developmental approach, even in his earliest writings. The current view, expounded most cogently by Lenneberg (cf. Lenneberg, 1967), that language develops because of an inherent biological propensity to assimilate and organize linguistic input, and that it progresses through ordered stages which form a constant for the entire species, is clearly congruent with Piaget's hypotheses that children's thought processes likewise are determined by innate factors and proceed through set and constant stages.

Lenneberg has set forth in some detail the relationship between linguistic development and the series of changes undergone by the brain in the course of maturation (cf. for example Lenneberg, 1967, pp. 142 ff., pp. 175-82). Although the correlation between the physical and the linguistic changes is not necessarily one of causality, it nevertheless is clearly significant and worthy of examination. The situation is essentially as follows: Language cannot be learned, according to Lenneberg, until a certain stage of maturation has been achieved (Lenneberg, 1967, pp. 127 ff.). The infant's inability to learn any language at all, except for some beginning vocalizations (probably not learned either), during about his first fifteen months is attributed to some physical cause. Lenneberg suggests that the cause is what he terms a general state of cerebral immaturity.

One of the more important processes taking place in the cerebral cortex of the brain as growth proceeds is that one side of it, generally the left (irrespective of 'handedness'; cf. Rossi and Rosadini, 1967, pp. 169-70), becomes markedly more productive in certain types of behavior than the other. Language generally comes to be localized primarily in the left hemisphere of the cerebral cortex, or at least certain component processes of language are so located (the situation is as yet far from certain). This is known, among other ways, because when damage to that portion of the brain occurs in adulthood, as from CVA or injury, then loss of some linguistic abilities frequently follows. In small children, the language function is not localized to one side of the cortex. It gradually becomes so over the first eleven or twelve years of life. As language becomes more definitely controlled by the dominant side of the brain, the ability to learn a first language decreases markedly. Not all children learn and retain their language normally in childhood, although nearly all do; some are deaf at birth and cannot be taught until later, some acquire brain damage which eradicates the beginnings of language early in life and they must be retaught. However, by the age of about eleven cortical lateralization is complete in most instances, and the prognosis for first-language learning or relearning past this point becomes much poorer.

If the small child receives injury to the left side of his brain, the functions of language can still be performed by the right side, or vice versa, presumably because no definite lateralization has yet taken place. But the brain appears to become functionally fixed as the child gets older, so that after eleven or twelve, brain injury may destroy language permanently because the undamaged side can no longer take over the functions of the other, or can do so only with the greatest difficulty. Rather than indicating that cortical lateralization causes language development, this merely indicates that some form of neurological development is prerequisite for such language development, and further that once brain development has more or less levelled off, language has usually been learned and cannot be learned in the same way again. Humans apparently have a so-called critical period for language learning, in other words, as for that matter they probably do for other forms of behavior as well.

This view of psycholinguistic development is clearly in accord with Piaget's model of the growth of reasoning and similar thought processes. Since this is so, it may be helpful to compare the stages of perceptual development as outlined by Piaget with those of brain development as presented by Lenneberg (neurophysiological material from Lenneberg, 1967, pp. 180-81):

Age	Piaget	Lenneberg
under 2	acquisition of perceptual invariants	perfect equipotentiality of brain at first; about 2, one hemisphere begins to dominate
2	pre-operational intuitive thinking	beginnings of functional lateralization of lang. to one cortical hemisphere (gen. left); but can still be switched if necessary. Polarization gradually established
3		
4		
5	first quarrels (5½)	
6	children play in groups of 2 (6½)	
7	genuine arguments (7½)	
8	presence of order in stories appears; ego-centric thought disappears (7½-8). language syncretistic children can work with others (8).	
9		
10		
11	formal, propositional thinking (11)	language markedly lateralized; can no longer be switched (11)

Although no startling conclusions can be drawn from this brief chart of correspondences, it does appear that an important developmental milestone occurs around the age of eleven. One might also generalize that the beginnings of cortical lateralization are also the beginnings of the child's rationality and organized reasoning processes, the time before this being devoted, among other things, to acquisition of the concepts of object-permanence, boundaries between self and others, and so forth. Again no causal relationship should be inferred. But it is interesting to note how different phases of the child's development co-vary.

As a final remark, one might note that one factor which increases markedly with maturation is the child's social awareness and need for others. Piaget maintains that the young child, strongly ego-centric and the center of his own world, engages in no real interchange or communication with others; only as he starts growing older does he begin to communicate effectively. But children do need the companionship of others; in fact, it appears possible that one cause of autism is the abandonment and rejection, whether real or psychological, experienced by the child. It has been shown many times that children, of our species and other primates as well, when deprived of love, attention and companionship, invariably develop abnormally (cf. Harlow, 1965, pp. 140-50, 158). Even the monologue behavior of small children, although not informative, does serve the purpose of integrating those in the environment with the child's activities. There is compelling evidence that companionship is essential in the development of the mind, that in fact the mind is an interaction system rather than a self-contained entity (cf. Houston, 1967). Piaget's model is relevant to this view. The child according to his description begins life ego-centrically, and unable to reason or operate logically. As ego-centrism declines with age, so do the reasoning faculties grow. The child's perceptions of himself as separate from the rest of the universe, and of objects as stable and permanent, originate too with his social development. The process of relating to others and deriving social interchange and companionship from them is concurrent with, or perhaps prerequisite to, the process of learning to ideate in a normal adult fashion.

APPENDIX TO CHAPTER 9: PIAGET AND AUTISM

Piaget's concept of normal behavior	... related to Bettelheim's autism
1. Early objects grasped, sucked; only later freely manipulated and utilized.	1. All objects may be conceived as "something to twiddle" or suck; only after these movements are freed does normal manipulation occur.

Piaget's concept of
normal behavior

. . . related to
Bettelheim's autism

2. Children (esp. during first 18-24 mos.) ego-centric, lack both self-perception and objectivity.

2. Same; acquisition of object-perception occurs at same time as acq. of self-perception. The autistic child does not believe he can affect his environment, remains inactive. Cosmos centered around unaware 'self'. (Children with these cstcs. may be pubertal or older.)

3. Concept of 'permanence of objects' vital to organization of space, time, causality. Acquired 18-36 mos.

3. Autistic child postulates and demands static, unchanging environment. Objects only exist when present or readily available. Child unconvinced of own existence, thus cannot believe in permanence of any kind. Change = catastrophe.

4. Permanence related to child's actions. To imagine an obj. he cannot touch or see, child must have acted on it in the past. Child must have reason to wish objects to be permanent.
➤ Must trust in benign intentions of reality.

4. Contradictory experience, emotions make child feel safe when objects (eg parents) are absent; child denies permanence of everything, except dead objs. If nothing has permanence, then neither has he. Existence constantly threatened. To believe in permanence of objs., child must interact with environm't. Ego-centric stance can only be dropped in favor of reasoned attitude based on self-acting-on-objs. ➤ Autistic child lacks trust in benign intentions of reality. Interaction = danger.

5. Socialized intelligence made possible by bond of language between thoughts and words, so child can use concepts.

5. Autistic child remains individual, isolated, tied to imagery, organic activity and movement. Acquisition of ability to tell thoughts to others or to keep silent deliberately is most vital to development of child's thought and logic.

6. Child becomes able to understand and plan how to deal with reality through inner symbolic manipulation or thought.

6. Constancy of objects not acquired as a concept.
➤ Novelty feared and avoided. Children can manipulate ob-

Piaget's concept of normal behavior

Must be able to represent displaced objects internally. Capacity for representational thought is a requirement for reasoning. → Child desires novelty before he finds it.

7. Syncretistic child drawing a man, puts in a few details, whether insignificant or essential, at random (eg, head, buttons, legs, navel). Details = general effect; association = causality.

8. Non-ego-centric thought develops only from repeated interpersonal interactions.

9. Pre-operational thought centered on one striking feature of an object, to the neglect of other features.

... related to Bettelheim's autism

jects but not abstract thoughts. Note: these are normally characteristics of the child of 18 mos. or younger.

7. Autistic child draws like a baby; one significant part, meaningful to him only, filled in with random detail.

8. Autistic child cannot interact with the world. Speech not adapted to needs of listener.

9. Autistic child's single-minded preoccupation with total fear of destruction arrests him at this same pre-operational level.

THE DEVELOPMENTAL APPROACH TO
LANGUAGE LEARNING

10.1. Although the stimulus-response model is applicable to acquisition of lexicon and to several other select areas of language learning, the complexity of language as demonstrated by modern linguistics necessitates the augmentation of this model. It has been shown that conditioning theory is insufficient to explain most facets of the language acquisition process, in part because of sizeable inbuilt capacity apparently instrumental in acquiring language and the resulting numerous linguistic and psycholinguistic universals. Current developmental psycholinguistics draws from conditioning theory and from other learning models as well; the material on cortical lateralization presented by Lenneberg and discussed in a previous section is a significant example of developmental psycholinguistic theory.

The modern field departs from earlier S-R-based work in several important ways, of which one is the recognition of a distinction between linguistic competence and linguistic performance. The linguistic competence is internalized, and therefore unobservable; it must be inferred from performance data. Chomsky says, for example, that "obviously, every speaker of a language has mastered and internalized a generative grammar that expresses his knowledge of his language", and further that this grammar consists in ". . . the knowledge of the language that provides the basis for actual use of language by a speaker-hearer" (Chomsky, 1965, pp. 8-9). The necessity for postulating this distinction arises from the notion of language as a system, within which exist complicated relationships not able to be deduced from the physical form of utterances. That a speaker can perceive such relationships indicates that he must have an internalized set of rules for understanding and producing language. Competence is not isomorphic with performance, but is rather the underlying framework for performance. It is essential to postulate, as has been pointed out, that such an internalized grammar exists at each stage of linguistic development; were this not the case, then children's utterances would not be patterned but rather random, and furthermore one would expect children's imitations of adult utterances to be far more exact rather than deformed as if to fit some specific structure. In addition, it appears that competence can develop even where performance is largely or wholly absent, as in the case of children who for one reason or another do not learn to speak and yet are capable of understanding language (cf., for example, Lenneberg, 1964, p. 67, p. 80; Lenneberg, 1967, pp. 284 ff. See also Chomsky, 1967, pp. 397-402; 1964a, p. 37).

To the modern linguist and psycholinguist, language is something other than a series of associative chains. Chomsky has set forth the following framework for the study of the structure of language.

The *grammar* of a language is a system of rules that determine a certain pairing of sound and meaning. It consists of a *syntactic component*, a *semantic component*, and a *phonological component*. The syntactic component defines a certain (infinite) class of abstract objects (D, S), where D is a *deep structure* and S a *surface structure*. The deep structure contains all information relevant to phonetic interpretation. The semantic and phonological components are purely interpretative. The former assigns semantic interpretations to deep structures; the latter assigns phonetic interpretations to surface structures. Thus the grammar as a whole relates semantic and phonetic interpretations, the association being mediated by the rules of the syntactic component that define paired deep and surface structures (Chomsky, 1967, pp. 406-07).

Clearly this concept of language is far more advanced than the simple associative model of positional categories related by stimulus-response connections.

It is generally accepted that all languages share certain deep-structure features or constraints on their possible form. These are referred to as linguistic universals. That these features are universal seems to preclude their having been learned in the usual sense of the word. Rather it is postulated that they stem from innate genetically determined factors common to the species (cf. McNeill, 1966a, pp. 100 ff.). The capacity for language acquisition, whatever its extent may prove to be, must be considered an inbuilt 'given'. The existence of universals is only one of many data supporting this hypothesis. The very complexity and open-endedness of language argue against acceptance of the S-R explanation of language acquisition so long taken for granted in its accuracy (cf. Chomsky, 1968, p. 2). One reason for this is that a finite amount of time is required to condition an organism to emit a given response. Even admitting the possibility of one-trial and latent learning, all the conditioning necessary to produce even one day's worth of typical adult utterances could not take place during the average lifetime, let alone acquisition of some additional capacity to produce novel utterances (for more on novel utterances, cf. Chomsky, 1967a, p. 76). But the young child by the age of four to six has mastered most of the syntactic machinery of his language, whatever the language may be, and generally has acquired a considerable lexicon as well. One has no choice but to assume, contrary to most learning theory explanations, that this can only be due to intrinsic properties of the learning mechanism which differ from mere ability to create stimulus-response chains or to be reinforced.

It should be noted too that the existence of physiological processes apparently coterminus with normal language learning indicates that some factors in language acquisition might be credited to maturation rather than solely to learning. The ethological concept of the open instinct is perhaps relevant; the open instinct is a behavioral capacity rather than a specific behavior, more or less equivalent to a program to learn such a behavior. For example, some birds are not born able to produce their particular song, but instead are born with the capacity to learn any one song pattern and then to sing just this one song for the rest of their lives (cf. Ardrey, 1966, pp. 23-28). This is in some ways analogous to the situation with human language; although humans can in some circumstances learn more than one language, there may be a critical period in which language must be learned and after which it cannot be, and in which, moreover, the human (if normal) will learn any language to which he is exposed. As a general rule processes which seem to be coterminus with stages of neural development may justifiably be suspected of being caused by something other than simple learning.

10.2. It is not too serious an oversimplification of conditioning theory to state that according to its precepts an organism learns by emitting 'correct' behavior and being reinforced for it, at least in operant or instrumental conditioning situations. There is, however, another learning process proposed as significant in concept formation. This is described according to the hypothesis theory of learning; it suggests that humans at least learn from errors rather than from correct guesses. Thus it is supposed that when an organism needs to determine the structure of some given data, the organism makes a series of guesses or hypotheses as to the nature of its organization. Each hypothesis is retained until proved wrong. As each is proved wrong, another is created from the information gained from the preceding tests. The hypotheses are derived from environmental information, processed according to innate perception pattern (as formulated by Gestalt psychology, for example) and abilities.

It has been postulated that the child learns language in much this way, by forming a series of trial grammars or hypotheses about how language operates. The hypothesis at each stage is a generative grammar, or a portion of one, which produces a set of sentences corresponding – at first rather badly – to the linguistic input. As discrepancies occur between the child's concepts and the data he receives, he alters his hypotheses accordingly (cf. Chomsky, 1968a, p. 66). This may mean that he expands his grammar, or perhaps that he eliminates portions of it entirely and substitutes new ones, the latter being a somewhat less tenable suggestion. The result is in any case adult native-speaker competence. It is of course the competence that is being altered at each stage of the process; alterations in the competence produce corresponding changes in the performance, although not necessarily at the same rate.

There have been a number of studies of how the child goes about constructing these hypotheses, which portions of language are acquired first and how rapidly and smoothly this learning progresses. It has often been assumed that children learn language mostly by direct imitation of their parents' utterances and thus acquire new words and also new syntactic patterns. This will be recognized as a key assumption of both Skinner and Mowrer. In order to determine whether children do learn language chiefly by this method, Brown and Bellugi studied the language development of two children, a boy aged two years and a girl aged one-and-a-half years (Brown and Bellugi, 1964). These experimenters noted that the children's mother seemed to imitate the children more frequently than the children imitated their parents. The parents' imitations tend not to be exact, but rather to be expansions of the children's utterances, or in other words repetitions with the addition of new material. For instance, when the boy said "See truck", the mother repeated and expanded the utterance as "Did you see the truck?" When the boy said "There go one", the mother said, "Yes, there goes one."

Expansions of the child's speech by the parent were found to be frequent enough that they might be significant in giving the child insight into how the language is structured. There is apparently considerable regularity in the construction of parent expansions of child language. Such expansions almost always follow the same word order as the child's sentence, for instance; examples: baby: "Baby highchair"; mother: "Baby is in the highchair". Baby: "Mommy sandwich"; mother: "Mommy'll have a sandwich". The mother seems to take word order to be a constant and does not disturb this order when expanding the child's utterance, as though she assumes in some way that the child means his utterance as spoken. The type of additions made by the mother are fairly constant as well; whereas the child uses mostly full-words or contentives, the mother tends to add form-words or functors, words with primarily grammatical rather than lexical meaning. These are words which do not normally occur at all in the young child's productive vocabulary. The mother's expansions serve to determine whether or not she has properly understood the child; but they may also serve as a principal source of linguistic information for the young child.[1]

Imitation of parent utterances by the child occurs as well as the reverse situation, however. But if the child is to learn principally by imitation, then his imitations must be progressive, that is, they must add new patterns to his corpus which he can thereafter practice. Although children do learn in this fashion, it may not be among the more important processes in language learning. This is because the child tends not to imitate verbatim sentences which are more complex than he can produce spontaneously at that stage (but cf. Fraser, Bellugi and Brown, 1963). Brown and Bellugi point out that the child usually imitates only portions of utterances that he hears, reducing the utterances in a regular manner, presumably in conformity to his own grammar of that stage (cf. also Slobin, 1968). Examples: mother: "He's going out"; baby: "He go out". Mother: "The same dog as Pepper"; baby: "Dog Pepper".

The child always preserves the order of words in the sentences he imitates, as the mother does when imitating the child. This may seem an obvious way to proceed, but it is not so simple; if one is required to repeat a string of digits, for example, he can usually remember the last few digits better than earlier ones, and so can probably repeat backwards for a few units more easily than forewards from the beginning of the list.[2] The Gestalt Law

[1] It is not known whether parent expansions of child speech are common in non-English-speaking cultures, or to what extent such expansions are essential to the learning process. It has also been proposed that a vital source of linguistic information for the child is the use of relatively simple linguistic structures by parents (cf. e.g. Fraser, 1966, p. 118; Fodor, 1966, pp. 108-09); on the other hand, this simplification, if a fact, may make the induction of syntax by the child more difficult.

[2] Although the so-called random digit span is a commonly used measure of, e.g., child language ability, in fact the type of learning as well as the type of forgetting which occur in the learning of random digit strings are

of Recency too indicates that the most recently perceived units will be best remembered and recreated. There is no *a priori* reason why the child should not follow a similar procedure with repeated sentences rather than preserving word order, and indeed adults may find such a procedure easier than preserving word order when repeating utterances in a foreign language. But the child's correct imitation is evidence for an internalized grammar, or at least an innate notion of the unidirectionality or vector properties of speech.

In English, as in other basically non-inflecting languages, word order has a syntactic function. If the child did not preserve the word order of the utterance repeated, and if he did not use some correct word order altogether, he would not be understood by adults. Brown and Bellugi mention the possibility that the child does not do this deliberately in order to preserve semantic and grammatical distinctions between sentences, but rather because this happens to be the way in which his brain functions. Slobin has noted (Slobin, 1966, pp. 133-35) that even in Russian, children tend to use a fixed word order for their early utterances – an order which is not necessarily the most common one in the adult language – and that they only later discover that word order in Russian is relatively free.

Since the preservation of word order in imitations, and the use of a constant word order in spontaneous utterances, by the child is not obviously deducible from the laws of learning, some explanation for it must be sought. Slobin suggests that since all languages use word order to some degree as a syntactic and semantic signal, including such inflecting languages as Russian, it is conceivable that fixed word order is a part of the child's language acquisition mechanism and a good first hypothesis for the child to try out on the language. In other words, Slobin postulates that the child somehow knows that word order is a language universal and an innate part of the device which causes the child's language development, a device which is called a

---

quite different from those obtaining in child linguistic imitations (cf. Houston and Kamm, forthcoming).

Language Acquisition Device or LAD, one of the standard terms for this hypothetical innate mechanism. It is Slobin's suggestion that LAD is naturally equipped with the ability to sense what features of the linguistic environment are language universals and to build these into successive hypotheses about the grammatical structure of the language being learned.

An alternative suggestion might be that word order is used by children not because it is a linguistic universal, but rather because its linear structuring is a natural process in child concept formation. An argument for this hypothesis is that serial ordering appears to be learned, or to function, prior to hierarchical or two-dimensional structuring, both phylogenetically and ontogenetically. Children may learn ordering behavior before classifying behavior as a general rule. Although it has been proposed that the neonate is neurologically incomplete (but cf. Kessen, 1965, pp. 83 ff., for evidence against such a view), nevertheless the neonate is born with a wide variety of abilities, among them the capacity for temporal organization. The alternative to fixed word order is inflection or concord, which presuppose hierarchical relationships in a way that word order need not. In other words, the function of fixed word order in languages which use it as a grammatical device may be unrelated to the function of word order in child language; since children do not commonly use inflection or concord markers, markers of complicated hierarchical relationships not yet present in their grammars, there is no reason *per se* to assume that they use word order in non-inflecting languages to mark these same hierarchical relationships. Word order in child language may thus be due to the tendency of children toward serial behavior rather than to any understanding of the grammatical significance of that behavior. Nor is the criterion of parsimony met by a theory which supposes that children first mark grammatical relationships in e.g., Russian by word order, and later eliminate this procedure from their grammars and substitute an entirely different one, namely that of inflection.

There are other characteristics of children's reductions of their parents' utterances besides fixed word order. It is notable too that the words omitted by the child in reduction are usually the same ones that the mother adds in expansion, namely functors or form-words. Most often nouns and verbs are retained in children's sentences, and somewhat less often adjectives. Children retain contentives in part because these are the items learned by ostension in connection with familiar objects and actions. Brown and Bellugi also postulate that the words imitated by the child are generally those most strongly stressed by the adult speaker, which nearly always turn out to be contentives. Adults hear weakly stressed items because they know that these items are there; perhaps the child does not hear them and so does not reproduce them. When given more than one-syllable words to repeat, children frequently repeat only the stressed syllables.[3]

Child language contains spontaneous utterances as well as imitations. Many such utterances were clearly not learned from the speech of adults. Examples (from Brown and Bellugi): "No I see truck"; "Cowboy did fighting me"; "Two foot"; "A this truck"; "A scissor". Some of these items are traceable to analogy, as are such errors as 'I runned' or even 'He stoled it'. But others do not so originate, nor are they random. The child has rules by which he produces both these anomalous-sounding utterances and other, more nearly 'correct' ones (for a note on determining which is which, cf. Klima and Bellugi, 1966, p. 183).

Most investigators of child grammatical structures have determined that the child starts with two main grammatical categories, frequently called (after Braine and others) the pivot class and open class. Some psycholinguists have proposed that this classification is formed on the basis of word order. Certain words in the child's typical two-word utterance (in English) have a definite position. That is, some words always occur first in such sentences and some always last, although the former is far more frequent. These words, which make up the smaller category, may be called

---

[3] It appears that semantic load and stress interact as factors underlying child reductions of adult speech, so that neither one alone can serve as the entire explanation of telegraphic speech (cf. Bradac, forthcoming).

pivot words, because the child's sentences pivot around them. The open class words are those for which no fixed position in the sentence has been determined. Possible sentence structures for the child have been described (McNeill, 1966, p. 23) as of two main types, P + O and (O) + O, in other words, pivot word plus open word, open plus open, or open word alone.[4]

Besides having fixed sentence position, the pivot class has relatively small membership compared to that of the open class, and higher frequency of occurrence than the open class. But the categories were originally defined on the basis of word order alone. This notion has been challenged, however, on the following grounds: each stage of the child's grammatical production ostensibly represents a closer approximation to the native-speaker mastery of the language. A grammatical classification based solely on word order is quite dissimilar to the criteria of the adult grammar; normally, grammatical classification is based on factors other than order privilege within the sentence, although this too is significant. But if order is the only factor attended to by the child, then his classes are likely to have rather random membership relative to the membership of adult grammatical classes, so that this would not be a good or efficient basis for the child's first hypotheses about the structure of the language.

There are other possible means by which the two classes might be formed. McNeill has suggested (McNeill, 1966, p. 23) that not only is word order not the definitive criterion in the child's grammar, but in addition the child probably does not operate with word distribution in parental speech either, since if the child's categories were formed on a distributional basis then they should be accurate from the beginning. McNeill does not credit the argument that the child observes only those distributional criteria

---

[4] Note that this explanation, like nearly all other generalizations about child language, derives from study of children learning English and to some extent Russian. It is not always easy to see how such hypotheses as the universality of the Pivot/Open distinction might apply to languages with a morphosyntactic structure differing greatly from that of English, as for example incorporating languages (e.g., Nootka, Eskimo) in which the concept of a 'word' is not viable at all.

which he needs, such as forming a class composed of adjectives, pronouns and articles because he has observed that all these may precede nouns. One does not presume to know how a child might come to observe this particular criterion in the first instance, or how he might even know that it exists.

The explanation proposed by McNeill is that the pivot-open class distinction of the child conforms to one of the distinctions found in the adult grammar, and thus represents an approximation to adult linguistic rules. He states that there is a hierarchy of grammatical categorization characteristic of adult speech, as represented by the following diagram:

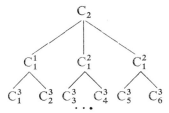

This hierarchy (adapted from McNeill, 1966, p. 34) represents the progressive stages of categorization in the child's grammar, leading to the final differentiation of categories found in the adult grammar (at a hypothetical lowest level of the diagram). Every possible string of words in the language, whether grammatical or not, can be generated by some stage of this hierarchy of categories. For instance, 'John plays golf' and 'golf plays John' are both represented here, at one of the upper levels before a distinction is made between animate and inanimate nouns. The distinction in well-formedness between these two sentences is not made at one of the higher levels of the grammar, because the levels represent successively finer differentiations within each class. The child's P-O grammar is a representation of one of the higher levels of this complete adult grammatical model, a level on which only broad distinctions between grammatical categories are made. As the child matures, he fills in progressively more advanced levels, that is, he acquires progressively more of the adult classificatory system until he has acquired the entire system.

According to McNeill, the LAD performs the work of language learning in the following steps (McNeill, 1966, p. 49): First, the LAD scans the linguistic input for distinctions which are found in the postulated universal hierarchy of categories, or in other words which are common to all languages. The LAD has a built-in cognizance of all the universal distinctions present in all languages, and searches what the child hears for representations of some of these distinctions. The primary linguistic data, or the earliest input heard by the child, is sorted according to these universal categories. Second, the LAD purportedly searches this preliminary linguistic data for certain sentence patterns which likewise correspond to basic grammatical relationships. McNeill states that "each pattern in the preliminary linguistic data that corresponds to a basic grammatical relation will suggest one or another hierarchical structure to LAD". Children are for all practical purposes born with all necessary distinctions, as e.g., subject-predicate, and need only scan the linguistic input in search of patterns which compose these categories. According to this theory, linguistic universals are a part of the child's neural equipment.

As an alternative suggestion, and one which assigns less material to the innate structuring, Slobin suggests that rather than being born with a set of preprogrammed categories, the child may instead be born with only the capacity to form such categories. Thus linguistic universals would be the results of an innate cognitive structuring rather than the content of this structuring. There may be inference rules, or innate discovery and decision procedures, but not innate grammar. Slobin feels that the child is not born with the concepts of plural, past tense, animate subject and the like, but rather with the ability to acquire categories of whatever nature.

It is perhaps worth noting that developmental psycholinguistics has re-emphasized the concept of innate linguistic (and other) ability, a concept more significant in itself than the decision as to how much is to be credited to this innate ability. One way of resolving this difficulty would be investigation of those factors which language has in common with other organizational systems, or in other words of suprasystemal universals, since unity of behavioral types tends to imply innate substructure (cf. Chapters 12, 13 of this work). It is at any rate highly probable that the capacity to form systems with certain gross characteristics is innate; among these characteristics are formation of the system from small units arrayed or mapped into larger ordered structures, having regular interrelationships among levels; expressability of such relationships by a number of combinatory and ordering rules at least theoretically finite; and non-maximal informativeness (e.g., language has redundancy, or predictability, or a measure of information per unit transmitted, and this redundancy is moreover relatively constant for all languages). It may readily be seen that these statements are characteristic of other forms of system besides language; the obvious example is music. But it is significant at the very least that they are in fact characteristic of all human languages, and thus are likely to be part of the innate language-acquisition mechanism.

11

THE BIOLOGICAL BASIS OF LANGUAGE

11.1. Much of the difference between early and later psycho-linguistics is traceable to differing estimates of the relative roles played by learning and maturational factors in language acquisition. It has been noted that the developmental psycholinguist postulates an innate language acquisition device responsible for the growth of language. Although there are divergent concepts of the extent and form of the LAD ranging from McNeill's suggestion that universal grammatical categories are innate to the LAD, to Slobin's hypothesis that the capacity for developing such categories rather than the categories themselves is innate, nevertheless the existence of some basic LAD is generally accepted. Modern psycholinguistics assumes a genetic basis for language, that it is a species-specific phenomenon resulting from evolutionary history rather than being a culturally instigated and learned activity. This view of the phylogenetic development of language is of course consistent with current descriptions of linguistic ontogeny: if it is presumed that children learn language because they are born with the capacity to do so when presented with the opportunity, then it is logical to study the history of this linguistic capacity and to look for signs of its presence in other (especially primate) species (cf. e.g. Kalmus, 1966; Premack and Schwartz, 1966).

Whereas the broadest issue of linguistic phylogeny, namely how and even where language originated, appears incapable of resolution (but cf. Diamond, 1965), it is feasible to inquire what is the evidence that language is a genetically motivated rather than a directed cultural activity. One way of conducting such an inquiry is to compare language with other forms of human behavior, namely those known to be either genetically determined or else culturally instigated, to examine with which category language seems to have most in common. In the most definitive such study, Lenneberg (1964a; cf. also Lenneberg, 1967, e.g., pp. 125 ff., pp. 371-95) notes that it is proper to speak of two essential alternatives in regard to language development, that is, that language either is genetically determined or else is purposive, deliberately created as a cultural phenomenon. This is not to suggest, of course, that the two factors are not each significant in certain aspects of language; nor is the proposed comparison strictly between learned behavior and inherited behavior, since all behavior has a genetic substrate in some sense – given a true *tabula rasa* as the neonate mentality, no learning whatever could occur.

Lenneberg notes (1964a) that the manner of species development is frequently misconstrued due to teleological concepts of the role of evolution in speciation. The notion of survival of the fittest is sometimes accepted as suggesting that species are somehow capable of developing precisely those traits which will insure their optimal survival in a changing environment, so that, for example, fish placed in a darkened enclosure will lose their sight because of their darkened surroundings. The author mentions the superficially reasonable statement that "the *purpose* of man's increased cranial vault is to house a large brain; and that the *purpose* of a large brain is the perfection of intelligence" (p. 580). As he explains, evolution takes place through intersection of the random process of mutation with exigencies of the environment and its alterations with respect to characteristics created by these mutations. Purpose is not relevant in such a connection. It is equally misleading to speak of the purpose of language development, as for example suggesting that language originated in order to facilitate communication. There are certain traits, such as larger brain capacity or the opposable thumb, which have adaptive value and thus have survived but there is no way for a species to use these traits in order to adapt better. Although this point may seem self-evident, misunderstanding of its implications

174   THE BIOLOGICAL BASIS OF LANGUAGE

frequently leads to resistance to findings suggesting the inherited nature of language capacity under the mistaken conviction that a higher purpose or species mind is somehow implied thereby. That language may be a genetically determined sort of behavior does not imply that man developed language in order to communicate, or as a means of expressing his emotions, or for self-defense or in fact for any other reason capable of philosophical specification.

The alternative to the genetic nature of language is that language be a part of cultural history, in which institutions develop because they are useful and serve a cultural goal. Lenneberg notes that culture itself may be thought of as the outgrowth of an hereditary trait, namely purposiveness; it is probably also due to an inborn need for companionship and at least bipersonal interchange. If it should turn out that language resembles such cultural activities, then explanation of its acquisition through associative conditioning precepts would be more valid. Since a behavior partially genetically determined is therefore not wholly learned, conditioning theory is not adequate in itself to explain a non-purposive language development. On the other hand activities developed deliberately and culturally transmitted, such as transportation techniques, folklore, machine technology, ordinance, orthography, must clearly be learned anew by those organisms which need to know them and are thus more susceptible to explanations based on learning theory.

11.2. To ascertain how the decision may be reached as to whether an activity is purposive or biologically given, Lenneberg (1964a, pp. 583 ff.) compares two activities about which such a decision has already been reached, namely bipedal gait, an innate behavior, and writing, which is learned. The comparison is made in terms of four main criteria, which Lenneberg names as variation within species, history within species, evidence for inherited predisposition, and specific organic correlates or lack thereof.

Intraspecies variation refers to the variety of forms which the activity in question may assume within the species. For example, humans have only one basic type of locomotion, namely upright on two legs. This is not subject to variation of a culturally determined sort. Writing, on the other hand, is a culture-bound activity, since orthographic systems vary widely and need not employ the same symbol-referent mechanisms. Further, the spread of writing can be traced geographically and be shown to follow cultural boundaries.

Likewise the history of writing systems is well known; most languages do not have corresponding native orthographies, and there are also relatively primitive orthographies, i.e., inefficient or ambiguous, and more efficient and advanced ones. Bipedal gait, however, shows no evidence of having evolved by stages throughout the history of human culture. Lenneberg points out that all humans have had about the same foot structure and have presumably walked upright as does modern man.

Evidence for inherited predisposition is self-explanatory as a criterion; "permanent and customary gait" cannot be taught if it is not biologically present. But the ability to write is not inherited, *per se*, and illiteracy is a sign of lack of training rather than of mental deficiency. There are finally a variety of verified organic correlates of walking ability, both central and peripheral, but there is no innate predisposition for writing – as Lenneberg states, a child does not begin writing automatically when presented with pencil and paper – nor are people who can write in any way organically different from those who cannot.

These four criteria can also be applied to language behavior (Lenneberg, 1964a, pp. 584-603). The first criterion, that of intraspecies variation, refers to the extent to which language behavior differs around the world. Lenneberg points out that all languages share three important features, which are approximately phonology, morphology and syntax; that all languages are apparently founded on the same classificatory principles is a significant linguistic universal. The basic levels of language classification do seem universal. For example, phonology is restricted to a finite group of sounds from the entire range of sounds that can be made by humans, although there is no *a priori* reason why this should be the case, and furthermore all languages have phonemes (cf. Chapter 12 of this work). There is also a theoretically finite set of rules defining the set of grammatical utterances in each language; or, put another way, all languages make a distinction between utterances which are well-formed or grammatical within the system and those which are not.

There are a number of possible explanations for the existence of such broad universals as these. Conceivably they exist because of coincidentally similar growth of language in many different places, although this seems empirically unlikely. Possibly, as an alternative, all languages are somewhat alike because they conform to some set of laws of optimal communication, or in other words linguistic universals establish the best type of communicative system and represent successive adaptations to cultural needs. However, it is not at all obvious that language has developed steadily toward an ideal communicative system. It is for instance not especially efficient for language to have the high degree of redundancy on most levels that it manifests; although redundancy may be of value, e.g. in noisy environments, many languages are still filled with what seem incredibly unnecessary complications of one sort or another. There are few ideally efficient or desirable features in most languages. A more likely alternative is that universal phenomena of language represent or reflect traits which are "related to the genetic mutation that has constituted the speciation of homo sapiens".

The second criterion for biological determination of language is history within the species. Language has no known evolutionary history; that is, there is no evidence that language ever existed widely in a more primitive stage than at present. To some extent this is because the history of language is necessarily the history of writing. But we do have writing which can be traced back about five thousand years, and linguistic reconstructions probably date back equally as far; yet no evidence has been found of the principle of phonemicization, for example, having developed from a simple and primitive stage to its present complexity. There are also indications that early grammar was at least as complex as present forms. The lack of developmental history is informative because phenomena known to be culturally determined typically do have such histories; cultural innovations are typically constructed by long trial-and-error practice, as the summation of accumulated knowledge and invention successively more complex at each stage. Speech, however, seems to have appeared much the way it does now, presumably because, as Lenneberg suggests, we have "a biological matrix or Anlage which forces speech to be of one and no other basic type".

It is difficult to determine the degree of inherited predisposition to language, partly because children's verbal stimulus input cannot be experimentally controlled. However, there are data which indicate at least an inherited predisposition for the behavior from which language develops. Lenneberg says that it is significant that in the absence of neural incapacity or injury, virtually all children develop language even in spite of grave obstacles to their doing so. Even where language performance does not develop, a highly structured competence is often manifested (cf. Lenneberg, 1962) so that the language acquisition device operates even when vocalization is inhibited.

It might also be noted that the component measured by most standard intelligence tests and often termed 'verbal ability' is presumed to be hereditary; skill at writing, speaking the native language without undue hesitation or nonfluency, glibness and so forth often seem to 'run in families'. There are several possible explanations for this, such as the fact that in some families the child hears and is probably highly reinforced for developing fluent and educated speech and stylistic elegance, so that environmental factors are also involved. There are people who have great difficulty in developing abilities outside of the verbal-based, however, a situation which does not seem to be dependent solely on early training.[1]

[1] On the other hand, it cannot be presumed *a priori* that the quantity measured by so-called verbal ability or verbal intelligence tests is in fact an aptitude rather than an achievement variable. This is because, among other reasons, the concept of linguistic competence differing from linguistic performance, so that a sample of the latter may not be representa-

The final criterion given by Lenneberg for differentiating purposive from genetic behaviors is the presence of specific organic correlates. The correlation between language development and neurological maturation has been discussed in a previous section; although this is not necessarily a causal relationship, it is worth noting that stages of ontogenetic language development correlate to some degree with stages of brain maturation. Lenneberg notes that all children start to talk at about the same age regardless of the language they are learning, that a normal child will learn any language with about the same degree of facility, and that a child who has failed to learn the language of his native country by the age of six or so could not learn "a foreign *simpler* language" with any greater ease (but cf. Slobin, 1966, p. 136). As comparison, writing systems clearly do not develop automatically from mere exposure, nor are all writing systems learned with anything approaching the same facility.

A most significant observation is that all children pass through identical stages of language acquisition. Children commence by babbling; they then develop a few words or phrases, mostly of one or two syllables, rarely more than three, typically referring to things, persons or events of direct concern to them. They often have a repertoire of stereotyped utterances, according to Lenneberg, and cannot combine portions of different utterances until a certain stage of maturation has been reached. Certain sentence structures never develop among English-speaking children until the age of three or so has been reached, for example conditionals

---

tive of the former, has been developed only recently and is not a basic assumption underlying the rationale for such tests. Thus these tests often seem to be measuring specific linguistic performance factors although they purport to be tests of 'language ability' (a prime example is the Illinois Test of Psycholinguistic Abilities or ITPA). Further, verbal ability tests incline heavily toward lexicon or vocabulary measures rather than tests of morphosyntactic competence. It should in general be noted that in order for a psychological testing instrument to be optimally acceptable, it must be reliable, valid and standardized; however, it is both possible and common for such tests to be standardized without meeting the other two criteria, particularly when the theory on which they were based is in some way deficient or outdated.

and subjunctives; and first sentences never include functors. The two-category grammar of the young English-speaking child is also fairly consistent. It must be emphasized that these are not the sort of factors likely to develop solely from environmental causes. Even the linguistic environment of children learning the same language may vary widely, and yet children generally develop grammar in the same way. Learning processes which remain constant despite greatly varying environmental conditions are frequently due to innate abilities.

11.3. It should be noted that despite the explanatory power of developmental psycholinguistics as presented by Lenneberg and others, there are still a number of alternative positions in regard to language acquisition, as for example that of Osgood. This is in part because in order to be considered maximally useful, it is generally expected that a scientifically created theory be based upon testable or measurable premises. There are certain difficulties created by a body of hypothesis apparently insusceptible of disproof; if any given set of results may be cited as favoring the hypothesis in question, and if further the crucial experiment is inconceivable, then the hypothesis may be equivalent to a belief system (for example, Freudian psychoanalytic theory has somewhat this character).

There is no single position on the role of maturational factors in language development precisely because no clear means of deciding the issue seem to exist. The environmental input of the child cannot be limited to maximize the influence of innate features on development. One may state that if language were wholly learned it might be expected to have a given set of characteristics, e.g., great variability in age of onset and stages of development; it does not seem to display these predicted characteristics and therefore one may conclude that it is not a conditioned behavior *in toto*. However, since there is no means to disprove the hypothesis, the reasoning is still aprioristic and although negative evidence exists from study of aphasia, delayed speech onset and other pathologies, it is not immediately clear what sort of evidence would tend to support the null hypothesis.

As in the case of evaluating grammars, however, suboptimum criteria must sometimes be accepted in the evaluation of socio-behavioral hypotheses. It is not generally advocated that psychoanalytic theory be discarded because of its seeming lack of disproof methods, for instance. In some situations a critical experiment may not be feasible, for reasons ranging from ethics to physical impossibility. This circumstance occurs rather often, especially when the material in question deals with such hidden or nonobservable processes as cognition and linguistic or behavioral phylogeny. When the strongest criterion of acceptability cannot be met, then a somewhat less powerful one may be necessitated. Of any new body of theory, it can reasonably be expected that the theory explain the relevant data better than any other existing theory, whatever this may prove to mean in the circumstances; that it be self-consistent and reliable; that its conclusions not conflict with those of proved postulates or descriptions; and that it serve to predict newly occurring relevant processes, so that confirming or denying evidence of some sort can be approached. From the field of General Semantics comes the analogy of a man compelled to describe the works of an unopenable watch; he may make a schematic diagram which would cause the hands to move at the desired rate, the watch to tick and so forth, but he cannot be certain that his creation is isomorphic with, or an analog of, the watchworks themselves. Although one may decide to accept that diagram which is simplest, or displays most technical sophistication, these criteria are not determined by tests against the data itself.

In the case of developmental and especially genetic linguistics, the situation in regard to crucial experiments is much the same at present. There does not seem to be any single given means of determining the nature and extent of the LAD, or the form of the adult linguistic competence. But it is noteworthy that current psycholinguistics is able to unify many facts previously thought of as random (e.g., the regular onset of language, cortical lateralization and its correlates, the hierarchical structure of utterances, linguistic universals and so on), and to predict stages of child language, ability to deal with varying sentence patterns and the like. It is clear that these theories supersede previous attempts at description of the language learning process; there is, for example, no reasonable explanation of language universals without postulation of inbuilt linguistic components. Despite immediate lack of any disproof method for these hypotheses, their explanatory adequacy has gained them wide acceptance.

It has been noted that alternative views do exist, however. For instance, the psychologist Chase suggests (1966) that either language is purposive in nature, or else that at the very least it developed in order to provide a communications system optimal in adaptability and versatility. Chase states that the plasticity or viability of human language distinguishes it from animal communication:

We observe in the course of evolution the development of greater plasticity with respect to the organization of communication systems. The advantage of such an evolutionary development is clear, as it allows communication systems to develop specificities of function that are particularly suitable to the environmental circumstances in which the organism must live. The ontogeny of communication capabilities that respect the fine structure of the environment in which the animal must live guarantees that the animal will not only be able to communicate information efficiently but in a manner appropriate to changes that occur in the physical and social environment (Chase, 1966, p. 261).

It is Chase's opinion, in other words, that the purpose of linguistic development was to provide us with a means of communicating about the environment even though the environment is subject to change. He states that "functional capabilities have evolved as a result of the efficiency and pertinence with which they mediate the requirements of biological growth and survival", or that language is basically adaptive. Chase states further that vocalization capabilities in each stage of individual language learning meet specific and different needs for information transfer at that particular stage. The infant's cry is purportedly an efficient means for transmitting what he terms affective experience; the early naming behavior is related to "the important psychological functions of exploring the surrounding physical universe and realization of the differentiation of self from this physical universe" (p. 262) and so has other functions than solely those of language acquisition. Finally, Chase states that Lenneberg's correlations between brain size, weight and specialization of function on the one hand and language growth on the other are not necessarily credible, and that

the fact that the human brain is of a particular size and weight and contains specific concentrations of certain chemicals at the time that language capability achieves a certain level of competence does not mean that the same degree of competence might not have been evidenced at an earlier stage of physical maturation if environmental contingencies had been other than they were (p. 263).

It is essentially Chase's position that communication is regulative of behavior and that communication systems are characterized by their capacity to transmit the right kinds of information. However, in examining the statement that vocalization capabilities at each stage of growth meet the needs of the individual at that stage, one must inquire as to precisely how the communicative needs of the individual are to be determined. If they can only be decided upon through observation of language behavior, then this observation cannot properly be used to support the thesis that behavior is developed to fit the needs.

Moreover, crying does not seem a strikingly efficient way of communicating either affective experience or other states. Since the infant's crying might indicate a variety of aversive stimuli besides, for example, hunger, the infant would be better advised to state 'I'm hungry' rather than to cry. Since mothers who come in response to their baby's crying frequently make some remark about the hunger of the baby, the baby presumably has the opportunity to acquire the relevant language from the environment and employ this language to meet its needs at that stage. One must inquire why it does not do so. It is not correct to state that babies are less intelligent than adults, in the same sense that one adult may be less intelligent than another and so fail to absorb environmental data efficiently; the trouble must rather lie with maturational causes. But this indicates that if language grows to meet the needs of the individual at each stage, then it does so rather poorly; or alternatively, the individual employs language as best he can at each stage to communicate about his current needs, rather than developing the language specifically to meet these needs. It is finally pertinent to mention that Chase's speculation concerning the possibility of language developing earlier in any given case if environmental conditions were different may be correct, but it lacks explanatory adequacy in that it provides no means of predicting how language development will proceed in any specific circumstances. Language appears to develop in the same manner regardless of environmental contingencies and over a considerable range of such contingencies, both in regard to physical and social environment and language being learned, so that one has difficulty in imagining how different the environment would have to be in order to alter language-acquisition stages as Chase suggests. It would appear once more that the hypotheses of standard developmental psycholinguistics provide more basis for prediction of observable phenomena than do alternative positions.

THE WHORFIAN HYPOTHESIS

12.1. Although the modern field of psycholinguistics tends to
focus on child language acquisition and the nature of the adult
language-production mechanism, there are additional, somewhat
more specialized facets of the psychology of language which have
been extensively investigated. For example, many works have
been concerned with the relation between language and cognition,
a problem which is in fact among the oldest areas of interest in
the field of language study.

There are many ways of approaching this subject; a standard
one is to inquire whether it is useful to differentiate language
from thought, and if so, whether their mutual influence is uni- or
bidirectional. The relevance of these questions to linguistics, psychology, philosophy and other fields of social and behavioral
inquiry is obvious; it is a central concern of all such fields to
determine how human reactions to the environment are influenced by verbal factors, for instance, or conversely how changes
in verbal behavior reflect corresponding changes in the nonverbal
environment. A demonstrated dependence of cognition on language would not only indicate an important source of intercultural
divergence and communicational malfunction, it would also carry
implications for the effects of verbal persuasion and influence on
behavior. Conversely, if language is shown to be shaped chiefly
by cognition, then this may indicate how linguistic operations can
be made more efficient through changes in ways of dealing with
environmental input. A further consequence of ascertaining the
relationship between language and cognition might be a clearer
concept of how to search for the presence of either among other
species.

Among the most significant works on this topic are those by Benjamin Lee Whorf, best known for his formulation of the Principle of Linguistic Relativity (also known as the Whorfian Hypothesis).[1] His hypothesis proposes essentially that speakers of different languages live in different worlds since their thought patterns are almost entirely shaped by the structures of their languages. Although the linguistic differences to which Whorf refers are part of what would now be considered surface structure, it is evident that he considers them to be fundamental or deep-structural facts about languages.

As the linguistic relativity principle indicates, Whorf believes that language is the most important factor in shaping the speaker's view of the world and his thought processes in general. In this connection he notes that "users of markedly different grammars are pointed by their grammars toward different types of observations and different evaluations of externally similar acts of observation, and hence are not equivalent as observers but must arrive at somewhat different views of the world" (Whorf, 1964, p. 221; subsequent citations in this chapter are from the same work unless otherwise noted). This view implies, according to Whorf, that the development of science as we know it (specifically Newtonian physics and other pre-Einsteinian scientific theory) was strongly influenced by the patterns of language and concomitantly of cognition common to Western science, patterns which he considers fairly uniform across all Indo-European languages and perhaps shared to an extent by those languages abutting on and influenced by IE as well. This group of languages Whorf calls Standard Average European (frequently referred to as SAE). Although he does not state that characteristic SAE scientific thought was caused by SAE language features, he does note that had our

---

[1] Although the linguistic relativity hypothesis is generally credited to Whorf, he was not the first to consider the issue; in particular, the anthropologist Edward Sapir's speculations about the relationship of language, culture and thought patterns apparently formed the basis of much of Whorf's work (cf. Sapir, 1921; 1929; 1949), although Sapir seemed much more skeptical than Whorf about the degree of influence language patterns have on cultural characteristics.

language been structurally different, our science would presumably have assumed a different form as well.

Whorf feels that language is significant to the totality of human behavior and cognition, in that without (or previous to) language the universe is perceived as an undifferentiated continuum of impressions, without temporal boundaries or distinctions between thing and event.[2] Stable perceptions are formed through the grammatical categorization of language, which also serves to erect boundaries between objects and between process and object. Such concepts are not proposed as being perceptual invariants stemming from psychological maturation, but rather ways of thinking brought about by language-motivated segmentation of reality. Whorf states that "it is the grammatical background of our mother tongue, which includes not only our way of constructing propositions but the way we dissect nature and break up the flux of experience into objects and entities to construct propositions about", which constitutes the logic of understanding and reasoning. He adds that

this fact is important for science, because it means that science *can* have a rational or logical basis even though it be a relativistic one and not Mr. Everyman's logic. Although it may vary with each tongue, and a planetary mapping of the dimensions of such variation may be necessitated, it is, nevertheless, a basis of logic with discoverable laws (p. 239).

Whorf thus believes that it is false to assert that science is a universal constant because the laws of space, time and matter are universal constants. On the contrary he feels both that the syntactic structure of SAE has generated Western science and that the syntax of other languages would have resulted in a different system. It might be remarked that science can be more logically

---

[2] Recent studies of neonatal and young infant perception development seem to indicate that this is not so (cf. e.g. Fantz, 1958; Weisberg, 1963). To the extent that infants show relatively undifferentiated reactions to environmental events, this is largely due to neurological immaturity; cortical activity is not present in humans from birth but requires a significant length of time, perhaps as much as several months, to develop. This is of course a physiological datum, quite independent of any linguistic variables.

regarded as influenced by the prevalent form of mathematical reasoning rather than by syntax, although perhaps Whorf would state that mathematics too is dependent upon language. It is at any rate difficult to see how Newtonian and Einsteinian reasoning can be based on the same set of linguistic structures, differing as they do in basic outlook; each is, however, based on a different mathematics even though both are formulated in SAE. Einsteinian mathematics especially seems foreign to the all-or-none rationality which Whorf considered characteristic of SAE languages.

On the relationship of language to consciousness, Whorf says that

the tremendous importance of languages cannot ... be taken to mean necessarily that nothing is back of it of the nature of what has traditionally been called 'mind'. My own studies suggest, to me, that language, for all its kingly role, is in some sense a superficial embroidery upon deeper processes of consciousness, which are necessary before any communication, signalling or symbolism whatsoever can occur, and which also can, at a pinch, effect communication (although not true agreement) without language's and without symbolism's aid (p. 239).

Whorf does in other words recognize the existence of some underlying perceptual and other cognitive framework which is common to the species and on which language is based. Language is presumably an overlay on this natural way of thinking and molds it into particular forms, in somewhat the same manner as physical science is an overlay upon the stratum of physical existence the phenomena of which it was designed to explain.

12.2. The most important facet of Whorf's hypothesis is that there is no justification for speaking of Language in the abstract sense:

The statement that 'thinking is a matter of *language*' is an incorrect generalization of the more nearly correct idea that 'thinking is a matter of different tongues'. The different tongues are the real phenomena and may generalize down not to any such universal as 'Language', but to something better – called 'sublinguistic' or 'super-linguistic' – and not altogether unlike, even if much unlike, what we now call 'mental' (p. 239).

so that only the most basic cognitive structuring is universal and all overlay on this is language-bound.

The Whorfian Hypothesis, especially as embodied in the passage above, postulates by implication far more than is expressed in the simple formula, 'different languages = different worlds'. Specifically it implies that, despite the basic biological cohesion of man as a species, one of the major behavioral systems controlled by the species – namely language – consists of a series of utterly separate and unrelated units. If this should indeed be so, then it would suggest a general nonstructuredness or entropy of behavioral systems. Whorf was demonstrably aware of the patterns of linguistic organization obtaining within each language, but he felt that structuring stops at the boundaries of the language.

12.2.1. If Whorf is correct in stating that speakers of different languages (who after all belong to the same biological species) are conceptually and behaviorally isolated from one another, then man is quite unique either in the random variation of his behavior or in the quantities of such behavior deriving from learning rather than from biological sources. Language, as the most striking of intercultural constants, should reasonably also be that most affected by genetic and neurological features common to *homo sapiens* as a whole, and so should not be characterized by major random variations in organization and by inter-unit incommensurability. One might further note that, if such divergence has developed within the behavior of a single species, then the prognosis is rather poor that other species may be found with which man might communicate.

12.2.2. Perhaps because its explanation of sociolinguistic divergence seems intuitively satisfactory, the Whorfian Hypothesis has generally found wide acceptance. Most current psycholinguists, however, in contrast to Whorf and other linguistic relativists, tend to feel that there are linguistic universals and that these universals reveal important facts about language and also about the cohesion of the species. They have been cited as one demonstration of the genetic basis for language, for example. Among the most significant universals of language is a basic pattern of organization which has been referred to as the phonemic principle. Pre-generative taxonomic linguistics presented the notion of language having levels of organization containing progressively larger units, the levels being phonological, morphological, lexical and syntactic. Each level is composed of a series of nonsignificant real units classified into a far smaller number of significant, presumably abstract or theoretical units. Thus phones, or the set of all speech sounds, are classified as or mapped into phonemes, or the set of all significant speech sounds. Phonemes, morphemes, syntagmemes and so on are basically distribution units, and it is they which participate in the patterning of language. Further, each level is constructed from units on the next lower level, so that morphs are composed of phonemes, words, of morphemes, and so on. The nonsignificant units in language are sometimes referred to as etic units, from the word 'phonetic'; the significant units, as emic units, from the word 'phonemic'. The pattern of etic/emic organization and the interrelationship of levels are characteristic of every human language.

Before the late 1950's, the reality of the phoneme was the subject of much debate within linguistics; it was asked whether the phoneme is an actual unit of speech or whether it is an artificial contrivance or a psychological concept available only through introspection. This is relevant to the Whorfian Hypothesis, in that the argument that the phoneme does not really exist is equivalent *mutatis mutandis* to Whorf's assertion that Language does not really exist.

In regard to the phoneme, it may be noted that the generalized characteristics which a group of phones (or morphs, etc.) have in common serve to label them as a discrete set, a complex unit called, in this case, a phoneme. There is no single physical manifestation of a phoneme, since specific individual sounds are only phones; the phoneme is a representational category. This is true of all etic/emic patterning. It has been pointed out that the levels of language may be cited respectively by the taxonomist as phonology, morphology and syntax, but the categorization need not stop at this point, for the following reasons. Whorf proposes that Language in the general abstract sense does not exist because only the manifestations of Language – namely languages – can be seen. However, languages can be considered as etic units and Language as the emic unit or abstract representation composed of the important overriding common characteristics of all languages. To speak of linguistic universals is then the structural parallel of speaking of the characteristics of a phoneme rather than those of a phone. Linguistic universals are those features by means of which all individual languages may be grouped together, just as the distinctive features shared by a group of phones serve to classify them as belonging to the same phoneme under the proper distributional circumstances.

It is frequently asked whether the principle of linguistic relativity is correct or incorrect. One might suggest, using this view of language classification as basis, that the principle is neither wholly correct nor wholly incorrect; this is because the similarities and the differences among languages are both significant in certain regards and in the same manner as the similarities and differences among phones are significant. The differences among languages are of course unstructured, so that it is not meaningful, for instance, to inquire why English developed a verbal system based on tense and Hopi developed a verbal system based on aspect. The differences among languages developed randomly, whereas the similarities are presumably due to characteristics of the species, in rather the same way as physical differences among humans are random whereas similarities indicate important structural features. Since languages are higher-level etic units, the similarities among them, as those among allophones, consist of a substrate of universal structuring; the differences among languages, as those among allophones, are a random overlay upon, or addition to, this structuring, significant only in that they are in fact random differences.

As an analogy to this situation, one might search for examples of similar hierarchical structuring in nonlinguistic spheres, since it seems a general enough principle to be found in many areas besides behavior. One may observe, for example, that the structuring of phylogeny seems to be organized hierarchically, with the levels phylum, genus, species arranged approximately in the same way as phonemics, morphemics, syntax. To extend the analogy, it is conceivable to postulate, as the phylogenetic emic unit corresponding to Language, a unit which one may call the organism or perhaps life in general – this is feasible because of the large number of characteristics shared by all forms of life on this planet, such as determination of heredity by DNA and RNA and of muscular movement by ATP, etc. If one may speak of only one language on Earth, from the structural-taxonomic point of view, then one may equivalently and analogously speak of one form of life on Earth, since the overriding common characteristics of each are significant and numerous enough to permit of their being grouped into such categories. The type of hierarchical organization termed etic/emic patterning seems, in other words, to be common throughout many types of extremely diverse systems; it is perhaps a kind of general systematizing principle or 'law', which may be universally expected rather as gravity is expected to obtain everywhere.

12.3. Although the implications of the Whorfian Hypothesis discussed above are those with the greatest general significance, Whorf makes other assertions more directly related to the study of language. It is his notion, for example, that the relationship between the thought patterns of speakers of different languages is dependent directly on the degree of structural differences between the respective languages. He states that not only are customary ways of viewing the world created by linguistic categories, but there are also a number of thought patterns peculiar to each language formed by categories that the speakers do not overtly notice.

Categories thus unmarked by a formal indicator, and therefore often unnoticed by speakers of the language in question, Whorf calls covert categories or cryptotypes, which he contrasts with overt or formally marked categories (cf. pp. 88-89). In some languages noun classes are overtly marked, as by a particular morpheme identifying the noun as belonging to the class. In other languages, such as Japanese for example, there is no formal linguistic marker of noun class; one simply must know to which class nouns belong and thus what sort of concord they take (this is of course largely true of gender in French, and in English as well). Nouns in Japanese, Navaho and other languages are classified by shape, for instance, as long, flat, bottleshaped, round or the like. But there is no formal indication of the category to which a particular noun belongs; therefore the category is a cryptotype. In regard to gender in English, Whorf notes that this category is unmarked but nevertheless present in co-occurrence restrictions; when we have referred to someone as 'Jane' we cannot thereafter refer to that person with the pronoun 'it'; we must instead say 'she'. If we call a goldfish 'Jane' we must say, 'Jane likes her food', not 'Jane likes its food', and likewise if we give the name to an automobile or a cannon. Thus the pronoun agrees with the name only, not with the experience (as noun classes by shape largely do) and not with the form of the word either. Whorf discusses overt and covert categories because he feels that they serve to demonstrate what is noticed and what is commonly taken for granted.

Whorf discovered that some languages have a different set of categories, both overt and covert, from those of the SAE languages. Among the most interesting data he gathered are those connected with the Hopi language, a language in which, according to Whorf, space and time are handled very differently from the SAE manner. For instance, Whorf notes that in SAE plurality and cardinal numbers are applied with equal facility to things which can in fact be enumerated and to those which in fact cannot: thus the SAE speaker says 'three men' and he also says 'three days', precisely as though the three days could be perceived strung out together or in a line all at once. Thus SAE describes cyclic occurrences (ten days, ten steps forward, ten rings of a bell) in the same way as aggregates (ten men, ten stones). Such speakers are aware of a subjective element in time and cyclicity, as the notion of 'becoming later and later', but for SAE speakers this falls in a different category of thought unrelated to the environment. Time spans are envisioned as countable arrays, so that the SAE speaker can refer to a length of time as easily as to a length of string. To Whorf this is not merely metaphor, but rather a basic process of perceiving the universe (cf. also Bright and Bright, 1965).

This manner of perceiving and talking about time is not the only one, however. Hopi has an entirely different linguistic situation:

Plurals and cardinals are used only for entities that form or can form an objective group. There are no imaginary plurals, but instead *ordinals* used with singulars. Such an expression as 'ten days' is not used. The equivalent statement is an operational one that reaches one day by a suitable count. 'They stayed ten days' becomes 'they stayed until the eleventh day' or 'they left after the tenth day'. 'Ten days is greater than nine days' becomes 'the tenth day is later than the ninth'. Our 'length of time' is not regarded as a length but as a relation between two events in lateness. Instead of our linguistically promoted objectification of that datum of consciousness we call 'time', the Hopi language has not laid down any pattern that would cloak the subjective 'becoming later' that is the essence of time (p. 140).

The Hopi, then, presumably does not view time as having an orderly division between past, present and future. The main distinction in Hopi temporal organization is between what Whorf terms manifested and unmanifest, or objective and subjective. The objective or manifested comprises everything except future; that is, past, historical present, present itself and so on. The subjective comprises everything that appears or exists solely in the mind, for instance wishes, concepts, all mentality and intellection and purpose, as well as the future. Thus the basic distinction in Hopi verbals is not one of tense at all; there is no 'when' involved in the automatic linguistic pinning down of an event, so to speak. The concept of distance is involved in this system as well as that of time, so that two events occur a long time apart in almost exactly the same manner as two villages are separated by a long distance. Whorf states that when many "periodic physical motions have occurred" between two events so as to cover much distance or accumulate magnitude of physical display in other ways, then the two events are far apart. The Hopi does not need to decide whether events in a distant village occur or exist at the same present moment as those in one's own village: events at a distance from the observer can only be known objectively when they are 'past' (that is, objectified, verified as definite occurrence), and the more distant, the more 'past'. What happens at a distant village, if actual (objective) and not conjectured about (subjective), can be known 'here' only later. If something does not happen 'at this place', it does not happen 'at this time'; it happens 'at that place' and 'at that time'. Whorf adds that

both the 'here' happening and the 'there' happening are in the objective, corresponding in general to our past, but the 'there' happening is more objectively distant, meaning, from our standpoint, that it is further away in the past just as it is further away from us in space than the 'here' happening (p. 63). ·

It is because of this same general conceptualization that the Hopi does not count days. According to Whorf, the Hopi sees tomorrow not as another day but rather as the same day returning. He does not prepare for tomorrow as the SAE speaker might ready himself for a new event, but in much the same spirit that the SAE speaker might say he can influence a later visit of a man by doing things when he is here at an earlier date. The bewildering effect of this explanation on SAE speakers serves to illustrate Whorf's basic point, namely that the SAE (or other non-Hopi) speaker can never fully comprehend the Hopi *Weltanschauung*. In SAE, time is seen as similar to a space of limited dimensions, or perhaps as a motion on that space, whereas the Hopi presumably could not conceptualize time in terms of space or motion. The same total lack of shared concepts would prevail between speakers of any two greatly divergent languages or language-family members.

13

THE WHORFIAN HYPOTHESIS:
INTERPRETATION AND EXTENSION

13.1. Since the material to which the Whorfian Hypothesis refers
is largely unobservable, and since the Hypothesis itself is stated
in impressionistic terms, relatively few actual experiments have
been devoted to confirming or denying it. Nevertheless there have
been attempts to proceed further with linguistic relativity, extending its implications (cf. e.g. Spier, Hallowell and Newman, 1941;
Hoijer, 1954; 1964) or codifying it in a form more scientifically
plausible. One such investigation was made by Lenneberg (1961)
and is concerned with color perception and recognition. Whorf
would presumably assert that people who segment the spectrum
differently – that is, have generic names for different portions of
it, or fewer or more color-names in their lexicon – should have
differing abilities to remember given colors and to recognize them
subsequently. This thesis is in accord with the psychological
principle stating that those objects and events for which one has
easily recognizable or producable names are best remembered, or
in other words that codability or ease in naming is a factor in
memory.
  Lenneberg's experiment was designed to investigate whether
speakers of two quite different languages show correlated differences in color perception. He performed the test with speakers of
English and Zuñi, languages in which the color-naming schemas
are different. Lenneberg discovered in general that although ease
of naming a color did appear to provide a good reference point
for describing the color to others so that they might better select
it from a group of colors, nevertheless having a simple name for
a color did not effect any significant difference in ability to remember and select the color from a similar group. How colors

are talked about in different languages does not seem to influence to any perceptible extent how they are recognized or remembered, which result tends to disconfirm one facet of Whorf's hypothesis.

13.2.   One major difficulty with the Whorfian Hypothesis is that it is not immediately clear what sort of evidence would tend to disprove it conclusively. This may be because the Hypothesis is not stated in terms which indicate methods of scientific inquiry, a point discussed by Osgood and Sebeok (1965, pp. 195 ff.). These psychologists note that the underlying assumption of Whorf's work, stated in psychological rather than linguistic or philosophical terms, is probably that "cognitive states are determinants of overt behavior – or more generally, that ways of perceiving and conceiving the world affect behavior norms toward physical objects and in social situations (culture)". Additionally they state that the relationship between language and cognition on the one hand and overt behavior on the other should be one of bidirectional rather than unidirectional interaction.

According to Osgood and Sebeok, in order to codify the concise proposition of Whorf in a manner lending itself to scientific examination, it might be effectively restated in the following four hypotheses (pp. 195-203):

1.   The cognitive states associated with stimuli influence the responses made to these stimuli.
2.   The behavior initially elicited by stimuli influences the cognitive states that come to be associated with signs of these stimuli.
3.   The form of codification of the language used to talk about stimuli influences the cognitions associated with these stimuli.
4.   The cognitions associated with stimuli influence the form of codification of the language used to talk about these stimuli.

The first of these hypotheses indicates simply that a response depends not only on a stimulus but also on the concepts or thought processes associated with the stimulus, in other words to the total stimulus situation as perceived by the reacting organism. This is a point to which the Gestalt experiments dealing with functional fixedness (cf. Chapter 2 of this work) are relevant. The second hypothesis, which presents the converse of the first, states in essence that how one perceives objects or events depends to an extent on how he reacts to them. Symbols of various sorts are seen as having meaning in terms of previous experience with them. This proposition and the preceding one attempt to formulate the influence of language structure on the world view, that is, perception, thought, memory and so forth. But the authors state that not only does language influence the world view, but also the world view influences and changes languages.

One might note an obvious difficulty in asking whether the world view changes language, namely that the question presupposes that people have innate differences in perception which do not originate with language. This is because clearly if perceptions are to influence linguistic behavior then they cannot be caused by this linguistic behavior. But in this case, from where do these perceptual differences stem? One reason this is a problem is that, disregarding similarities in deep structure, the differences among linguistic surface features are very great. It cannot be proposed that different cultures have different inherited characteristics corresponding to their respective *Weltanschauungen*. Nevertheless there are striking differences in linguistic behavior between any two languages no matter how closely related (cf. Steiner, 1969). It is clear that languages influence the way their speakers perceive the environment, and select those features of the environment to which they pay habitual and customary attention. It is not immediately obvious how to describe the nature of the influence in the other direction on any but an idiolectal basis, or having done so, how it might be tested or experimentally investigated.

The third proposition advanced by Osgood and Sebeok is that the form of codification of the language used to talk about stimuli influences the cognitions associated with these stimuli, or in other words, that the way in which a situation is referred to or encoded changes behavior toward it. Previous to his entering the field of linguistics, Whorf worked as investigator for a fire insurance underwriter, in which position he investigated many hundreds of claims following fires and inquired into the causes of these fires. Often he found that people had behaved carelessly around potential fire-hazards, in a manner which would be inexplicable unless one were to take into account the manner in which they referred to and consequently perceived these hazards. Whorf cites, for example, the case of a man who threw cigarettes into gasoline drums filled with gasoline vapor, thereby causing a fire. Whorf proposes that this occurred because the men spoke of these containers as 'empty gasoline drums', thus ignoring the fact that the containers were in actuality 'filled' with vapor. This resulted according to Whorf from the meaning of the word 'empty' in English, since it presumably led its users to disregard the actual contents of an empty-appearing container. However, as Osgood and Sebeok comment, the man's perception of the drum as empty or as non-dangerous cannot with certainty be attributed to his use of the word 'empty' to refer to it; the label might better have been explained as the result of, rather than the cause of, the perception.

The final supposition of Osgood and Sebeok is that the concepts a speaker has concerning objects and events influence his verbal codification of them. Some of the 'cognitions associated with stimuli' referred to by the authors are experiential, while others are the results of what Hebb terms psychological maturation (Hebb, 1966, p. 157). Presumably linguistic distinctions resulting from the latter sort of cognitions will be linguistic universals. Thus it has been postulated (Campbell, 1966), that most languages will distinguish between 'tree' and 'branch' rather than between 'upper part of tree trunk' and 'lower part of tree trunk', or between 'man' and 'boy' rather than between 'man of 30-40' and 'man of 40-50'. Research on this topic would probably best be directed toward determining which concepts are most easily and therefore universally discriminated, and correlating the results with the discriminations marked in languages. Perhaps also relevant in this connection is the widespread notion which holds that cultures have many words for objects and events about which they must talk frequently or which they must differentiate finely, such as types of rice for the Chinese, or words relating to the fishing industry for fishing cultures.

There are a number of difficulties in the investigation of how innate perceptions influence language, if language is to be viewed at any but the idiolectal level. Again this is because of the previously discussed great differences among languages in regard to surface structures at least. If innate perceptions are to be regarded as a species constant, then the core of distinctions common to all languages may be the result of these perceptions, whereas the differences among languages are caused by other factors such as random generation of characteristics. On the other hand, one cannot justifiably suggest that wherever distinctions are found in language, they are indications of perceptual differentiation processes. Thus it is apparently reasonable that languages differentiate 'man' from 'boy' (although even such an SAE language as German has some difficulty with this distinction), and that they not differentiate 'man of 45' from 'man of 55' by means of pure lexical contrast. But it does not seem reasonable in the same sense that a language use different lexical items to indicate 'your wife' and 'my wife'. One may propose that it is in fact necessary and reasonable, because the language in which this distinction obtains (Japanese, for example) has a cultural or sociolinguistic system in which this distinction is perceived as significant just as is 'man/boy' in SAE. However, this is not an innate perceptual differentiation but rather a learned and culture-bound phenomenon. It may be that categories of classification, or methods of forming such categories, are the universals rather than the fillers of such categories.

13.3.   There have been other approaches to the subject of language and cognition besides that taken by Whorf. For example, the Russian psychologist L. S. Vygotsky has worked on the topic from a more Gestalt-oriented point of view. Like Lenneberg (and Whorf also to a degree), Vygotsky is concerned with the genetic basis of language and thought, and tends to feel that systematic linguistic behavior is basically species-specific (cf. Vygotsky, 1962;

cf. also Lenneberg, 1967, pp. 33-72). Vygotsky, however, does not believe that other species show no approximations to language or to human cognition; instead he notes that in animals, "speech and thought spring from different roots and develop along different lines" (p. 33). In apes, for example, although there is no linguistic behavior per se, Vygotsky states that the ape's rudimentary use of tools, social behavior and beginnings of reason seem to constitute a sort of prelinguistic behavior. Moreover, he adds that one may find in the chimpanzee "a relatively well-developed 'language' in some respects – most of all phonetically – not unlike human speech. The remarkable thing about [the ape's] language is that it functions apart from his intellect" (p. 34). In their gestures too Vygotsky feels that apes demonstrate prelinguistic behavior.

In regard to the development of thought and language in the child, Vygotsky states that early speech, especially babbling, has no relation to intellectual functioning, since speech does not become associated with cognition until about the age of two. This turning point, at which the child feels the need for words and discovers their symbolic function, is marked by new curiosity about words and questioning about the names of objects, and by concomitant rapid increase in lexicon acquisition. Vygotsky proposes that neither does language cause thought nor does thought cause language; instead the two originate independently and then at a certain stage become bound together.

In the adult, insofar as there is influence between thought and language, Vygotsky tends to agree with Whorf that the perceptual categorization derives from the linguistic patterning. He feels that the relationship between a word and its referent is not static but dynamic, a constantly changing process. He states, for example, that "thought is not merely expressed in words; it comes into existence through them. Every thought tends to connect something with something else, to establish a relationship between things" (p. 125). Further, he notes that for children especially, a word may be indistinguishable from its referent; a child will say that a cow is called a cow because it has horns, and when told to call a dog 'cow' and then asked whether now a 'cow' has horns will persist in saying yes even though the referent of the word 'cow' has been altered (cf. Piaget, 1967, p. 63 f.).

13.4. As a conclusion to this discussion of Whorf and the language/cognition relationship, one might consider briefly the extent of linguistic relativity as viewed by Whorf himself. The amount of universal patterning credited by Whorf is rather greater than is frequently imagined. He says, for example,

[We have seen] that, in linguistic and mental phenomena, significant behavior . . . [is] ruled by a specific system or organization, a 'geometry' of form principles characteristic of each language. This organization is imposed from outside the narrow circle of the personal consciousness, making of that consciousness a mere puppet whose linguistic maneuverings are held in unsensed and unbreakable bonds of pattern.

But to this he adds,

And now appears a great fact of human brotherhood – that human beings are all alike in this respect. So far as we can judge from the systematics of language, the higher mind or 'unconscious' of a Papuan headhunter can mathematize as well as that of Einstein; and conversely, scientist and yokel, scholar and tribesman, all use their personal consciousness in the same dimwitted sort of way, and get into similar kinds of logical impasse. They are as unaware of the beautiful and inexorable systems that control them as a cowherd is of cosmic rays (Whorf, 1964, p. 257).

These remarks may seem paradoxical but they are in fact straightforward; Whorf probably intends to state that, although the effect of individual language systems is to shape the cognitive patterns of their speakers differently, the fact that all languages operate in this way and that all cognitive patterns are thus derived may be regarded as a universal. This interpretation is confirmed by his following remarks:

Without a serial or hierarchical order in the universe it would have to be said that these psychological and linguistic experiments [i.e., those which demonstrate universal ways of linking experience] contradict each other. In the psychological experiments human subjects seem to associate the experiences of bright, cold, sharp, hard, high, light (in weight), quick, high-pitched, narrow and so on in a long series, with each other; and conversely the experiences of dark, warm, yielding, soft, blunt, low, heavy, slow, lowpitched, wide, etc., in another long series. This occurs whether the *words* for such associated experiences resemble or not, but the ordinary person is likely to *notice* a relation to words only when it is a relation of likeness to such a series in the vowels or consonants of the words, and when it is a relation of contrast or conflict it is passed unnoticed. . . . What is significant for our thesis is that language, through lexation, has made the speaker more acutely conscious of certain dim psychic sensations . . . (p. 267).

Thus language produces a universal set of concepts or, better, of relations between concepts, which remain relatively unaffected by individual linguistic experiences.

14

BILINGUALISM: NATURALLY ACQUIRED
BILINGUALISM

14.1. Bilingualism, as a special case of language acquisition, is clearly of interest to the psycholinguist attempting to create a comprehensive model of the language learning process. Because of its relevance to second-language teaching, the topic has most frequently been studied by applied linguists, who tend to concentrate on the verbal behavior of the accomplished bilingual rather than on the process by which he acquires the languages in question. There have been few significant examinations of the situation of children learning two languages; among the most widely known is that by Leopold (1939-47).

The bilingual speaker is generally defined as one who speaks, or understands, or knows two (or more) languages; the difficulty in determining precisely what is meant by knowing a language, or what degree of proficiency in each of two languages is required in order to call the speaker a true bilingual, causes some imprecision in the definition. It may be useful to refer to two general types of bilingual speaker, namely the speaker who learns two languages in a natural speech situation, whether consecutively or concurrently, as contrasted with the one who studies a second language formally, as in school. These may be termed respectively primary and secondary bilinguals.

The major study of primary bilingualism, and that which has most influenced later works on the subject, was written by Weinreich (1964). In this work Weinreich's main emphasis is on the problems faced by the bilingual attempting to maintain two separate language systems, and on the factors governing which of his languages such a speaker will use in a given context. The basic linguistic problem besetting such a speaker is interference, or the detrimental influence of one of the speaker's languages upon the other. Interference may be primarily phonological, morphological or syntactic, although one may also find it helpful to consider the possibility of semantic and pragmatic interference. Interference is apparently an inevitable concomitant of bilingualism, since at least in theory anyone who speaks two languages demonstrates some influence of one upon the other regardless of circumstances of acquisition; the interference may be uni- or bidirectional in primary bilingualism and would tend to be unidirectional in secondary bilingualism.

In general, a bilingual is said to have one of two principle systems by which he organizes his two languages, namely compound bilingualism and coordinate bilingualism. The difference between these systems, although it may be defined in various ways, appears to be one of relationship among a word in language A, the corresponding word in language B, and the referents of each. If a speaker considers a word in language A as having the same meaning or reference as the corresponding word in language B, then he purportedly has a compound system – in other words, if he is a speaker of e.g., Hungarian and English, he will view the English 'book' as linguistically equivalent to the Hungarian *könyv* so that both words have the same meaning or set of referents to him. If on the other hand the speaker perceives the English 'book' as a sign distinct in meaning from its Hungarian equivalent, the system is coordinate. There is also the possibility of a mixed system, in which one of the words is perceived as meaning the other rather than referring directly to the object or event in question, as if for example the speaker were to view '*könyv*' as a translation or encoded version of the English word 'book' rather than as a direct symbol of the object *book*.

14.2. Since interlingual interference is far more striking a problem in secondary than in primary bilingualism, and since the topic has so often been investigated by linguists interested in its applications to second-language learning and teaching, most studies of bilingualism have concentrated on describing the role played by interference in compound and coordinate bilingualism and occasionally proposing means by which such interference might be overcome (cf. Lado, 1957). In a true coordinate bilingual system there would be no interference, since in this system each language is theoretically a separate and discrete entity in its relation to referents. It has even been proposed that in a pure coordinate system the languages would remain mutually uncontaminated to the degree that they would be totally incompatible and thus their speaker would be unable to translate from one to the other (cf. Lambert, Havelka and Crosby, 1958). It has not been demonstrated, however, that such a situation can occur, and for this reason the utility of the basic compound-coordinate distinction has been seriously questioned (cf. Diller, 1967). Note that coordinate or compound bilingualism are functions of the speaker's own behavior rather than of any genealogical or other linguistic relationship between the languages; the same two languages may be compounded for one speaker and coordinated for another. Types of bilingualism also occur irrespective of the learning situation, so that the monolingual studying a second language in school is presumably capable of forming a coordinate system from his first and second languages, which is in fact the goal toward which modern foreign-language teaching is directed.

Interference may take place at any level of language. It is best regarded as a syndrome rather than a unit process, and it usually has a whole host of contributory factors. Applied linguists hypothesize that language students will have difficulty at points of difference between the native and foreign languages whereas points of similarity will facilitate learning; on the other hand, apparent similarities may be more confusing than obvious differences. The most common type of linguistic interference is probably phonological, i.e., interference between the sound systems of the speaker's two languages (cf. Weinreich, 1964, pp. 14 ff.). It is assumed, as will be discussed presently, that most bilinguals are more fluent in one language than in the other; the former is called the speaker's dominant language, and it is usually this language which interferes with the second language rather than vice versa. So the speaker for whom language A is dominant may fail to distinguish differences in language B which are not recognized in his dominant language. For example, the speaker of Spanish and English for whom Spanish is dominant (this includes the Spanish speaker beginning to learn English) may fail to recognize the difference between English 'bet' and 'bait', a difference which is not phonemic in Spanish. Contrariwise, such a speaker may make overly fine distinctions in language B, imposing these distinctions from his dominant language A in which they are phonemic; thus an Arabic speaker might interpret English front [k] and back [ḳ] (as in 'keep', 'cool') as belonging to different phonemes, because the distinction is phonemic in Arabic.

Other types of confusion besides under- and overdifferentiation obtain on the phonological level. A speaker may also substitute phonemes from the dominant to the non-dominant language, as for instance a Russian-English bilingual who says [xauws] for the English 'house'. Sound-system interference may occur in non-segmental areas as well; the most persistent interference, in fact, is frequently in intonational patterns. This feature of language is frequently overlooked in the secondary bilingual situation, primarily because teachers tend to be unaware of the problem or incapable of adjusting students' faulty intonation. In many languages this does not make a practical difference, since intonation may be redundant within a given context and at any rate speakers of most languages are accustomed to intonational distortions in speech otherwise marked as foreign and make allowances for it. On the other hand, in languages such as Chinese in which tone is phonemic, teachers or other native informants are likely to direct the student's attention to pitch levels so that they will not be consistently ignored. There are also languages in which the status of tone is not so clear-cut, however; Japanese, for example, may have phonemic pitch, but there is sufficient doubt about this to insure that it not be taught as such in the great majority of cases. Perhaps more significant is the fact that in Japanese, as in some other languages, men's and women's speech are differentiated markedly by intonation and other paralinguistic differences, although there is a levelling process taking place in the language. Students having only male or only female informants to copy will invariably learn only one set of patterns, since it simply does not occur to an informant of one sex to attempt the paralinguistic features of the other, and such students will thereafter make errors which appear highly puzzling or even offensive to the native speaker.

Morphosyntactic interference, a category at least as typical of secondary bilingualism as is phonological interference, frequently seems to be caused by attempts at literal translation (i.e., word for word or morpheme for morpheme), especially in languages which do not seem structurally incompatible to the speaker. It may also be due to attempts at rendering a distinction in one language peculiar to the other only; or alternatively, to attempted analogy, especially between related languages. Thus a Danish-German bilingual for whom the former language is dominant, may say in German, *Kennen Sie ihn *zufälligweis?* instead of *–zufällig*, on the model of Danish, *Kender De ham tilfoeldigvis?* Or, he may say, **Hat er gehabt Ferien?* from Danish, *Har han haft ferie?* which is normal word order in Danish but not in German. Morphosyntactic interference is prevalent in most instances in which the speaker learned one of his languages in childhood and the other in adulthood, as is normal in situations of emigration. The interference is frequently predictable, so that, for example, non-English-speaking emigrants learning this language may be stereotyped according to the errors expected of their particular linguistic origin – thus Herman and Herman (1943), in a manual instructing radio performers on the art of dialect imitation, note that a Japanese speaker will say 'Thank you not to do so' instead of 'Please don't do that'; a Russian, 'Was many people in lake' instead of 'There were many people in the lake'; a German, 'He was by the house upstairs' instead of 'He was upstairs in the house'. It is not unusual for such interference-produced errors to be understood with little difficulty by native speakers of the language being spoken, due, among other causes, to the high degree of redundancy in language. In contrast to e.g., distortions of intonation and other paralinguistic phenomena, it appears that morphosyntactic errors are more likely to produce loss of communication (signalled most often by requests to repeat the utterance) than specific misunderstanding or misinterpretation, a point deserving of investigation.

14.3. There have been a number of psychological interpretations of bilingualism, many designed to explain the influence of control of two languages on the thought processes. The French psychologist Epstein proposed in 1915 the notion, still rather widely held, that bilingualism hampers ideation (Epstein, 1915; discussed by Weinreich, 1964, pp. 71-72). Epstein stated that there are three main variables involved in bilingual systems, namely a word in language A, the corresponding word in B, and the idea to which the words refer. There is purportedly a bond formed between each word and the idea; it is Epstein's thesis that the two bonds are likely to interfere with each other and cause confusion in thinking. For each idea thought about by the bilingual, the concurrent word associations conflict in this manner, so that both thinking and fluency of expression are inhibited. This theory has stimulated a number of experiments comparing the intelligence of monolinguals with that of bilinguals. The results of these experiments have been widely diversified. The notion of bilingualism inhibiting intelligence is still so common that Carroll notes (1964, p. 42) that "there is no good evidence that . . . bilingualism retards mental development". It is difficult, in fact, to define the concept 'mental development' in such a way that the sort of retardation presumably inflicted upon it by bilingualism might be tested, and there is no palpable evidence whatever that such retardation exists. If bilingualism does affect the development of perceptual abilities, for example, then one might conceivably expect it to produce greater sensitivity to environmental changes and to different viewpoints because of the experience of dealing with two linguistic systems instead of one.

14.4. It is generally to be expected that the exigencies of the environment will determine which language is predominantly used by the bilingual speaker. However, Weinreich notes (pp. 73-74) that two main factors influence bilinguals' language behavior irrespective of the speech situation. These are the speaker's aptitude, and his switching facility.

For bilinguals who have learned their two languages consecutively with a wide separation in time between the two, ability to learn a foreign language will be an important factor in determining language performance in both the first and the second languages. To a speaker bilingual from early childhood, neither language is foreign, and a different type of ability must be involved. Some linguists feel that early bilingualism is a handicap in the learning of yet a third language, while others feel that it is beneficial. However, since language learning in the child is qualitatively different from language learning in the adult, regardless of the number of languages involved at either time, childhood bilingualism will have no consistent effect on later ability to learn languages, although the nature of the particular languages in a given instance may produce more or less interference. It does not appear, in other words, that basic language-acquisition aptitude is affected by the number of languages learned at any particular time, although there is rather a lack of data on this point. A reliable means of testing language aptitude is still a strong desideratum within linguistics (but cf. Lado, 1961).

Switching ability, as the name implies, refers to the bilingual's facility at changing from one language to the other when appropriate (cf. e.g. Lambert and Preston, 1967). This should exclude switching back and forth when inappropriate, as for example in the middle of an utterance. The latter form of switching occurs commonly, however; a bilingual speaking language A who cannot think of a correct word and inserts its equivalent in B may find himself continuing the conversation in B without being aware that he is doing so. This may be due to environmental circumstances (such as the conviction that the hearer understands both languages), to learning context, or perhaps to a combination of these and innate factors. It is further the case that the bilingual may not always know either what language he is speaking or in what language he has been addressed, although practiced speakers of two or more languages often become conditioned to responding in the language in which they are addressed without conscious effort. A proficient multilingual who must deal with speakers of many languages (e.g. at the United Nations) may classify them by the group of utterances proper to use with them without labeling each by language – that is, his reaction to meeting an acquaintance may be the equivalent of, 'That is the person to whom I say *Jó napot*', rather than 'That is the person to whom I speak Hungarian'. This is a question of orientation rather than of speaking ability. The same situation may prevail in regard to reading and writing, so that it is possible to begin reading a text, for instance, without noticing for a few seconds in what language it is written.

On the other hand, there are bilinguals who cannot switch back and forth between languages save with the greatest difficulty, if at all. The proficient multilingual may frequently be this sort of speaker, since the ability to learn a large number of languages may be necessarily concomitant to the ability to keep them all separated and not confuse them or even connect them to any extent. Note that the oral interpreter must however keep both his languages clearly in mind at all times; this skill may effectively prevent him from mastering more than two or three languages since he might tend to confuse a larger number.

14.5. As was mentioned previously, in most bilingual situations the speaker is more fluent and at ease in one of his languages, and shows less interference in this language, so that it may be termed dominant. One of the factors instrumental in determining which of the bilingual's languages will be dominant is his relative proficiency in the two; he is likely to use with more confidence the language he speaks better, and far less likely to show interference from his other language to the one in which he is more fluent. It is in turn useful to inquire why the bilingual should be more proficient in one language than in the other. Often this comes about because he learned the dominant language first and spoke it all his life, adding the second only later. Most speakers do not show interference from their second to their first language. If both were learned in childhood, then relative proficiency, if marked, is the result of factors such as emotional attachment, relative social importance and so on; since all languages are learned by the child with about the same degree of ease, learning difficulties in childhood are rarely responsible for lack of fluency. Of course the bilingual may have had less childhood opportunity to acquire one of his languages.

In regard to a second criterion of dominance, Weinreich notes that "the visual reinforcement in the use of a language that a bilingual gets by reading and writing it may put that language in a dominant position over a purely oral one" (p. 75 f.). If the bilingual is literate in only one of his languages, he will *ceteris paribus* make this the dominant language. Visual skills are relevant to all language learning, including formally presented secondary bilingualism, contrary to the thesis of some applied linguistic methods that reading and writing should be learned much later than speaking (cf. Rivers, 1964, pp. 99 ff.). Bearing on this topic is the fact that material presented in multiple input modes (i.e., visual, auditory, tactile etc.) is generally retained better than that presented in only one.

Order of learning is a third factor in determination of language dominance, and it is often the most important factor. Weinreich states that "the distinction of having been learned first is so great that the first-learned language, the 'mother-tongue', is generally considered dominant by definition". This is especially true in the initial stages of bilingualism, although some bilinguals may acquire great proficiency in a second language to the extent of losing some of their ability in their first.

Weinreich states also that there is a certain emotional involvement with the mother tongue which is rarely if ever transferred to the second language. In those few cases of bilingual aphasia on record, often the mother tongue was recovered first, and this is usually said to be at least partly due to the greater emotional attachment to it (cf. Lambert and Fillenbaum, 1961, on bilingual aphasia). One would need extensive information on such cases – difference in time between learning of the two languages, relative proficiency, extent and localization of injury – in order to explain the reported results. Note that even when the two languages are learned concurrently in childhood, one frequently becomes established as primary very early, so that greater attachment to it may be built.

There are a number of additional factors mentioned by Weinreich as determinants of dominance in the bilingual situation; some of these are usefulness in communication, function in social advance, literary value. Clearly, the more a bilingual is required to use one of his languages, the more prominent it will become; likewise if one of his languages is rarely used, or is used only with groups of low status or prestige to him, then its use and prominence will decline. The children of bilinguals are often resistant to learning the native language of their parents once they have immigrated. This situation can be observed among immigrants to America; the attitude is reasonable from the point of view of the children, since they cannot use the language to their American friends, they are not understood if they attempt to speak it to strangers, and they are instructed not to use it in school. This has even been known to influence the parents to cease using the language at home when they discover how strongly their children are opposed to it. Native bilingual speakers may share the problem. American Indians, bilingual in their own language and English, tend not to use the Indian language in towns in which they are discriminated against for being Indians, which severely limits its use overall. Since the Indian languages have low prestige, relatively speaking, many Indian children refuse to learn them or at least to display speaking knowledge of them, a circumstance which causes great friction within Indian families.

Weinreich notes too that environmental factors influence how a bilingual speaker will use his two languages. For example, in speaking to a monolingual, the bilingual often makes an effort to limit his interlingual interference and borrowings between languages. This is called interlocutory constraint. When speaking to someone who handles both of his languages, the result is often an interlingual mixture comprehensible to the parties to the discussion but to no one else. A further influence upon language behavior is called by Weinreich the "departure from specialized uses of a language". For instance, a child learning both languages in his home environment may be able to discuss everyday matters in both; but if he studies certain subjects in a monolingual school he may have difficulty in transferring his knowledge from this language to the other, due partly to lack of specialized lexicon. Some bilinguals are accustomed to using only one language to a given person or category of persons and thus find it difficult to speak the other language to them. This phenomenon seems quite pervasive, and may account for the tendency of speakers of certain languages to reply in (albeit broken) English when addressed in non-native versions of their own language, a tendency which often causes misunderstandings and ill will. It is not necessary that both languages be native for this lack of transfer to occur; advanced students of foreign languages who study specialized subjects taught in the language they are studying (e.g., Germanic linguistics taught in German) may have difficulty communicating about these subjects in their native language.

The final determinant of language use noted by Weinreich is emotional stress. A person under great emotional stress may tend to revert to his mother tongue even if he has not spoken it in many years. So during nightmares, bilinguals may cry out in their first language and may thus become involved in a variety of unpleasant situations. The propensity of bilinguals to use their native language when under stress was especially useful to intelligence operations during the last World War. Thus agents often trapped spies into using their mother tongue by this fact, a technique which sounds somewhat simpler than it actually is. An interesting account of such an occurrence is given by Oreste Pinto, in writing of his work in British Intelligence during the war (Pinto, 1952). He details his attempts to coerce a German spy posing as a Belgian into revealing his knowledge of German (which under his cover story he could not possibly have had).

Pinto, morally certain that the man was in fact a spy, tried directing him to count quickly, which he did in French; shouting *"Feuer!"* at him to see if he would panic, which he did not do, and so forth. Finally, in a sort of desperation, Pinto called the man in and said to him without warning, *"So, jetzt bin ich zufrieden. Sie können gehen. Sie sind frei."* The spy's obvious and involuntary signs of relief at being freed demonstrated his knowledge of German, and led to his execution. It is very likely that there are neurological as well as psychological factors involved in determination of dominance and perhaps in use of one of the two languages in times of stress as well, although there are as yet insufficient data to demonstrate this.

15

BILINGUALISM: BILINGUALISM AND THE
FOREIGN LANGUAGE CLASS

15.1. Much of the data collected from study of the primary bilingual situation is also relevant to problems of secondary bilingualism, or bilingualism brought about by formal study (generally in adulthood) of a foreign language. The goal of modern foreign language teaching is to create within a limited time competence in a foreign language approaching that of the native language, or in other words proficient coordinate bilingualism. In the past, various other goals of foreign language teaching have been thought important, chief among these being the imparting of so-called reading knowledge in the target language; however, both the current Audio-Lingual Method and the older Direct Method of language teaching concentrate on speaking and understanding almost to the exclusion of literary skills during the early stages of instruction. Since the topic of applied linguistic theory and methodology is open to discussion from a wide variety of viewpoints, the treatment here will concentrate on two main aspects of it, namely, whether it is in fact feasible to try to create true bilingualism in the classroom, and what special problems are faced by the student who must learn two or more foreign languages through formal study.

In order to ascertain whether it is in fact possible to learn a foreign language in school in such a way that one may be considered bilingual in it and the native language, it must clearly first be decided what are the various characteristics of bilingualism and how these may be tested for or measured in the classroom. No one single standard of proficiency rating in language aptitude or achievement has yet been developed; individual proficiency goals are generally set by language teachers, so that a certification of knowledge of a language may indicate a variety of different ability levels. A widely employed language achievement rating is that developed by the Foreign Service Institute, whereby the speaker is classified on a scale ranging from S1 to S5 according to the topics he, can discuss fluently in the language. The lowest level indicates minimal competence; the highest. native-speaker competence. However, even under this system the tests are not standardized but are based mainly on the discretion of the tester.

It is likewise difficult to measure proficiency in the usual classroom situation. In foreign language classes, it is possible to specify at the outset of the course precisely what should be the terminal behavior of the students; alternatively one may define the objectives less precisely (e.g., by stating that the students are expected to 'know French' by the end of the course) or even not at all, preferring merely to teach as much as possible of the language in the allotted time. The specification of terminal behavior in foreign language teaching is a relatively modern development, instituted by proponents of the Audio-Lingual Method (cf. Rivers, 1968, pp. 44 ff.). Under the ALM precise statement of goals is standard procedure; such statement is based on the material to be presented to the students, and may appear in such forms as,

The students by the end of the course are expected to have learned the 250 dialogues in the lessons, and to be able to carry on a conversation with a native speaker on the following topics (list) with the vocabulary they have learned and following the syntactic patterns demonstrated in the dialogues.

The main reason for such precise specification of goals is that if no statement of this sort is prepared at the beginning, there is in effect no way of judging whether the students have succeeded in learning what they should have learned. Knowledge of the language, or ability to speak the language, are so vague as course goals that practically any level of attained proficiency might be said to fulfill them. When terminal behavior consists in having learned a specific set of data, it becomes no problem to determine whether students have met this terminal behavior goal. But it is necessary to have a clear concept of how the fixed terminal behavior relates to one's notions of bilingualism, especially bearing in mind that true bilinguals are rarely equally proficient in both languages, that fluency in the native language varies considerably, and that it is probably not possible to impart adult competence in a language in the brief time available to schools and training programs.

It might be well to inquire, for example, whether true bilingualism is approached by the memorization of a set of dialogues and the ability to use some vocabulary within the syntactic limits set by these dialogues. If it is accepted that, as Chomsky states, "every speaker of a language has mastered and internalized a generative grammar that expresses his knowledge of his language" (Chomsky, 1965, p. 8), then one must seek to determine whether in fact the input data specified by the ALM and other modern language-teaching techniques is sufficient and/or necessary to the creation of such a grammar. Since the ALM is based on the assumption that language is a form of habit (cf. e.g., Lado, 1964, pp. 44-45; Rivers, 1968, pp. 76-78), an assumption that has been shown to be largely untenable (cf. for example, Chomsky, 1966), it is not at all certain that ALM techniques are suited to creation of the type of linguistic competence demonstrated by actual bilingual speakers.

Another way of specifying the goals of foreign-language instruction is to state that the students should eventually be able to think in the target language, instead of having to translate from the native language to the foreign for production and vice versa for understanding. There are methods for testing whether the student seems to be thus translating or whether he can manage without doing so. One way of determining whether the student can think in the given language is to ask him, as Scherer and Wertheimer have stated (1964, p. 155); other ways are to engage him in rapid conversations in the language, call him suddenly in the language and see whether he responds in it automatically, compare his hesitation phenomena in the native vs. the foreign language, induce him to talk in the language on topics for which he does not have the requisite lexicon, to see whether he can extemporize as he could in his native language, and the like. There is of course no objective determination of how to interpret the results of these and similar methods, but they are suitable to ad hoc testing for such purposes as the administration of grades or certificates of competence.

15.2.   An alternative means of approaching the subject of bilingualism and second-language learning is to consider the neurophysiological correlates of such learning, insofar as they are known or projected. It has been noted previously that the completion of cortical lateralization (around the age of eleven to fourteen) is approximately coterminus with the ability to learn a native language. This is a physical process, standard across the species, not affected by such environmental conditions as what language is being learned. Perhaps the major implication of this theory for applied linguistics is that language learning in the adult (i.e., the post-pubertal individual) is qualitatively different from language learning in the child. If the adult is unable to acquire a native language after the age of eleven or so, then it would seem to follow that the type of learning process with which he treats a foreign language must be different after this age also.

For the child, there are no foreign languages; that is, the child will learn any language in whose environmental he is placed, and will learn it as a 'native language'. Indeed children cannot help doing this. However the child goes about learning his first language, he follows the same procedure with other languages learned during childhood as well. It is presumed that after the age of eleven or so the brain becomes functionally as well as structurally changed in such a way that it cannot process linguistic input automatically as it previously could. This may well mean that the adult learns a foreign language with a different portion of his brain (i.e., area, pathways or other sets of neural structures) than that with which he learned his native language. The adult does not ordinarily learn a foreign language at all; the language is usually fed in and stored as a collection of learned data, somewhat on the order of multiplication tables or a list of Kings of England, put through completely different pathways than are used for the native language. One might propose to define true language behavior as specifically left-hemispherical (or right-, where this is the dominant hemisphere); right-hemisphere or perhaps non-native-language-pathway language behavior is not language behavior at all in the same sense, but merely a form of higher-level cognitive functioning commonly employed for most other forms of learning as well. Thus when an adult student says that he cannot think in a foreign language, his remark might be interpreted to mean that he is not handling it as a language; he is actually not thinking in it but merely about it, using his native language to classify concepts in it.

One might additionally comment that the terminology of compound vs. coordinate bilingualism is directly opposed to the physiological situation. A speaker with so-called coordinate bilingualism can handle his languages equally well, and is equally at home in either (note that this is not especially a function of the quantities of each language known by the speaker). He can in other words think in either. This indicates that both his languages are of native-like status to him, that both are controlled by the same neural area or pathways. To the compound or mixed bilingual, on the other hand, only one language, his first, is a genuine language; he thinks in his first language about his second, or treats his second language as ordinary learned data. He is not using the same neural equipment to handle the second language as the first. Thus the conventional coordinate bilingual actually might be said to have a neurophysiologically compound system, whereas the conventional mixed or compound bilingual would have a neurophysiologically coordinate or separated system.

Although the exact facts of cortical lateralization and its influence on language acquisition are not yet known, nevertheless the existence of this developmental process is apparently a kind of in-species constant, which persists whether or not it is taken into account in the creation of language teaching techniques.

Without discussing at length the implications of this theory for foreign language teaching, one might mention merely that despite the change in learning potential, it is clear that adults can in fact learn foreign languages, on occasion so well that they become able to think and otherwise function easily in them. The situations vary considerably, but typically this occurs when an adult has been living in the country where the language is spoken and using it constantly for a number of years. Presumably what takes place in such cases is that the foreign language acquires native-language status, which may mean that its control has somehow become allocated to the native-language neural pathways. This is approximately the situation which one might wish to effect in the classroom, in a briefer time period. It probably cannot be done by attempting to differentiate the foreign language from the native by contrastive techniques; students will learn to regard the foreign language as so much nonlinguistic data anyway, if left to their own devices, and contrastive techniques according to the present theory do not seem designed to correct this tendency. One way to prompt the student to handle the foreign language on the same level as the native is to expand the boundaries of the native language, as it were, and add a group of new elements to it, rather than trying to impart a new language system intact. This is done essentially by forming a controlled *mélange* of the two languages, for which purpose a technique is currently being developed by the present writer.

15.3. An interesting and little-studied facet of secondary bilingualism is the circumstance of the student who must study more than one foreign language during adulthood. In academic circles this situation is rather common, since most students must have at least reading knowledge of two languages in order to pursue work toward graduate degrees and a large number must in addition attain speaking competence in two or more languages.

For the adult students of two or more foreign languages, problems of interlingual interference are greatly complicated. The speaker of language L learning a foreign language, A, already has the problem of L-A interference; but students who have mastered the first foreign language then have the added difficulty of A-B interference, which can not only prevent them from acquiring any degree of skill in B but also impair their knowledge of A. Difficulties are apparently worsened where A and B are closely related. The types of interference between A and B are often somewhat different from interference occurring between the primary bilingual's first and second languages. Confusion between A and B is more frequently lexical than is confusion between the native language and either of the two foreign ones. This seems to be because the native language is compartmentalized separately insofar as lexicon is concerned; L-A or L-B interference is most likely to be phonological. The latter form of interference is the most persistent type; insofar as the learner transfers grammatical patterns from his native language to one of the foreign languages, he is likely to be susceptible to correction and not to make the mistake again. It is not certain what causes this greater plasticity on the syntactic level: perhaps grammar is paid closer attention than phonology; perhaps phonology is more a habit below the conscious level than is syntax; perhaps the closer a category is to the bottom or read-out line of an internalized generative schema of language, the less vulnerable it is to alteration.

In the acquisition of two foreign languages after the native language has been mastered, two courses may be followed: the languages may be studied consecutively, or else they may be studied concurrently. Where the latter course is followed, great obstacles are presented to the student, especially if he is not particularly high in language aptitude. Such study often entails several hours of work in each language per day. It is not justifiable to expect the average learner to be able to switch back and forth between languages, since this is a specialized ability often incommensurable with the learning of several languages. Moreover language textbooks are often constructed along similar lines, so that the lesson plans and particularly the lexicon in the two languages are often just dissimilar enough to form a kind of interlocking web for the student, so that he will not always remember to which language each set of words or patterns belongs.

Little can be done to aid such a student within the ordinary language classroom, in which it is scarcely possible for the teacher to take time to discover whether any of the students are studying other languages and what difficulties this may be causing them. A possible solution, advanced on the theoretical level, is teaching both languages together in a coordinated program utilizing a double class period of about two hours a day, divided into thirds. The first third of this time might be devoted to instruction in language A; the second, to comparison between A and B relative to the specific points covered in the day's lesson; the third, to instruction in B. It is presumed that the material in A and B will be not identical but rather comprised of approximately the same material, with similar lexicons and with the occurrence of cognates in related languages emphasized instead of ignored. A major advantage of the method is that it presents a controlled learning situation; the parallels between languages A and B can be overtly presented, so that instead of realizing that such parallels exist, trying unsuccessfully to ignore them and thereby thinking consciously about them to the detriment of learning, the student may be able to see the parallels as well as the divergences in their proper perspective as part of the language *in toto*.

The student who must learn two languages consecutively has a rather different set of problems from those of the student learning them concurrently, since the former already has a background of language study to help or hinder him as the case may be. In order to teach this student a third language, an approach is required which concentrates on imparting proficiency in language B while not ignoring his knowledge of language A, and which in fact should ideally utilize his learning set without permitting him to feel that the patterns he has seen in A are those of all foreign languages in general, a not uncommon attitude among students who have learned one foreign language. Perhaps the best method might be one which would permit the student to strengthen his knowledge of language A while learning B. A technique which seems to meet these requirements is the teaching of the second foreign language using the first as a base, with all texts, lectures, explanatory material, lexicon translations and so forth in language A instead of in the students' native language. So for example a student who has studied French for three or four years and wishes to learn Spanish would take a course in Spanish using a standard French teaching grammar of the Spanish language, with a teacher who speaks only French when not speaking Spanish. Any spot translations found necessary would be from Spanish to French rather than Spanish to English.

One justification for such a proposal is that the student should in the main not be troubled by A-B interference by this method, since he will not need to attempt to repress A patterns when studying B. Instead, he will have the A equivalents of B words presented to him. He need not, for example, attempt to correct the habit of thinking of the word *homme* when he sees the Spanish *hombre*, since *hombre* will be presented as meaning *homme* instead of as meaning 'man'. Additionally, the student should not need to forget his knowledge of A or to confuse A patterns with those of B. The parallels and skews between A and B will be shown in the most graphic manner possible, and thus the student will be able to learn B without either having to suppress A or to lose his proficiency in it.

It has been noted that the goal of much language instruction is to induce students to form a series of linguistically coordinate systems of their foreign and native languages, so that each language learned would be a system in itself independent of other foreign languages controlled by the speaker and of his native language as well. The natural procedure for students in such a situation is to form a series of compound systems L-A, L-B and so on, with each foreign language referring to the native language. The associative schema provided by this technique, however, should prove more efficient in the long run. This is because the student who has learned one foreign language presumably has formed a compound system between it and the native language; but if his next system is formed between foreign languages A and B instead of B and the native language, then he will in effect have learned to operate entirely in foreign languages, a new form of behavior for him. Note that the goal of foreign language instruction might be phrased as the attempt to teach students foreign language behavior, rather than foreign language *per se*, since it might be hypothetically desirable for students to learn as many new forms of behavior as possible in order to be more adaptable to environmental changes whereas the requisite two years of foreign language instruction in most schools probably adds little to their knowledge, abilities or general perspective. It is at any rate postulated that the presently proposed schema may eventually lead to the student's being able to think in language B without associating the latter with either A or L. In addition, the necessity of absorbing explanations and other such material in foreign language A will probably strengthen his knowledge of this language as well, so that it will take on the aspect of a genuine means by which to deal directly with reality. By forcing the student to work with foreign language A as though it were his native language, it is expected that he have the same orientation toward it as he has toward his native language, which may affect his entire set of attitudes toward languages. A final advantage of this method is that the student who lacks confidence in his language-learning ability may be reassured by the realization that he has after all been able to learn one language, namely A, well enough to use it for learning a second. This may provide a continuous reinforcement for his language-learning behavior.

It is justifiable to inquire whether the student will in fact be able to learn a third language in this fashion. If the student has been taught his first foreign language in such a manner that he has acquired the habit of mental A-L translation, then he may at first have great difficulty working directly from B to A, and may try to translate both languages to his native language prior to comprehension and instead of using either as a unit in itself. But it appears that the ability to associate one of the foreign languages with the other develops with necessity, in much the same manner as one becomes accustomed to seeing correctly through lenses which invert the image. Of course, in some cases it may

be easier to relate B to A simply because of objective relationships, as is the case with an American student learning Italian
and Spanish or German and Russian. At any rate, if no L is ever
spoken in class, the student's A-L channels will begin to be in
conflict with his new A-B ones and thus will probably be eliminated through necessity. It is likely that the student in such a
class may become a true bilingual in some sense.

16

EXTRALINGUISTIC FEATURES OF
COMMUNICATION

16.1. It is necessary for discussions of how humans communicate to go beyond the bounds of the utterance, as did Skinner in his attempts to analyze the speech episode rather than the single verbal response. This is because much human communication must be considered nonlinguistic in both structure and function. Mahl and Schulze state (1964, pp. 51-52) that

> when an individual speaks he engages in a special class of behavior – linguistic behavior. The immediate purpose of this behavior is to communicate with another individual, to interact by means of messages. From the strictly linguistic standpoint, speaking behavior is determined by two things: (1) the code itself and (2) the intention to communicate a particular message in that code. These linguistic factors, however, do not fully determine the behavior of the speaker. One important qualification is that the code does not completely mold or restrict the content of the behavior. There may be variations both within the linguistic behavior itself and in accompanying non-institutionalized behavior. . . . Another important qualification to the strictly linguistic determination of speaking behavior is that, beyond the immediate communicative intention, other psychological states or processes are simultaneously operative. Of necessity, or adventitiously, or both, they enter into the determination of *both* linguistic and nonlinguistic behavior.

The type of phenomenon of which these authors write is frequently termed extralinguistic, since its explanation does not derive from analysis either of the linguistic code features or of message features. When considering extralinguistic features of communication, it is useful to think of language not as dichotomized into code and message but rather as tripartite in some sense, as indeed some psychologists have sought to do. For example,

Morris (1938) interpreted communication as divisible into study of the relationship of sign to sign, called syntactics; of sign to thing, called semantics; and of sign to elicited behavior, called pragmatics. One might alternatively wish to speak of the divisions of language as code, message and medium (from most to least concrete respectively), whereby code subsumes structure features, message is concerned with that which is communicated by the code (roughly semantics), and medium refers not only to modality of communication (i.e., oral, written, etc.), but also to all communication in the communication situation or episode not expressable by code or message rules. The study of extralinguistic phenomena is equivalent to the study of medium features of communication. Note in addition that the usual transformational grammar model has a syntactic, a phonological, and a semantic component. This terminology is somewhat differently employed than the above, since both the syntactic and the phonological components of the transformational grammar pertain to the realm of syntactics. It is in fact necessary that a generative grammar have a syntactic or code component (including phonology, both segmental and suprasegmental), a semantic or message component, and also a pragmatic or, more generally, a medium component. The latter is possible, assuming only that one accept interpretation and production of medium features to be replicable, or statable in formal terms. In this regard it is clear that, insofar as interpretation of medium features is consistent, it is replicable and therefore can be formally described. Insofar as interpretation of medium features cannot be replicated, it is inconsistent and therefore not within the province of the communication system. Much the same thing could be said of the interpretation of syntactic and semantic output. This is not meant to imply, of course, that inconsistent interpretation resulting from what might be termed structural ambiguities of medium features cannot be explained by the grammar, since this would render the grammar inadequate.

16.2. The main topics in extralinguistic research are frequently cited as paralinguistics and kinesics, although the field comprises a number of other studies as well. Paralinguistics is basically concerned with the relationship between the medium and the code of language. It is the study of such features as ratio of specific grammatical categories to the total lexicon, rate of speech, duration of utterances, hesitation phenomena, voice quality and rhythm and the like. Kinesics is the study of gestures and other bodily movements and attitudes which enter into the communication process.

In general, extralinguistic studies are directed toward those features of language not under the deliberate or conscious control of the speaker. Since the speaker does communicate unintentionally by his gestures, tone of voice and so forth, the listener can often infer certain conclusions about the speaker's values, concepts, state of health, mood and the like which might not have been revealed in consciously motivated or directed speech. There are idiolectal extralinguistic phenomena (and probably dialectal as well), and there are further sets of extralinguistic phenomena common to entire cultures or language groups. Although lack of comprehension of the latter group especially can cause serious misunderstandings of an entire communication situation, often with grave international consequences (example: American misunderstanding of the Khrushchev shoe-banging incident at the UN), these phenomena have been but sparsely studied. One reason for this is that extralinguistic activity seems to operate on a continuum, or to be basically analog rather than digital, so that it is difficult to find an adequate unit of analysis. This difficulty can be overcome, however – as indeed it must be in order to construct a medium component for a formal grammar – in a number of ways. It seems tentatively that a promising approach might be to follow the procedure suggested by Katz and Fodor (1963) in reference to semantic theory, namely setting up markers and distinguishers[1] to represent pragmatic 'entries'. An alternative

---

[1]   As Katz and Fodor state, "The semantic markers and distinguishers are the means by which we can decompose the meaning of one sense of a lexical item into its atomic concepts, and thus exhibit the semantic structure *in* a dictionary entry and the semantic relations *between* dictionary entries."

would be to create a theory of substantive medium universals (cf. Chomsky, 1965, p. 28; cf. also Chapter 17 of the present work), in which case it would presumably be possible to represent medium features in the grammar as types throughout the grammar (whatever the language in question) and as tokens in the final read-out or terminal string only[2] (cf. Herdan, 1960, pp. 14-17, for definitions of these terms).

16.3.   As Mahl and Schulze state (1964, p. 53), two main methods of analysis have been employed with reference to extralinguistic phenomena of speech. These methods may be termed behavioral and paralinguistic:

Those investigators who use Behavioral methods are less concerned with interpreting every instance of the phenomena they are studying; they tend to focus on a few specific phenomena; and they usually employ statistical tests to evaluate relations between certain theoretically-suggested assemblages of extralinguistic phenomena and other behavioral phenomena. Those investigators who use Paralinguistic methods of analysis usually are more concerned with individual – that is, discretely identified – instances of certain features of utterances,

---

Markers may be such items as 'Male' or 'Female', 'Animal' or 'Human', 'Young', 'Liquid', 'Dependent' (cf. Bolinger, 1965) and the like. Bolinger states that the distinguisher is "the idiosyncratic remainder of a given sense when all the markers have been stripped away".

On the general subject of the code/message/medium distinction, one might note that this trichotomy is useful in a variety of technical and non-technical situation. An example of the latter is the judging of formal speeches, for instance in oratory contests such as the Kirk. Such speeches must be judged on many usually unclassified criteria such as content, logic (e.g. presence of so-called fallacies of reasoning) and persuasive technique, continuity of presentation, appropriateness of topic for occasion and of style for topic, literary quality and erudition, syntactic construction, avoidance of repetition and of endless enumeration, and so forth. It is helpful in such a situation to judge the speech separately on code features (syntax, whether correct or anomalous; balance of constructions; etc.), message features (appropriateness of ideas conveyed to the intend of the speech; logical construction; rationality, etc.), and medium features (fluency; appropriate rate of speech; voice modulation; appropriate gesture; frequency of hesitations and other nonfluencies, etc.).

[2] In general, 'type' can be interpreted as an emic unit, and 'token', as an etic unit.

including deviations from characteristic patterns. Usually an exhaustive analysis is made, in which scorers attempt to identify *all* instances of *all* phenomena included in the entire classification system of Paralanguage.

Mahl and Schulze present, in outline form, the topics comprising extralinguistic study of the two types described above, as follows (p. 54):

I. Behavioral Methods of Analysis
    A. Language style
        1. Verb/adjective ratios
        2. Parts of speech
        3. Verb tense
        4. Other
    B. Vocabulary Selection and Diversity
        1. Type-Token Ratio
        2. Rank-frequency
        3. Other
    C. Pronunciation and dialect
    D. Voice Dynamics
        1. Voice quality and rhetorical features
        2. Rhythm
        3. Continuity
            a. Silent pauses
            b. Non-fluencies
            c. Intrusions, including speech mannerisms
        4. Speech Rate
        5. Other temporal phenomena
            a. Duration of utterances
            b. Interaction rates
            c. Latency
        6. Verbal output, productivity
II. Paralinguistic Methods of Analysis
        1. Voice qualities
        2. Vocalizations

Both language style and vocabulary selection and diversity are often considered the provinces of stylistics or text analysis. Language style includes the ratio of verbs to adjectives, nouns to adjectives, etc. in a language sample, relative frequencies of various verb tenses, and so on. These factors apparently tend to be constant throughout the speech and especially the writing of an individual, so that in some cases authorship may be determined by use of these and similar statistical measures. Also, these as well as most other paralinguistic phenomena have frequently been studied in the context of psychological and psychiatric interviews, to determine whether they tend to correlate with particular attitudes or emotional states of the speaker – for example, it has been hypothesized that a high ratio of verbs to adjectives in speech connotes forceful and dramatic imagery, perhaps expressive of anxiety or tension. Paralinguistic measures often correlate with nonlinguistic measures of anxiety.

According to Mahl and Schulze, type-token ratio, the first category under vocabulary selection in the outline above, refers to the ratio of different words or types in a sample to the total number of all words or tokens within the sample, or, in other words, variety in lexicon. Rank-frequency curves are measures of the frequency of occurrence of each word in the sample. These items typically are tested in interview settings, with the subjects either engaged in natural conversation or else speaking on specified topics (e.g. associating to a set of diagnostic drawings or pictures). Since anxiety is considered to inhibit the variability of behavior (Mahl and Schulze, 1964, p. 82), it has been predicted and experimentally demonstrated that the type-token ratio should be low in cases of emotional disturbance or nervousness; the more nervous or anxious the subject, the more he is inclined to repeat rather than to innovate lexically. This may well be true on the syntactic level as well; it would be worthwhile to investigate, for example, the number and complexity of transformations per unit of speech in normal as contrasted with disturbed conversation.

Variations in language usage by polyglots are included in the category of pronunciation and dialect. It is not surprising to find that studies in this area have indicated that the multilingual or -dialectal speaker tends to use the variation of language with which he feels most comfortable and secure at the time (cf. Chapter 14 of this work). This is presumably the case with both bilinguals and bidialectals, if such exist (cf. Houston, 1969). Choice of language or dialect is said to be influenced by the speaker's desire to avoid anxiety and find the 'good', socially acceptable or least marked form of speech within a given environment. It is actually rather an overextension of the concept of paralinguistics to include the specific language being used; perhaps use of an inappropriate language might constitute an extralinguistic communication in itself, but it is difficult to see how use of appropriate language would do so.

Pitch and stress changes are characteristic of voice dynamics; more significant and more interesting, however, are the various types of pause, hesitation and nonfluency behavior (cf. Goldman-Eisler, 1961; 1968). There are two main categories of speech interruption, namely silent pauses and filled pauses. The silent pauses are otherwise called hesitation phenomena. In order to be classed as extralinguistic, they must of course be medium rather than code phenomena; there are pauses in the linguistic code, namely junctures, which are a part of syntactics and are generated as such. There are a number of criteria for determining whether a brief silence is a code pause or a medium pause, for example preceding and following pitch, position of occurrence in the sentence and so forth.

Mahl explains the occurrence of hesitation pauses as follows:

Theoretically, silence (and perhaps speech disturbance) may be regarded as a defense motivated by anxiety invoked by ideational events or by the nature of the interpersonal relation. Speech disturbances and short hesitations may also be conceived as predominantly indirect linguistic consequences of anxiety that do not have the instrumental function of reducing anxiety. This notion is based on the assumption that one effect of anxiety, regardless of its source, is to disrupt *all* ongoing behavior, irrespective of its behavioral relation to the source of the anxiety (p. 85).

For a speaker to hesitate, it is not necessary that he be upset or anxious concerning the subject of his discourse. Mahl states that nonfluencies "do not have the instrumental function of reducing anxiety"; they may on the contrary tend to increase anxiety by adding speech-fright and embarrassment to the speaker's concerns. There are several varieties of filled pause. Some of these are 'Ah-pauses', sentence change or anacoluthon, repetitions, stuttering, omission, sentence incompletion, slips of the tongue, and intruding incoherent sounds, according to the authors. Two main categories, namely Ah and non-Ah pauses, may conveniently be proposed, since they seem to vary separately within most parameters and to be influenced by different factors. For example, experimental interviews featuring controlled stress on the interviewee tend to produce a higher non-Ah ratio but not a higher Ah ratio. Perhaps more than most other extralinguistic portions of the speech stream, the filled pause is likely to relate to anxiety or disturbed emotional state. However, such nonfluencies may also be constant idiolectal features of a speaker rather than manifestations of situational anxiety. This is frequently the case with speech mannerisms, for instance repetition of a phrase such as 'you know', 'or the like', 'see', 'I don't know', or similar formulas. The speaker is apparently rarely conscious of repeating these phrases, which serve only to allow him to think of the next thing he wishes to say. They are more distracting to the listener than are 'Ah's' and can in fact draw attention completely away from the message being communicated. Such speech mannerisms may also increase numerically with anxiety.

Although speakers of English tend to think of filled pauses as being of the 'uh' or 'umm' type, there actually many different ways of filling a pause; perhaps 'ah' is most common among speakers of English. The filler for this sort of pause is not a natural or innate reaction to anxiety, any more than the exclamation /áwč/ is a natural reaction to mild pain, but rather is language-bound. Speakers of different languages may have markedly different hesitation phenomena; there is, for example, apparently a Russian-Polish hesitation pause which sounds like [mm nyə:], at least an idiolect feature of several Slavic speakers. This is striking to the English speaker because it has two syllables, which English hesitation phenomena almost never do. Japanese also has a standard two-syllable hesitation pause, namely [ánoo] with falling pitch on the final syllable. This does not have the exact status of the English 'mm . . .', however; it is basically an intonation contour with superimposed phonation, and the contour can and frequently does appear in conjunction with lengthening of the final vowel of the preceding word with or without a brief pause, minus the segmental phones. This particular pause has quasi-morphemic status as a paralinguistic unit, functioning somewhat in the manner of the American significant clearing of the throat to indicate disbelief, puzzlement, stunned surprise or mild or strong disapproval; used in this form the utterance is /ánoo née/ with variable intonation depending on the meaning to be expressed. It does not typically occur sentence-initial, as the English 'uh . . .' may followed by a pause while the speaker considers the situation, somewhat as a student called on in class may have an initial 'Well . . .' presumably because he feels the necessity to begin talking instantly even though he may not have formulated his utterance yet. Japanese does have other units more commonly used in this latter function; a frequent one is /sore karaa/, which is also a legitimate lexical item.

Speech rate, articulation rate and similar factors interact to a great extent with those phenomena already discussed, notably pauses. Variations in speech rate are largely determined by variation in duration or frequency of pauses. There is some evidence that speech is normally filled with a great many micropauses, which can be edited out to produce a kind of compressed speech many times faster than normal; speech is fully understandable under these conditions (cf. Cherry, 1957, pp. 45-46). Such micropauses are not properly classed as paralinguistic, since they are more or less constant for all speakers within a language group. Speech rate tends to decrease when the speaker is in a state of anxiety, although this may depend on situational and personality factors.

16.4. Whereas the study of paralinguistics is frequently quite molecular in outlook, kinesics and the remaining medium-feature studies are somewhat more molar, partly because it is difficult to quantize such behavior. These topics have most often been examined by sociolinguists or anthropological linguists such as Hall and La Barre. La Barre notes (1964) that cultural kinesics may study such matters as different ways of walking in different cultures; gestural differences such as ways of pointing or indicating contempt and ethnic gestures; cultural attitudes toward time and appointment keeping, and so on. In reference to the study of gesture, for instance, one may inquire into ways of expressing affirmation or negation; nodding in the former case and shaking the head in the latter are not universal. In some place in India, shaking the head is a sign of affirmation; the Arab may express negation by tossing his head quickly back once, and so forth. Gestures of contempt provide a varied field of study as well. La Barre states that the well known Mediterranean *mano cornudo* (first and little fingers of the right hand extended, other fingers and thumb folded) was originally and still may be used to ward off the evil eye, although it has long been a gestural insult and one taken most seriously (implying lack of manhood and the 'horns of the cuckold'). A common Greek gesture of contempt is made by extending the hand palm outward toward the insultee, fingers and thumb widely spread; this is purportedly an ancient insulting gesture dating to the days when wrongdoers were paraded through the streets on donkeys, to be jeered at and have things thrown at them (although this explanation may be folk etymologized).

There are also ethnic differences in gesture. La Barre states that the difference in gesture vocabulary between the Italian and the European ghetto Jew is considerable and can be charted; for example, the Italian's gestures are on the whole more sweeping and made with the whole arm, whereas the Jew's gestures are more confined and tend to be made with the elbow instead of the shoulder as pivot. Although perhaps no significant correlation of such facts with other cultural characteristics can invariably be cited, it is nevertheless worthwhile to gather such data, if only to demonstrate that gestures are not common to all speakers but are rather learned and differ among languages. Lack of knowledge of this point not infrequently creates incorrect attitudes toward para-linguistic behavior of other groups, and serious misunderstandings may result. These matters should certainly be communicated to prospective tourists, for example.

Hall has devoted considerable study to the ways in which time and space can be used to communicate (cf. also Hall, 1967). He notes, for example (1961), that an American asked the time will feel a compulsion to state it exactly (e.g., '8:57'), whereas a Latin American, on the other hand, might well say 'It's nine' if it is actually five after eight, or a quarter to ten, perhaps. American attitudes toward when to arrive for appointments or invitations are also considered by Hall; as he states, Americans, who worry about being on time for things, have differing periods of lateness which may be called 'mumble something' periods, slight apology periods, mildly insulting periods requiring full apology, rude periods and downright insulting periods. Twenty-five minutes past the time of invitation is approximately standard for arrival at an American cocktail party, especially one that has no speci-fied limits; the same lateness at a dinner party would be con-sidered very rude unless there is a drink before dinner, in which case the lateness would presumably only be mildly insulting. On the other hand, twenty-five minutes' lateness for a morning busi-ness appointment is considered almost inexcusably rude. Else-where in the world, values are quite different. According to Hall, in Latin countries forty-five minutes is only the beginning of a reasonable waiting period instead of the very end; someone kept waiting for this period in America would be incoherent with rage. Likewise to an Arab, the distinction between waiting a long time and waiting a very long time is meaningless, since he does not view time in this fashion at all. Nor do other cultures share the American urgency to complete projects; in many countries, things get done when they get done, since the future does not have the same meaning that it has here. Such assertions might be taken as lending support to the Whorfian Hypothesis (cf. Hall, 1961, pp. 128-45).

Space communicates as well as time; the study of proxemics is concerned with speakers' relations to each other in terms of distance. The ordinary American comfortable distance for non-intimate two-person conversation seems to be about 25-30 inches whereas the distance for many foreigners is considerably less (Hall, 1961, pp. 162-64). Hall mentions having seen an American backing down the full length of a corridor in an effort to maintain a comfortable conversational distance from his foreign inter-locutor. He adds that there are specific distances for conversa-tions associated with different tones of voice (e.g., 3-6 inches, whisper; 20-36 inches, soft voice, low volume; 4½-5 feet, full voice, information of nonpersonal matter; and so on); these fig-ures are of course different for other cultures. A great deal more data is needed on this and similar topics since, for example, the American conversational distance is often interpreted as indicat-ing hostility and aloofness; it is especially important that those in the diplomatic and similar services be apprised of the more significant paralinguistic divergences between this and their target culture in order to avoid needless and nearly always irreparable misunderstandings of this sort.

17

LINGUISTIC UNIVERSALS

17.1. Of major importance to any aspect of current language theory is the topic of linguistic universals, features common to all languages. This is chiefly because it is assumed that linguistic universals represent knowledge, or perhaps capacities for the acquisition of knowledge, brought to the language learning situation by the child. They are universal because they constitute characteristics of the human species.

It has been shown in a previous section that the extent of the universal pre-programmed language capacity is not yet certain: some linguists hold that within the Language Acquisition Device or LAD which contains or is isomorphic with linguistic universals, a set of actual grammatical categories exists, so that the child's main linguistic task is to discover which of these categories are represented in the language which he is to learn; others believe that this view credits too much to innate capabilities, and that it is rather the capacity for inducing and working with these categories which is built in and not the categories themselves. Much of the theory of linguistic universals was formulated by Chomsky (e.g., 1965, pp. 27 ff.; 1966, p. 112; 1967, 402 ff.), who seems in general to feel that the innate component of the LAD is quite extensive. Chomsky states, for example, that the basic theory of linguistic universals hypothesizes that

the child approaches the data with the presumption that they are drawn from a language of a certain antecendently well-defined type, his problem being to determine which of the (humanly) possible languages is that of the community in which he is placed. Language learning would be impossible unless this were the case (1965, p. 27).

The most frequently used classification of linguistic universals, likewise developed by Chomsky, divides these features into formal and substantive categories (cf. also Chomsky, 1968, pp. 4-5). He states that "a theory of substantive universals claims that items of a particular kind in any language must be drawn from a fixed class of items" (1965, p. 28), as an example of which he cites Jakobson's theory of distinctive features, which asserts in essence that each output of the phonological component of a generative grammar can be described in terms of a small number of universal phonetic features, irrespective of the particular language concerned. There are also theories of syntactic and semantic substantive universals.

In regard to formal linguistic universals, Chomsky says,

Consider a claim that the grammar of every language meets certain specified formal conditions. The truth of this hypothesis would not in itself imply that any particular rule must appear in all or even in any two grammars. The property of having a grammar meeting a certain abstract condition might be called a *formal* linguistic universal, if shown to be a general property of natural languages (1965, pp. 28-29).

For example, he notes that it has been proposed that the syntactic component of all grammars must contain transformational rules; or that "the phonological component of a grammar consists of a sequence of rules, a subset of which may apply cyclically to successively more dominant constituents of the surface structure (a transformational cycle, in the sense of much recent work on phonology)". This is a different sort of rule from that involved in, e.g., distinctive feature theory: "Substantive universals such as [those cited] concern the vocabulary for the description of language; formal universals involve rather the character of the rules that appear in grammars and the ways in which they can be interconnected."

Both formal and substantive universals are regarded, by Chomsky and others, as part of the general definition of human language (cf. Chomsky, 1968, e.g., pp. 43-44). They are either innate or due to processes such as Hebb's 'psychological maturation'; so that if one accepts that there is a complicated underlying structure common to all languages, then this

... suggests that the structure of the grammar internalized by the learner may be, to a presently quite unexpected degree, a reflection of the general character of his learning capacity rather than the particular course of his experience. It seems not unlikely that the organism brings, as its contribution to acquisition of a particular language, a highly restrictive characterization of a class of generative systems (potential theories) from which the grammar of its language is selected on the basis of the presented linguistic data (Chomsky, 1966, p. 112).

Thus linguistic universals present basic facts not only about languages but, more significantly, about their speakers; and in addition they provide a set of criteria for determining whether a particular non-human communication system can properly be called a language.

17.2.   The search for linguistic universals, both formal and substantive, may be undertaken from a multitude of directions. Historically, more attention has been devoted to collection of substantive linguistic universals (cf. for example Ferguson, 1963; Cowgill, 1963), or the type of feature characterized by Osgood (1963, p. 238) as phenotypic rather than genotypic. Whereas all universals are interesting in that they inform about the contents and capabilities of the LAD (cf. McNeill, 1966, p. 101), the most significant are those which might be considered criterial for language systems in general. Frequently these turn out to be formal rather than substantive. At the most theoretical level, such features form a kind of defining set by which it may be determined whether a given communications system can be called a language at all and whether it can further be called a human-like language to the extent that humans could conceivably either learn it or communicate with its speakers by other means.

The most widely applicable set of defining criteria for language has been developed by Hockett (1960 and 1963), who also has some relevant remarks on the definition of the universal itself (his remarks appear to apply chiefly to substantive universals, it might be noted). He points out, for example (1963), that the assertion of language universals depends on definition, empirical evidence and also extrapolation. It cannot be based on empirical evidence alone, as he states, because complete evidence on all languages past and present does not exist, thus necessitating generalization from the known to the unknown; it likewise cannot be based solely on evidence and extrapolation therefrom, because decisions must always be made whether when a system is found which does not contain the feature in question, one should classify the feature as non-universal or alternatively classify the system as non-linguistic. Hockett states that such decisions are in fact definitions of both what constitutes a universal and what constitutes a language; and notes that widespread or universal features are most apt to be important if they recur against a background of diversity, and if they are not readily diffusable among languages:

Given a taxonomy, if we find that languages of the most diverse types nonetheless manifest some feature in common, that feature may be important. It is not apt to be, however, if it is an easily diffusable item. Thus the fact that many languages all over the world have phonetically similar words for 'mama' is more significant than a similarly widespread general phonetic shape for 'tea' (1963, p. 4; subsequent citations are also from this work).

Hockett stresses as an important function of linguistic universals the differentiation of languages from other forms of communication, especially that of other species. It is his hypothesis that specific features can be cited which seem to be found in every human language, and each of which seems likewise to be lacking in at least one known animal communicative system (p. 6). The following are the features listed by Hockett as constituting a basic defining set (pp. 7-11):

1. Vocal-auditory Channel
   Broadcast Transmission and
2. Directional Reception
3. Rapid Fading
4. Interchangeability
5. Complete Feedback
6. Specialization
7. Semanticity
8. Arbitrariness
9. Discreteness
10. Displacement
11. Openness
12. Tradition
13. Duality of Patterning
14. Prevarication
15. Reflexiveness
16. Learnability

By stating that human language is limited to the vocal-auditory channel, Hockett in effect excludes writing as a kind of language. This is done purposely, for the reasons that spoken language is "part of the 'common denominator of cultures'" and of undisputed antiquity, whereas writing is more recent and is not universal; that writing as a communication system lacks several of the remaining characteristic attributes in the list, notably rapid fading; and that writing systems, which seem to vary far more than spoken languages, are difficult to describe in a uniform consistent manner as a single phenomenon. Writing is clearly a derivative or second-order system based on spoken language (cf. Lenneberg, 1964a; cf. also Chapter 11 of the present work), although the relationship between written and spoken language is difficult to specify precisely and varies among writing systems. (cf. Gelb, 1952). Some animal communication systems are not vocal-auditory, for example the communicative behavior of beavers in slapping their tails on the water to warn of danger, or the socalled bee dance in which other sensory modalities (tactile, visual, biochemical) are used.

The effect of broadcast transmission is that a communication is audible all around the communicator rather than, e.g., only in front of him as though he were to yell through a pipe; of directional reception, that one can generally tell from where a communication originates. Hockett says that "these properties are the consequences of the nature of sound, of binaural hearing, and of motility", and are implied by the existence of the vocal-auditory channel. If language did not have this attribute, it would presumably be necessary for speakers to sign on, as it were, with a characteristic signal to identify caller and location, as do shortwave operators. But note that utterances tend to carry some means of identifying the person to whom they are addressed, so that this is not usually ambigous even where directional reception is for some reason impaired.

Rapid fading indicates that linguistic signals are transitory rather than permanent, so that one must listen at the time something is being said in order to hear it. As Hockett states, this means that

messages already transmitted do not clutter up the channel and impede the transmission of new ones (as happens sometimes when one has a blackboard but no eraser). Thus, emergency signals can get through. On the other hand, it implies that the import of a message has to be stored internally in the receiver if it is to be stored anywhere at all. The 'attention span' required of human hearers to take in a long and involved sentence is considerable, when measured on the general animal scale (Hockett, 1963, p. 13).

The attention span, insofar as concerns perception of speech, is probably due to learning as well as to inherited capacity. Some languages habitually run to longer utterances than do others; it is well known, for example, that German during the early part of this century had a comparatively high frequency of long sentences and also of syntactic devices requiring a somewhat extended attention span (e.g., constructions such as *der von mir gestern gesehenden Mann*).

Interchangeability refers to the capability of all members of a linguistic community for transmitting and receiving communications. As Hockett points out, this is not true of some animal communications, for example the system of the crickets in which only males chirp although both males and females respond to the chirping of others. There is a surprisingly common mistaken belief to the effect that some languages have different sublanguages for males and females, so that they cannot understand each other at all. In its pure form this would seem a rather nonfunctional distinction; it is true, of course, that there are often great differences between male and female speech (and cf. e.g. Haas, 1964). In many languages, for example, a portion of the lexicon may be taboo to women (example: so-called swear words in many segments of Western culture), or taboo to men (example: such words as 'cute', 'lovely', 'darling' as general descriptive adjectives); some lexicon may be unknown to women (e.g., much technical vocabulary in many cultures) or to men (e.g., descriptive terms for clothing and many color-names in our own culture); a type of communication may be taboo to women although known to them (e.g., Mazateco whistle language); or there may be structurally significant paralinguistic differences between men's and women's speech, as still is the case to some extent in Japanese. However one cannot in such instances speak of lack of ability to engage in certain forms of communication but rather cultural rules prohibiting free exchange of linguistic forms.

Complete feedback refers to the speaker's reception of his own message, in non-pathological instances. This is helpful in that with such feedback the speaker can adjust the message to his inner conception of how it is supposed to sound; he can, for instance, speak more loudly if the environment is becoming so noisy that he cannot hear himself. One also knows what he is saying during the message itself and presumably before he begins to speak (as against having to wait and hear what one is going to say before knowing the content of the message), so that this provides a different sort of internal check.

By specialization Hockett means that only certain features of the communication are significant; that is, for instance, the direct energy connected with speech serves no communicative purpose, since only the triggering effects are important. He notes that "even the sound of a heated conversation does not raise the temperature of a room enough to benefit those in it" (p. 8), although it appears that there may be a perceptibly significant rise in body temperature during anger. Hockett notes further that physiological phenomena may form a portion of the main communication in some other species, for example sticklebacks. It is not possible for humans to attend to all features in a communication (even excluding such matters as body temperature), although the linguistic medium (cf. Chapter 16) is probably more significant than is generally realized. Linguistic redundancy (approximately information communicated per unit transmitted, or predictability; cf. Weaver, 1963) is a formal linguistic universal; phonological redundancy is around fifty percent, and redundancy on other levels is probably about the same amount. This means practically that one need not listen all the time, which of course could not be done in any case, and this in turn means that communication is possible even in fairly noisy channels. The less specialized language becomes, the more there is to attend to, and therefore the lower the redundancy. If all of each utterance were significant, even on the level of segmental phonology, communication would have to be slowed greatly in order to remain commensurate with the short-term memory limits, which are probably dependent upon units received rather than time elapsed since the message commenced. If, on the other hand, e.g., the exact pitch and decibel level of utterances were significant, there might be a concomitant reduction in other features of language now used to make important distinctions, since systemal redundancy is presumably an innate characteristic of the language processing device and humans are severely limited in how much they can attend to at one time.

Semanticity refers to the fact that all languages have a mechanism for reference. Hockett says that "linguistic signals function in correlating and organizing the life of a community because there are associative ties between signal elements and features in the world; in short, some linguistic forms have denotations" (p. 8). All human languages appear to have denotative, connotative and grammatical meaning. Presumably only denotative meaning is a clear necessity. Animal communications do not have semanticity, nor do they specifically lack it; the term is simply irrelevant to animal communications, which seem to be constructed on a different basis altogether (cf. Chapter 19 of this work).

Arbitrariness refers to the lack of direct connection between a word and its referent. A system in which there is such direct connection is called iconic or analogic, the latter term in contrast to digital. Hockett says that "the relation between a landscape painting and a landscape is iconic; the relation between the word *landscape* and a landscape is arbitrary" (p. 8). In an analogic system, for example, the word 'one' might be represented by '|'; two, by '| |'; three, by '| | |'; and so on. Since in bee dances, the direction of the source from the hive is directly represented by a direction of dancing, this form of communication is iconic or analog.

Discreteness indicates the possibility of quantization of the speech stream; that is, language consists of meaningful units which are conjoined rather than in a continuum, so that "any utterance in a language must differ from any other utterance of the same length by at least a whole phonological feature". A continuous system can represent only by orders of magnitude of the signal; as Hockett notes, in a continuous semantic system the semantics must thus be analog or iconic rather than digital or arbitrary. If there were an analog linguistics, each continuum would probably have a separate reference point, or stand for a separate set of concepts. This is not the way in which human language operates at all, nor do humans tend to view phenomena as continuous. It is possible to conceive of organisms for which the reverse might be true, but they would not be high forms of life by present definitions.

Displacement is defined by Hockett as the ability of language to refer to things remote in time or space, or both, from the site of communication. Much of human communication is concerned with absent objects and events. If language could not refer to the future, then humans could not plan; if language could not refer to the past, then humans could neither learn inductively nor teach, nor have historical reference. This might lead to (or, be caused by) a concept of time as an object rather than a process, something like living with the first derivative of the present world, so to speak.

Openness means the possibility of coining new messages and talking about newly occurring events and objects, transmitting and comprehending novel utterances. Other primates do not do this, although Hockett feels that bees probably do; there is some doubt as to what may legitimately be called a novel utterance, however. Hockett states further that the characteristic of openness has two subcategories, namely that every language has grammatical patterning which allows for coining of new messages by blending, analogizing upon or transforming old ones; and that new idioms constantly come into existence in all languages, or that "either new or old elements are freely assigned new semantic loads by circumstances and context". A non-productive or non-open language would function only in an hypothetical static environment.

Tradition refers to the fact that humans are taught a language and learn it, rather than acquiring a specific language biochemically as do many other species. It is apparently rather widely thought that children are in fact born with the propensity to learn their specific language, so that the notion is not inconceivable; it would mean, however, that humans would have greater genetic differentiation than they now have, a suggestion which carries far-reaching implications.

Duality of patterning indicates the possession by every language of phonology and grammar, a small number of meaningless or quasi-meaningless elements which are built into larger structures by regular and nonrandom rules. Animal communication systems do not have duality. This is of course an entire principle of hierarchization, not mere concatenation of phones into phonemes, phonemes into words, words into sentences; a language cannot have words without having the whole structure. Such structuring is not essential in any communication system; one could imagine a communication system wherein each unit would be indissoluble and refer to a specific object or event, but this would be quite cumbersome given the limited human vocal repertoire. One could alternatively imagine a theoretical organism composed of projector-like components with unit schemas to represent utterances, in a kind of combined Chinese logography and 'chop'-type personal symbols, but it would be difficult to label such a system a language.[1]

---

[1] The concept referred to is that of a communications system possessed by organisms which transmit their communications visually, by projecting them on large screens somewhat like TV screens with large computer memories. One would suppose such communications to be schemas rather than phonologically based words; each communication would be a total picture rather than a phrase, sentence or other readily classifiable unit. The language might have about zero redundancy under these circumstances. It might also be based on continua rather than discrete units; that is, there would be no quantization of the speech stream (in fact no real speech stream at all). Such a picture-projection language would be basically analog rather

Prevarication, which is related to displacement, indicates the ability to communicate false or meaningless messages. Hockett notes that he can assert "that it is ten miles from the earth to the moon, or that the interior of all opaque solids is green until exposed to light" (p. 10). Lying is either rare or nonexistent among other species. Although all languages contain the mechanism for prevarication, it is apparently not a universal custom; speakers of some Amerind languages profess to be unable to say 'I have a horse', for instance, if they do not have a horse, indicating that lying is a culturally instigated phenomenon. Hockett might also have noted that he could say 'every statement I make is false', or even, 'it is raining and it is not raining'. The property permitting of such statements is in logic called expressive completeness, or the ability to phrase within a system all propositions with which the system must operate. Humans can utter misinformation and can classify it as such (although there is no consistent method of dealing with paradoxes, in formal logic or elsewhere). The inability of animals to lie is implied by their inability to abstract. Animal communication is signal rather than symbolic; this probably includes the bee dance. Animals cannot utter meaningless statements in the human sense, that is possibly grammatically well-formed but semantically anomalous utterances.

Reflexiveness refers to the ability of a linguistic statement to communicate about itself; language can be about language, although a bee dance cannot be about a bee dance. Hockett says that language has universality, equivalent to expressive complete-

---

than digital; that is, one unit language would represent one unit of environment. The language would not depend on temporal organization; it would not have rapid fading, and would effectively say everything it has to say about a situation with one picture. Further, one might propose that the language have a continuum-type representation of affect or of paralinguistic phenomena (human analog representations of affect are paralinguistic; human terms for affect are of course digital); the communications might be lighter or darker, drawn with thicker or thinner lines, to represent different degrees, not different states, of affective or emotional continua. Finally, one might suppose what seems to be true of all analog communications schemas (as noted e.g. by Gregory Bateson, in conversation), namely that such a language would be incapable of lying.

ness, although this does not mean that every language has a word for every concept. The assertion of universality probably cannot be tested, as he says, since there may be things of which we are unaware simply because we cannot communicate about them. There are also things of which we are aware but about which we cannot communicate, or cannot always communicate with equal success; this appears to be the case, for example, with what is termed bad writing (especially bad fiction), since bad fiction completely, not partially, fails to communicate certain aspects of the situation. Additionally human languages do not have extensive vocabularies by which to communicate sensory data such as tastes and tactile impressions, and must therefore resort to metaphor. This is largely true of emotional states as well, as indeed it would have to be in all save a telepathic species.

Learnability, the final item on Hockett's list, indicates that humans can learn new languages. One might point out that, e.g., a gibbon could not learn the communication system of a lion, irrespective of the difference in peripheral articulatory mechanism, but of course this is cross-species and therefore scarcely surprising. It is presumed that, although there are attested regional dialects in some animal communication systems, the construction of each such system is constant throughout the species. The discussion of linguistic universals in human language in fact serves to demonstrate that a similar proposition might be advanced in regard to the latter (cf. Chapter 12 of this work), that the property of learnability is a result of the basic similarity of all human languages. Hockett makes the point that, if languages were genetically determined, then speakers of one language might not be able to learn another, or only with the greatest difficulty. Likewise, since formal and substantive linguistic universals seem to be genetically determined, it can be postulated that humans cannot acquire systems based on different principles, or can do so only with the greatest difficulty.

17.3. An alternative method of undertaking the search for criterial characteristics of language is to attempt to isolate those

250 LINGUISTIC UNIVERSALS

cognitive processes which seem to underlie language and related systems. For example, a tentative list of some such processes might include concept identification, in turn including analysis and synthesis; hierarchical perception and serial behavior; temporal and spatial organization; abstraction and symbolic behavior; capacity for imitation; capacity for affect expression; and perhaps a separate number concept. At least these systems, and undoubtedly others as well, participate in forming language or the capacity for language. Synthesis is one process involved in lexicon acquisition, for instance, insofar as ascertaining that different members of one concept group belong together in a single category; concord is also a synthetic process, whereas the basic process involved in decoding linguistic input is analytic. Hierarchical and serial behavior have been discussed in previous sections, as has abstraction. The necessity for temporal organization clearly stems from the fact that utterances have a duration, or are strung out in time. Imitation is included, although it is not a unit process, because it must apparently exist in order for there to be language transmission between generations; imitation functions in Hockett's learnability, although imitation might be considered a characteristic of the speaker whereas learnability is a characteristic of the language. The necessity for affect and for a number concept is far less certain; both appear to be present in all human languages, although perhaps merely by accident – number especially may be an entire system or group of components in itself.

It is at any rate important to study universals, both formal and substantive,[2] among other reasons because they are significant in

---

[2] A brief sampling of substantive linguistic universals might include the following (Greenberg, 1963):

All human languages have both intonation and non-intonational phonological features.

All languages have proper names (although in some they are seldom used).

All languages have functors or elements of grammatical rather than lexical meaning.

All languages have first- and second-person referent words.

All languages make a basic distinction between topic and comment.

testing hypotheses about the language acquisition device. As Chomsky states (1965, p. 55),

A theory that attributes possession of certain linguistic universals to a language-acquisition system, as a property to be realized under appropriate external conditions, implies that only certain kinds of symbolic systems can be acquired and used as languages by this device. Others should be beyond its language-acquisition capacity. Systems can certainly be invented that fail the conditions, formal and substantive, that have been proposed as tentative linguistic universals in, for example, Jakobsonian distinctive-feature theory or the theory of transformational grammar. In principle, one might try to determine whether invented systems that fail these conditions do pose inordinately difficult problems for language learning, and do fall beyond the domain for which the language-acquisition system is designed.

In languages with declarative sentences with nominal subject and object, the subject almost always precedes the object.

If a language is exclusively suffixing, it has postpositions; if it is exclusively prefixing, it has prepositions.

If a language has gender, it has number also.

A language never has more gender categories in the plural than in the singular.

No language has 'proper verbs' as well as 'proper nouns'.

All languages seem to be able to express negation and to ask questions.

All or most languages have some onomatopoetic words.

All or most languages seem to have some color terms (even if only two).

18

APHASIA AND OTHER LANGUAGE PATHOLOGIES

18.1. Much information about normal language learning processes can frequently be gained by studying the malfunctioning of these processes. There are many ways in which linguistic behavior can be abnormal or disturbed, and such disturbance may be caused by a variety of factors; the field of communicative disorders includes, for example, study of the linguistic behavior of the deaf, articulatory problems caused by paralysis or apraxia, stuttering, mutism and delayed onset of speech, aphasia and similar problems. Of most interest to psycholinguistic theory are those language problems brought about by neurological damage, namely aphasia and related disorders, and in fact most current knowledge about neurological correlates of linguistic abilities has come from study of such disorders.[1]

Aphasia is a rather general term, not so much denoting a specific condition or set of conditions as referring in general to language disability resulting from organic brain damage. The damage in aphasia is always physical, typically resulting from brain injury, cerebrovascular accident or disease; psychological or emotionally motivated speech disturbances are not properly categorized as aphasic, nor are those caused by peripheral damage or disability such as laryngectomy, apraxia, etc.[2]

[1] The reader should be aware that the study of language pathologies such as aphasia is an extremely broad subject on which a library of literature has been written. The present chapter should be regarded as no more than a very brief summary of some common definitions and theories concerning these disorders.
[2] There are of course a number of functionally rather than organically caused language disorders, such as those resulting from autism or functional schizophrenic conditions, as well as language disorders caused by such factors as generalized retardation. None of these are to be considered as

Although one can specify those disorders which do not belong under the heading of aphasia, it is somewhat more difficult to describe precisely what type of loss has occurred in a particular case. For this reason among others, it has proved nearly impossible for all practical purposes to create an orderly and consistent typology or taxonomy of aphasic disturbance. One problem is that brain damage may be either localized or more generalized, and either sort can have a notable effect on language abilities. Theoretical description would be simplified if language could be conceptualized as a localized unit controlled by one portion of the brain; there is, however, little evidence to support such a notion since general brain damage may cause some loss of linguistic ability even when not concentrated in one of the supposed speech areas. Additionally there is rarely a case in which language impairment is the only symptom, so that there is no set method of predicting what type of loss will occur from most specific types of injury, nor of extrapolating the nature and extent of injury from observation of the language impairment. The most frequent cause of severe language disfunction is extensive injury to the dominant (usually the left) cortical hemisphere, but this too has its exceptions (cf. Lenneberg, 1967, pp. 57-67).

There have been many attempts to form a classificatory system of language disabilities, since being able to state which of a finite number of disorders is manifested by a particular aphasic patient would be useful both in predicting what sort of behavior he is likely to demonstrate and in indicating possible directions of treatment or training. A popular theory was advanced by Roman Jakobson (1961), who first offered the hypothesis that, at least insofar as concerns aphasic articulatory loss, "aphasic regression has proved to be a mirror of the child's acquisition of speech sounds; it shows the child's development in reverse" (p. 421). According to this view, the first sounds learned by the child will be the last to suffer from aphasic loss, whereas the most recently acquired abilities are most likely to show immediate loss upon

---

aphasia. The distinction is highly significant, because all these different disorders must be treated by widely different techniques.

injury. The same process is postulated although more tentatively as occurring on the syntactic level, a postulate which would currently be taken to mean that the aphasic should show evidence of a less particularizing level in the hierarchy of grammatical categories than the normal adult speaker (cf. Chapter 10 of the present work), the limiting case of which would presumably be return to the pivot + open class grammar.

Although the hypothesis that aphasic progression is the reverse of child language development is sometimes correct, there is no indication that aphasia invariably operates in this manner. Loss of language abilities may be spotty and irregular from the standpoint of learning order, or the loss may cut across this categorization entirely, since the patient may for example manifest total impairment of the capacity to form grammatical sentences but still be able to find and use single words of a non-childish variety. Further, if one presumes that language learning is in some sense a concomitant of neural development, which is an irreversible process insofar as is now known, there is no readily discernible means by which a return to earlier states of the process could be effected. On the syntactic level language is not merely learned and remembered but is probably acquired through formation of successive hypotheses of language structuring, so that regression would mean return to an earlier hypothesis. This does not seem to take place. In addition the neural development of the adult cannot be represented as equivalent to that of the child plus a quantity of anything; the difference is clearly qualitative as well as quantitative, so that brain damage must effect its alterations on the final stage of adult language development rather than returning the brain to a childlike state through simple subtraction. One would assume that parallels between aphasic speech and child language are analogies rather than true analysis.

In addition to his hypothesis about the nature of aphasic loss, Jakobson postulates two main categories of aphasic disturbance corresponding to two types of relationship found in normal language. These relationships he terms similarity and contiguity. The concept of similarity is that which permits creation of grammatical classes; that of contiguity allows concatenation of elements, as in sentences. To these correspond the two types of aphasia which Jakobson calls similarity disorder and contiguity disorder. The patient able to handle contiguity but not similarity will for example be unable to find synonyms for a given word and will also be unable in some cases to think of the word belonging to or referring to an object (this is frequently called loss of word-finding ability). The patient who can no longer operate with contiguity will manifest agrammatism or inability to construct well-formed sentences. It is this latter type of aphasia which Jakobson feels demonstrates the most systematic regression toward earlier use of language (pp. 422-26).

18.2. Perhaps the most widespread and useful classification of aphasic disturbances is that originated by Weisenberg and McBride (1935), who described the disorders observed among their aphasic patients thus (from Schuell and Jenkins, 1961, p. 429):

1. *Predominantly expressive*. Disturbances varied from slight defects to almost complete loss of expression. Receptive processes were impaired, although less severely than expressive.
2. *Predominantly receptive*. Impairment of understanding varied from slight to severe, but there was never an absolute loss. Jargon and paraphasia were present, and writing reflected defects found in speech.
3. *Amnesic*. Fundamental difficulty was evoking words. Receptive processes were relatively satisfactory.
4. *Expressive-receptive*. Very severe limitations were present in all language performances.

Expressive aphasia is empirically defined as difficulty in speaking; receptive aphasia, as difficulty in understanding spoken language; and amnesic aphasia, as difficulty in thinking of specific words. The categories show much overlap; specific cases are rarely typical examples of one single category, and nearly any given case might justifiably be diagnosed as expressive-receptive. This overlap is significant, since although it is not of primary importance to attach a label to the syndrome caused by a brain injury, nevertheless classification based on differential analysis of symptomatology should indicate methods for treament and prognosis for cure in an unambiguous manner. In regard to his classificatory system, it appears that aphasic symptoms are arranged on a continuum, which suggests (as noted by Diller, 1967, in regard to classification of bilingual behavior) that the classification is an artificial one superimposed on the data.

A third useful means of classifying types of aphasia is presented by Jones and Wepman (1965), who distinguish three types, namely semantic aphasia, syntactic aphasia and pragmatic aphasia (cf. Chapter 16 of the present work). The authors state that

the disturbance we would call semantic aphasia is marked by the inability of a patient to call forth signs that represent given objects, actions, or events. . . . Word usage by patients with this disorder tends to be limited to the more frequent words of the language. . . . Notably, there is retention of some grammatical form and function. Speech is frequently interrupted by pauses, word-finding attempts, and circumlocutions.

This disorder corresponds to Jakobson's similarity disorder. Further,

in the syntactic aphasic patient, the ability to nominate at least some of the substantive symbols of the language remains relatively intact, but he displays a loss of the grammatical functions of language. Thus there tends to be a reduction from the expected number of occurrences of at least some of the highly frequent function words of the language. Syntactic aphasic patients tend toward a telegraphic style of speech. . . . These same syntactic patients also may fail to properly use inflection, tense or gender,

although the authors note that these difficulties, even when taken in the aggregate, may not seriously interfere with the ability to communicate effectively. The final type of aphasia, namely the pragmatic disorder, is least specifically described; it is pointed out that in this condition

there is a disruption of the ability of the individual to obtain meaning from a stimulus and use it as a basis for symbol formulation. Analysis of the speech of pragmatic patients suggests only slight constriction of vocabulary. However, words and neologisms apparently unrelated to the stimulating situation are commonly found. Meaning of the patient's utterance typically is severely disturbed.

Whereas pragmatic patients do not typically show loss of phonological accuracy, they tend toward breakdown of the self-regulatory mechanism on other levels of language, so that they are frequently unaware of their own failure to communicate (pp. 243-44). One might note, while on this topic, that it would no doubt be worthwhile to investigate the comprehension and production by aphasic patients of extralinguistic or medium-feature data.

18.3. Much extant work on aphasia treats the subject from the applied point of view rather than from the technically descriptive; that is, such literature deals with methods of retraining the aphasic patient. In therapeutically-oriented works the emphasis is frequently on description rather than classification. A useful guide to elementary understanding of aphasic disorders, and one fairly broad in scope, is that of Granich (1952). Following is his description of the various disorders comprising aphasia and related disabilities (pp. 8-37):

18.3.1. *Dysarthria.* – Dysarthria, although included in the general description of speech disturbances, is generally traceable to apraxia of the mouth parts and so is not a genuine aphasia. It is sometimes confused with motor aphasia; however, the latter is a central rather than peripheral disorder.

18.3.2. *Motor aphasia.* – Motor aphasia is among the most common forms of speech disorder. In contrast to dysarthria, it is not manifested as difficulty in pronouncing specific sets of sounds, since the list of sounds with which the motor aphasic has difficulty may vary from day to day. Granich notes the apparent lack of kinesthetic feedback in motor aphasia, such that the patient may be aware of the sound or word he wishes to articulate but be unable to produce the correct output or to recognize it if he has produced it. The prognosis for recovery from motor aphasia is relatively good especially for young patients, once the patient has been led to experience kinesthetic feedback again by one of several therapeutic measures.

18.3.3. *Difficulty in oral word formation.* – This differs from the previous category in that word-formation difficulty is manifested solely on the word level, so that the patient may be able to pronounce isolated sounds but cannot integrate them into words. This is because, according to Granich, there is more involved in pronunciation of a word than the so-called kinesthetic-motor set or concept of the muscular movements corresponding to the articulation of the word in question. The patient must also be able to re-auditorize the word or visualize silently how it is supposed to sound. The motor set may serve to carry him through short and very frequent words; and if nothing else will avail, the patient may develop the ability to paraphrase longer words which he is unable to conceptualize as auditory patterns. This disorder is also called verbal apraxia, which Darley (1964, p. 32) defines as "a specific difficulty in performing the oral acts involved in articuating speech sounds and ordering them sequentially into words, although understanding of speech is adequate and the patient respond meaningfully in writing". Sometimes such patients are in fact able to imitate a word they hear although they cannot pronounce it spontaneously, an ability of no particular benefit to them when trying to pronounce the word on their own.

18.3.4. *Agrammatism, or difficulty in sentence formation.* – The agrammatic patient uses single words only and cannot utter well-formed sentences. Granich notes that this is sometimes confused with word-finding difficulty, since the speech of the agrammatic patient is slow due to the necessity for him to search for the single word which best expresses his meaning. Differential diagnosis is not especially difficult, since the agrammatic will at best use only childlike sentence types, omitting functors, although he is able to use some complex words in isolation. Agrammatism, which rarely occurs as an isolated symptom, appears to be a difficulty with the ability to handle high-level hierarchies; it is not complete inability to deal with hierarchies, however, since the use of words implies at least retention of phonemic distinctions. It might be of interest to check other concomitant disorders of the agrammatic patient, for example, acalculia and change in music comprehension and production.

18.3.5. *Amnesic aphasia, or difficulty in word finding.* – Amnesic aphasia is one of the standard categories and is a common type of aphasic disorder. Granich describes the characteristics of this difficulty as follows:

> Words are affected in a characteristic order of difficulty – not the order in which they were learned in infancy, nor the order in which they would appear in a psychometric vocabulary scale (a scale of relative difficulty), but an order determined by the psychology of the brain-injured. Proper nouns go first, certain common nouns next, then certain verbs and adjectives. I would suggest that a single factor determines the order of difficulty of words ... namely, the extent to which the word has come to be, in the individual's private thinking, an intrinsic attribute of the object or concept itself; or conversely, the extent to which he must regard it as an arbitrary symbol imposed on him by the social group for purposes of communication. An emotional exclamation is almost identical with a strong inner experience. But a stranger's name has little *natural* connection in our minds with his appearance or his behavior or his personality. In [amnesic aphasia] the most difficult words to recall are proper nouns, the symbols arbitrarily set by the social group to designate people and places. Then come common nouns, words which have in our private thinking become somewhat identified with objects; then words identified with experiences which are largely subjective, such as running and laughing, bigness and prettiness; and finally ejaculations, those identified with strong inner experiences.

It might be noted that the facet of verbal memory with which normal speakers appear to have most difficulty is the proper noun; facets of aphasia often seem to have counterparts in normal linguistic behavior. Granich's hypothesis here is interesting, although one must point out that there seems to be little way to verify it.

18.3.6. *Anomia.* – Anomia consists of loss of ability to handle nouns. Granich states that anomia produces the most familiar type of circumlocution associated with aphasia, in which the patient calls a pen 'what you write with', and so forth. This difficulty, although frequently present in cases of amnesic aphasia, is not necessarily so and therefore is treated separately. It is nearly inconceivable that anomia should exist without other severe aphasic symptomatology, since one has the greatest difficulty in postulating a type of brain damage which should wipe out only the ability to deal with nouns. The process of class inclusion or concept identification instrumental in formation of nouns is also central to formation of verbs. If in fact it appears that anomia does occur in isolation, this might well indicate the need to reconsider the nature of the internalized language-production mechanism.[3]

18.3.7. *Receptive aphasia.* – Receptive aphasia is generally defined as difficulty in understanding spoken language. It is frequently manifested most noticeably as difficulty in keeping track of long or complicated sentences, and may be measured by, e.g., the standard Random Digit Span test, since there is a pathologically low digit span or ability to remember consecutive digits in receptive aphasia. This disorder may also be termed auditory aphasia, or sensory (as contrasted with motor) aphasia.

18.3.8. *Alexia.* – Reading disorders are frequently grouped under the heading of alexia, which in itself refers to general inability to comprehend the written word. Alexia is not uncommon, and there is some slight evidence to suggest that a form of it may be genetically determined. Note that there is also a quasi-aphasic reading disorder known as reduction of the visual field; this disturbance, which corresponds in kind to dysarthria, is manifested by a blurring of print after a period of reading, due to breakdown of compensatory eye adjustments. Large type may be helpful to a patient with this difficulty, although there seems to be no cure for it (cf. also Lenneberg, 1964a, p. 593).

18.3.8.a. *Visual recognition difficulty.* – This is the inability to perceive letters or words clearly, and may be diagnosed with recognition tests featuring geometric forms or designs. In a number of cases the problem is that the patient sees letters as though they were in motion or at an angle. These difficulties are often brought on by fatigue and are alleviated, according to Granich, by rest or change of activity.

[3] One might note that present psycholinguistic models of language are for all practical purposes quite inadequate to deal with the fact of anomia.

18.3.8.b. *Loss of phonetic associations or letter-sound connections.* – This is the commonest form of alexia, consisting basically of loss of association between visual-recognition areas and sound-recall areas of the brain according to some modern explanations. Very probably it would come about by subcortical as well as cortical damage. Granich states that the loss is not one of symbolism *per se* but rather of evocation of auditory association by the letter. He notes also that retraining may be accomplished by phonetic association of whole-word form with sound of word, which is then recognized by its sound; or by visual-to-visual association of whole-word form, in the case of nouns at least, with revisualization of the object; and finally by using phonetic associations from letter form to sound.

Visual-to-visual association consists in associating the entire word with the object it represents. Some aphasics may be taught familiar nouns by this method, but they may tend to read the word 'drive' as 'car', or 'ocean' as 'sea'. "The patient functions, so to speak, in a dead-silent world. He recognizes a word form, evokes a picture or perhaps a 'meaning', then names the picture or idea." Alternatively, the patient may be taught to sound a few letters, by constant repetition and imitation; then he may be able to read a word by sounding the first few letters until he recognizes the word he is sounding and then can pronounce the whole word. In the long run, this method must be combined with others. Granich recommends the rather laborious method of teaching the patient to make a certain specific mouth movement upon seeing a letter (e.g., "Having seen the letter *m*, he learns to form his mouth for a humming sound"). The patient hears the sound he makes, although he cannot recognize that it is appropriate to the letter given, but he can listen to his vocalizing and try to recognize the word. A final method of training, for the patient who seems entirely unable to grasp phonetic associations, is to print flashcards with common words (e.g., 'the', 'in', 'room') and with a distinctive border or pattern on each card, and have the patient identify each card by its name ("as if the words were names and the cards separate objects"). Then when the patient sees a word he has thus learned in a printed text, he will revisualize the appropriate card and so recall the name. One cannot help speculating upon what form this disorder, and its treatment, might take in languages with logographic writing systems such as Chinese and Japanese.

18.3.9. *Agraphia and other writing disorders.*

18.3.9.a. *Difficulty in letter formation.* – Difficulty in letter formation may be due to pathology in the 'motor strip' or motor control areas of the brain. Granich comments that even writing one letter involves a series of events comprising a serial performance, and thus requires kinesthetic set and repeated feedback relays, constant awareness and checking of the changing state of affairs. It is conceivable that any of these functions, or any group of them, might misfire. One would expect other disorders to accompany agraphia, depending on precisely what mechanism or set of mechanisms was actually at fault. Where the condition is caused by hemiplegia or paralysis of the preferred hand, retraining may be effected.

18.3.9.b. *Difficulty in formation of the written word.* – Granich states that "this is due essentially to loss of sound-to-vision associations. . . . The patient cannot associate from a sound, either heard or imagined, to a revisualization of the letter required". Writing requires motor habits, ability to revisualize the entire word, and phonetic association of sounds with the corresponding letters. If one or more of these abilities is impaired, loss of ability to write is the result. The patient may be able to visualize only the first and last letters of the word, for instance, or may scramble the letters of the word much in the manner of typing errors. The patient is sometimes unable to write nonsense syllables, since he cannot utilize a familiar word to aid him in this process and is unable to use the sounds directly to produce the proper spelling. Note that, in reference to typing errors, these may represent an area of presumably normal functioning analogous in certain ways to aphasic failures; typing errors most frequently are not due to lack of motor coordination, as is often assumed, but rather are of several distinct sorts some of which may be tunings-out of word-formation mechanisms.

18.3.9.c. *Failure to revisualize the word.* – In this case, the patient is only too able to connect sound with writing; the patient suffering from this difficulty tends to spell phonetically, since he cannot check the correct appearance of the word with any inner visualization of it. It might be mentioned that the concept of inner visualization is a schematic representation of what occurs in language production, a hypothetical rather than a verified process accepted because of its utility in explaining this sort of disorder.

18.3.10. *Acalculia.* – Acalculia is a separate category of disorder, nearly always appearing in the company of other forms of aphasia proper rather than in isolation (although a surprisingly large number of normals or non-aphasics claim total disability in this area). It refers to specific difficulty with calculation or arithmetic. There are many different processes at work in arithmetic, and so general mental deterioration often produces loss of arithmetical ability because some of these processes, although not necessarily all of them, have been damaged. Granich states that

because of the high level of concentration required for calculation, most individuals learn to attack arithmetic in several different ways, resorting to a secondary approach when the first approach is fatigued. Even in normals we find a tendency to verbalize problems when fatigue sets in after a period of calculating at sight.

Granich here describes a significant set of conditions, one true of many activities besides arithmetic. Error in processes for which there are several different approaches or attacks may be due to overlap in approach rather than to fatigue of the particular approach being used at the time; most frequently more than one attack is employed at a time, and these may become, for one reason or another, temporarily out of phase. Any process containing associative chaining as well as a number of other methods for generating performance, and which is liable to a high percentage of errors or misfirings, may be suspect of being thus composed. Again, typing is an example.

In regard to the general prognosis for aphasic patients, Lenneberg (1967, p. 143) states that

in contrast to normal small children, the adult patient does not relearn language. Neither training nor conditioning procedures are guarantees for the restoration of language to the patient with a well-established aphasia. This is understandable because his problem is not that he does not know language but that he can no longer make use of language that he has learned. A patient with aphasia has not lost other, more general abilities to learn; he is not demented and not psychotic; he may continue to make new associations, to build up new expectations, to make new inferences and, generally, to give signs that his nonspecific learning capacities have not come to an end. Thus, the language disorder is not a learning impairment.

Lenneberg notes further that

aphasias acquired during adult life, that is, after the age of eighteen, may recover within a three-to-five months period. There are reasons to believe that this is due to physiological restoration of function rather than a learning process. Symptoms that have not cleared up by this time are, as a rule, irreversible.

Perhaps the most serious obstacle to treatment is that usually one cannot be certain what sort of damage has occurred or how extensive the loss of ability may be. The goals of retraining must always be practically oriented (e.g., toward helping the patient recover his former ability to manage in society) rather than based on neurological concepts, since there is invariably great difficulty in determining what portion of the brain has been damaged, what portion might best take over the function of the damaged areas and especially how it might be induced to do so. It is felt that injury to the right (or non-dominant) portion of the brain alone almost never produces aphasic symptoms (cf. Russell and Espir, 1961), but damage does not tend to be localized on the left portion of the cortex only but is more often generalized and subcortical as well as superficial. That children are better able to recover from aphasia than adults seems to follow from the development of the localization of language function, although this remains hypothetical. Recovery from aphasia is a complex matter; for instance, although it is not necessarily true that the more languages a person knows the better are his chances of recovery from aphasia, it does seem to be the case that a bilingual recovers his second language first after onset of aphasia. Lambert postulates (1961, p. 456) that "co-ordinate bilinguals would be more likely to show aphasic damage in one language system, while compound bilinguals would be more likely to show aphasic damage in all languages known". It is likely that this depends to a great extent on when the languages were learned, the interval separating their learning, and the extent and locale of the damage, probably irrespective of the learning context; possibly bilinguals who learned both languages in childhood would tend to show aphasic damage in both, whereas those who had learned one language in adult life would tend to show such damage in only one language (which one depending on localization of the damage). However, there is little evidence as yet bearing on these and other such hypotheses.

19

LANGUAGE AND COMMUNICATION:
ANIMAL LANGUAGE

19.1. The structure and function of communication in other species have long been of interest to psychologists and linguists. As has been noted, one reason for studying linguistic universals is that these may provide a set of criteria by which it may be determined whether a non-human communications system can in fact be called a language. The biological bases of language are also relevant to the topic of animal communication; if it can be demonstrated that general laws of learning apply to language acquisition, as proposed by e.g., Skinner or Mowrer, then the possibility exists that other species have either a form of language or else prelinguistic behavior. Contrariwise, if the capacity for language acquisition and production is genetically determined and species-specific, then it is most unlikely that genuine language behavior could be found among animals. Nevertheless it is clear that all species show communicative behavior, sometimes of a rather complex sort, so that the topic is one which bears further investigation irrespective of one's position on the extent of the innate linguistic component in human language.

The subject of animal communication has been rather intensively examined by biologists, anthropologists, ethologists, psycholinguists and scientists in other fields as well. There seems to be widespread belief, especially among nonlinguists, that at least some animals are capable of understanding human language and of communicating in a humanlike manner with one another and with humans as well. This belief is in fact so common that it has frequently tended to influence studies of animal communication; this is an area in which the bias of the experimenter has a pervasive influence, so that those ethologists who happen also to be very fond of animals, and to have worked extensively with them, often seem determined to find the traces of linguistic behavior from the outset. This is presumably the explanation of, for example, those reports which claim to present six words in the vocabulary of the horse. But descriptions of complex communicative behavior among animals are so frequent and occasionally so compellingly linguistic in character that they cannot be dismissed without at least attempted explanation. Following are a selection of possible questions which one might pose in connection with animal communication:

(1) Do any animals have a language in the same sense as humans; if so, which?

(2) What is the best procedure for deciding whether a given communication system is in fact a language, or, alternatively, an approximation to language?

(3) If no animals can be considered to have a language, then what is the nature of their communications, if any, and how can these be compared with human communication?

(4) If no animals have a language, is there a possibility that some extant species may be in the process of developing a language?

19.2. Since dogs are the most common house pets, they are the animals about which it is most often asserted that understanding of human language exists. Many dog owners believe that dogs are capable of obeying commands which they have never heard before, and thus, by extension, of understanding human language in general. It is also sometimes claimed that dogs and other pets express a variety of human emotions through their particular communication, and presumably that they do so deliberately in order to communicate with their owners. Packard states, for example, that "dog-owners known that their dog utters a wide range of meaningful sounds. A dog in its bark can express surprise, pleasure, pleading, alarm, playfulness" (1950, p. 158). Although it is most probable that such interpretations are the result of animism or anthropomorphism, animals (perhaps especially dogs) do produce utterances not designed to communicate with others of their species, and such sounds are presumably expressive of something rather than randomly generated. There is to date no evidence to indicate that dogs have the same range of affect as humans, of course, but comments such as these by Packard do not seem to be gross misinterpretation.

Dogs are demonstrably capable of acquiring complex behavior patterns in response to human language. There is, for example, a verified instance of a dog which will sit by the table of its owner begging for scraps until told to go away, at which point it moves off a little distance; when told that this is not far enough, the dog backs off still further, and so on for the length of the room. When finally told to leave the room, the animal does so. The owner states positively that the dog was not deliberately trained toward this behavior, nor is it known specifically how the behavior was acquired. One may be relatively certain that the conditioning process which led thereto developed gradually over a long period and was not noticed until the behavior was completely shaped. If a dog is told in a loud, scolding voice to do something and does not do so, the dog is generally punished, so that the dog might tend to heed the loud voice next time. A typical reaction to aversive stimulation is to withdraw from it; if a loud and scolding voice became a secondary negative reinforcement to the dog (in a process such as Mowrer's fear conditioning), the dog might well tend to withdraw upon hearing it, especially if rewarded for so doing. If the direction 'Leave the room' or the like were to accompany the scolding tone of voice, for which the dog had already learned the behavior of withdrawing, then this verbal direction would tend to become a CS for the same behavior. The training process in such instances is generally straightforward enough, although when training is not carried out deliberately the results may appear puzzling.

There has seldom been a serious attempt to credit dogs, or other common animals, with higher-level communicative abilities, at least in regard to their behavior toward humans. No animal such as dogs, cats, horses etc. has ever demonstrably learned any features of human language; every instance in which this has been claimed has turned out to be a case of simple operant conditioning. This includes such famous animals as 'Der Kluge Hans' ('Clever Hans'), the so-called talking horse displayed by von Osten of Berlin around the turn of the century. Hans purportedly could answer questions and especially solve arithmetical problems by tapping his foot. But the horse was only able to do this when his master was present; when questioned by others, Hans's linguistic ability would vanish. Packard describes the performance thus:

The master had not been cuing Hans *deliberately*, but nonetheless there had been slight clues that the sharp-eyed Hans had responded to, to get his lump of sugar. As Hans began tapping, Herr von Osten would become tense and count silently with Hans. When Hans had tapped out the right answer, the master would relax slightly and Hans – cued by the relaxed posture – would stop tapping! It was found that Hans knew nothing about spelling, mathematics, music or anything else, but only knew how to follow the cues given unconsciously by his master (1950, pp. 85-87).

Von Osten did not have any explanation of the ability of his horse, and seemingly had not trained the animal deliberately. There remains no doubt about how Hans effected his performance, and the process has no relation to language.

19.3. Bees and talking birds have been the most frequent candidates for postulated linguistic behavior. In reference to the latter, it must be inquired whether the imitative behavior of birds can be considered akin to human language, a question which in part hinges on whether the birds can employ their vocabulary in human-like ways. It has been asserted by some naturalists that talking birds may learn to say 'good morning' and 'goodbye' only at the appropriate times, and the ethologist Lorenz describes two incidents in which birds (a parrot and a crow) learned and used utterances which they had heard only once or twice (Lorenz, 1952, pp. 95 ff.). Although he was not present during the actual learning of these remarks by the birds, the nature of the remarks was such that they could not have been repeated very often in the normal course of events.[1] Claims of extant linguistic behavior in birds are always directed to this mimicking ability; bird songs are rarely described as linguistic behavior in the sense of human language, although they are communicative. The ability of birds to imitate human utterances is rather striking, although it is considered natural since it is so commonly demonstrated, and so one often fails to notice that this is the only thing birds do which resembles human language behavior. In a sense dogs exhibit more responsiveness to human language than do birds. The bird's imitative behavior is not evidence of possession of language any more than the seal's horn-blowing activity is evidence of musical genius; language does not consist solely in phonation, so that one would hesitate to call the behavior of, e.g., an English-speaking phonetician imitating an Aranta utterance genuine language behavior.

The best-known intraspecies communication, and that which has received the most learned speculation, is the bee dance. In brief, upon locating a source of nectar, a bee returns to its hive and communicates the location of the food source to other bees in the hive, by means of a series of wiggling and circling movements commonly termed the bee dance. The Austrian zoologist Karl von Frisch, after many years of study, discovered that the bee's directions to its fellow hive-members are based upon the approximate distance of the nectar from the hive and its location

[1] Lorenz also discusses the communication of dogs in this section of his book, and notes that in some respects the dog is more receptive than humans: "Everybody who understands dogs knows with what uncanny certitude a faithful dog recognizes in its master whether the latter is leaving the room for some reason uninteresting to his pet, or whether the longed-for daily work is pending." Lorenz also notes that his own Alsatian was practically telepathic in her knowledge of which of Lorenz's visitors annoyed or were disliked by him, and would attack only those people. This type of understanding, which he does not regard as especially uncommon, is credited to the dog's powers of observation and sensitivity to minute movements of expression. Lorenz, who is of course a highly trained comparative psychologist and ethologist, does not feel at all that this constitutes, or approximates, language.

in relation to the position of the sun. He determined further that when the food source is within 50 to 100 meters of the hive, the circling dance is used; for longer distances, the wiggling dance is used. So much for the significance of the two types of motion. The wagging dance contains more information than the circling dance, which is to be expected since the further the food source from the hive, the more precise directions are needed to get there. The number of turns per second made by the dancing bee varies with the distance; in experiments, when the food was 100 meters away, the bee made about 10 short turns in 15 seconds, and when the food was 3000 meters away, the bee made 3 long turns in about 15 seconds. At considerably short distances from the hive, the bees are less likely to be accurate in going directly to the source, presumably because the scout bee communicates less information than if the source were further distant. The method of navigating by the sun is rather complicated; it has been found that the bees can do this even when the sun is hidden by clouds, or when the hive is placed in an unknown location (cf. Krogh, 1955, pp. 47-53).

The analysis of the bee dance necessitates consideration of the difference between signal and symbolic communication. In most cases of animal communication there is no symbolism involved, a fact probably universally true among nonhuman species with the possible exception of dolphin communication. However, bees do seem to communicate about physically absent objects. Since the distinction between signal and symbolic communication is often considered crucial in deciding whether a communication process is to be regarded as a language, one may either say that the bee communication is symbolic in fact and therefore perhaps linguistic, or alternatively one may propose that the bee dance not be considered an instance of true symbolic behavior. Note that signal behavior is not considered to be species specific, although symbolic behavior generally is, so that if bee dances are found to be symbolic the decision as to species-specificity of language capability must be rethought to some extent.

It is often difficult to judge whether a communication is about an absent event or not, since this is a relative matter. Language does not especially reflect obvious physical processes in the environment; different linguistic codes direct attention to different portions of the environment and cause these to stand out more than others. Whorf has noted (1956, p. 63) that to the Hopi speaker the concept of simultaneity of events in two places is different from ours; something happening at a distant place happens by definition at a distant time, since it can be known about only later by report. This is a different view of the absence of the event from that of the SAE languages, and it thus demonstrates that the significant matter in language is not so much what is really the true state of events, which is problematic in any case, but rather the linguistic representation of events from which notions of reality are to an extent derived.

It is not meaningful to inquire whether to a Hopi speaker events really take place at the same time or not; it is rather important that according to this language the concept of such simultaneity is inconceivable. One may likewise wish to postulate that it does not matter whether or not nectar is actually an absent object for the bees. That it is responded to in invariant and genetically determined ways indicates that the nectar is treated in some sort of signal rather than symbolic sense. Bee dances are always about nectar; they represent the same data in the same ways in different locales and from generation to generation; they are further responded to in invariant ways (as has been demonstrated by experiments with bee-shaped puppets manipulated in bee-dance patterns); and they are apparently inherited intact rather than learned. These are not commonly listed among characteristics of a language, a fact which, taken in conjunction with the relatively low phylogenetic position of *Hymenoptera* and lack of proper neural equipment for a language system as we know it, seems to imply that bees do not engage in linguistic behavior or in symbolic behavior either. Nectar, in other words, may justifiably be said not to constitute an absent object to the bee any more than the sudden appearance of the hunter constitutes an absent object to a tail-thumping beaver. The functioning of the *signifié* within the communication system, rather than its position in the real world, is the crucial factor in determination of linguistic properties, nor must the two be obviously related.

19.4. Perhaps the most interesting possible exception to the rule that most animal communication is relatively uncomplicated and signal in nature is the group of marine mammals called cetaceans, and in particular the dolphin or porpoise.[2] There have apparently been stories illustrating the intelligence of these animals for many years; in ancient Greece storytellers mentioned that dolphins occasionally formed friendships with human children and rescued the children from drowning or being marooned. The dolphin was so considered a friend to man that it frequently was portrayed in sculpture and other decorative work. In more recent times, sailors have told of being guided through narrow channels by these animals, which seemingly knew that the ships were in trouble and sought to help. There have been a number of popular works on the dolphin (e.g., Lilly, 1962 and 1967), and such works often mention definite linguistic ability as well as general intelligence as characteristics of dolphins.

Since dolphins make a good deal of noise naturally, it is not difficult to find utterances to study (it is appallingly difficult to record and reproduce them, however). The social interaction of dolphins or porpoises, whatever its nature may turn out to be, involves a fair amount of concomitant communication. These animals whistle over a large acoustic range, and are capable of emitting sounds of over 100 kc, whereas human hearing is limited to about 20 kc. They also produce clicks or pulses, either isolated or in pulse-trains, primarily for the echo-location which is the

---

[2] Dolphins and porpoises are actually different animals, distinguished by the shape of the teeth and of the head and by size, among other features. There are many more varieties of dolphin than of porpoise, and it is almost invariably the dolphin which is used in experimentation (most frequently the *Tersiops Truncatus* or bottle-nose dolphin); however, they are often called porpoises anyhow since there is a common fish also known as the dolphin (*Coryphaena Hippurus*). The terms are used interchangeably in this section.

dolphin sonar system.[3] Dolphins also can make various other sounds, such as squawks produced through the blowhole, but whistles and clicks (which can be produced simultaneously) are their principle forms of communication. The whistles may be subdivided into about six main types with three or four subtypes each. In communication situations, when one animal whistles another is likely to respond with a whistle in the same main category, so that these classifications are basically behavioral, but it is not yet known what the significance of the categories may be. It might be noted that, despite claims to the contrary (e.g. by Lilly, 1962, pp. 116-17), it does not appear that dolphins have any ability to mimick human words or sentences.

The most fruitful studies on dolphin language and culture are those sponsored by the U.S. Navy (studies with which the present author worked for a time). There were two main centers of porpoise study affiliated with the Navy, one at the Oceanic Institute in Oahu, Hawaii, and one in California. The Hawaii studies are of the sociolinguistic sort, designed to determine the nature of porpoise group dynamics (and cf. Pryor, 1969). An interesting theory of animal behavior connected with this project and proposed by Gregory Bateson (personal conversation) states that all mammals, including porpoises, communicate with each other and with humans solely about relationships; for example, the meowing, purring kitten is not asking for milk but is rather asserting a dependency relationship, and the wolf leader guarding his harem from other pack members is in effect saying, 'I am your superior' or perhaps, 'I am your surrogate parent', and so on. Communication about relationships is the most immediate form of signal communication, since it concerns only the participants in the communication situation and totally omits reference to the environment. Bateson notes that porpoises seem to show this typically mammalian communication about relationships. However,

---

[3] Although the vision of dolphins is quite adequate, they tend to depend for the main portion of their activity on the auditory sense. The auditory area of the dolphin's brain is about six times as large as that of man, in proportion to the rest of the brain.

he also indicates that they probably have some communication features peculiar to their species and dissimilar to those of human communication, for example lack of paralinguistic or facial kinesic features and thus purely digital rather than analog communication. Bateson also hypothesizes that porpoises are basically capable of forming only dyadic relationships, or in other words of perceiving themselves in relation to only one other Gestalt. This is based on the observation that their social groupings typically have a stable two-animal core.

The dyadic relationship is probably common to all mammals if in fact it is a real grouping among porpoises, and very likely humans also tend to form bilateral relationships. Although such an hypothesis might be difficult to prove, since anything with which a dolphin or other animal interacts might be described as consisting of one Gestalt from the animal's viewpoint (although the Gestalt may be complex one), nevertheless the proposition implies some interesting notions about what sort of language these animals might manifest. For example, one might speculate that a creature capable only of dyadic relationships would express only first and second but not third person, and also would tend to view things vertically, or ordinally, rather than horizontally, or cardinally, in much the manner of the Hopi view of time as described by Whorf.

Some of the most psycholinguistically interesting experiments with dolphins are those conducted by Jarvis Bastian, whose investigations are designed to induce informative communication between two porpoises. A typical research design is as follows: Two animals are placed in adjacent tanks, with hydrophone connections between the tanks so that the animals can hear but not see each other. Animal A has been trained to push either the left or the right of two paddles in its tank, depending on whether a light it sees is flashing or steady; the training has taken place prior to this phase of the experiment. Essentially, what takes place is that animal A sees its light, either flashing or steady, and then must accordingly communicate to animal B (who has no lights, only paddles), which paddle B should push in its own tank. If B makes the correct choice according to what A has communicated, then A also pushes its own paddle. In other words, the sequence is: A sees light; A communicates with B; B pushes paddle; if B was correct, A pushes paddle.

The results of this experiment are surprisingly positive: B pushed the correct paddle most of the time, when A had communicated properly with B. Bastian and others had expected that the porpoises' whistles would carry the requisite information; instead it seemed that the clicks or pulse trains were almost surely the significant portions of the utterance. The whistles of animal A only served to indicate to B when the experiment was commencing so that B should be alert – to mark the beginning of each run – rather than to communicate about the lights.

Although it is believed by the experimenters that genuine intent to communicate and to receive is being demonstrated here, and that symbolic communication is taking place, there is not yet enough evidence to warrant an assumption of linguistic capability; since this would be the most complex possible explanation of the results, a kind of limiting factor or terminal assumption, other possibilities must be investigated before commmunication with intent is adopted as the explanation. Note that intent to send information on the part of porpoise A does not necessarily imply intent to receive on the part of B, nor vice versa. It is possible, for example, that B had been trained (that is, conditioned) to listen for the information he needed, and that this information was merely an incidental accompaniment to A's performance rather than a deliberate broadcast by A. It may be that the noises made by A and upon which B depended are some sort of natural reaction to the choice-situation, rather than being purposive in nature. This possibility can be tested by recording the vocal behavior of animal A when it is simply required to choose a paddle itself, not to communicate its choice to another animal, and ascertaining whether it makes the same sounds it made during the experiment. An alternative possibility is that A and B were both working from some sort of cue not perceived by the experimenter; this might be tested by reversing their roles, so that B must communicate to A. Finally, it might be interesting to re-construct the experiment so that the animals are rewarded only when A selects and pushes a paddle prior to B and then must direct B to push the opposite paddle, a test which might aid in determining whether the animals are in fact capable of abstract communication.

With the present limited evidence and lack of a standard decision procedure, it is difficult to indicate whether or not there seems to be a possibility that dolphins have a language or are capable of developing one. Although Bastian and others have studied the intent to communicate as well as the presence of symbolic behavior among dolphins, the former is probably more significant than the latter; one might in fact state that all animal communications are purposive, that is, uttered with the intent to communicate, since clearly not all animal noises are emotive or randomly emitted and this seems to be the only other alternative. It is likewise difficult to propose a crucial experiment to test whether a group of animals has a language. With dolphins the difficulties are even more acute, since they are aquatic and are also primarily auditory- rather than visual-oriented, these factors limiting the types of experiments which can be successfully used with them. There is no present evidence to suggest that dolphins have an intrinsic language system, in the sense of human language. As has been indicated, it is not justifiable to search for words in the utterances of the porpoise or dolphin, or other animals, since language is by definition a multilevel system the whole of which must be present if any one level is to be found. If there are etic/emic distinctions in dolphin communication, they have not yet been discovered; the utterances of these animals do not quantize in any natural, regular manner.

On the other hand, it is very likely possible to test the general intelligence of dolphins in linguistically-oriented directions, even if one cannot directly tap symbolic behavior and other pure language processes; for example, one might attempt to test a series of cognitive processes considered as instrumental in composing language, such as analysis, synthesis, serial and hierarchical behavior, and so forth (cf. Chapter 17 of this work). There are many kinds of experiments which might be helpful in this procedure. For example, one might attempt to teach the dolphin random numbers, which in dolphin terms can be expressed as a random series of left-right alternations. It has been noted (by Bill Powell, director of Navy porpoise research in California) that in discrimination experiments in which the animal selects from two choices a particular material, sometimes placed on its left and sometimes on its right according to a table of random lefts and rights, the experiment should not re-use the same series of ten trials because the animal might be capable of learning the list. This would be an interesting fact, since it would indicate not only good memory but also the type of temporal organization which might be significant in linguistic behavior (i.e., that involved in remembering a list in order). To test this ability, the animal might be trained to discriminate between two metals, for instance copper and aluminum, which it is easily capable of distinguishing by sonar. It could be trained to go to the copper plate, for example, whether this is on its left or on its right. The same series of ten left-right alternations would be used repeatedly in placing the two materials before the porpoise. Then materials would be substituted which the dolphin cannot discriminate, and it would be expected to follow the left-right pattern previously practiced and reinforced for this behavior.

Another experimental possibility would be to teach the dolphin addition and subtraction of a sort. Essentially the animal would be reinforced for fetching a specified number of convenient objects, say three hoops. It would be given three hoops and trained to retrieve all three when they are thrown into the tank. Then six or eight hoops would be thrown out, and the animal required to bring back three only. When and if this is mastered, the animal would be given one hoop and see six or eight others tossed into the tank, and be expected to bring back two only to complete the group of three. If given three hoops, it would bring back none from the larger group, and so forth. Once this has been learned, the same procedure might be tried with a larger number of hoops for the critical number, say five. There is every reason to expect that the animal could be conditioned to bring back two hoops when given one, for example, a fact which would indicate little in itself. It is significant to discover whether any generalization of principles takes place, however, so that a correct addition could be made without any prior training to that particular problem. There are many factors involved in arithmetical behavior, and the animal demonstrably capable of carrying out such behavior might well be examined further for evidence of higher-level communicative ability as well.

19.5. It is essential to bear in mind the distinctions between language and general communication when studying the latter process in other species. Presence of communication does not imply presence of language. It has been pointed out that intra-species communication exists among all living species; members of a species must at the very least communicate their mating readiness in order that the species be continued, and mother-offspring communication is also necessary if only for a short while. Animal utterances are frequently specific and purposive, rarely random. Animals communicate for many reasons; among them, mating, challenges to rivals, indications of territoriality (cf. Ardrey, 1966), calling their young, and so forth. There are also solitary or noncommunicative utterances, such as bird songs, but the majority of animal utterances are communicative (cf. Huxley and Koch, 1964, for further information on the variety of animal communications).

Although animals do communicate with one another, this communication is not generally spoken of as language. Animal communications are invariably about concrete and physically present objects or 'about' (that is, because of) biological drives. This is one strong argument for suggesting that they do not constitute genuine linguistic behavior. Too, insofar as is now known, animal communication never is hierarchically organized or systemal, nor does it contain etic/emic patterning on any level, so that it cannot be represented as can language by orderly rules which map its levels into one another and build its units into utterances. Finally, it is undoubtedly necessary that some utterances within a genuine language may be characterized as well-formed, thus implying the existence of another set of utterances which may be labeled as less well-formed or as non-well-formed, so that not every possible sequence of noises is a good or grammatical utterance within the language. Animal communications are presumably all well-formed, and do not in general contain the possibility of producing non-well-formed utterances (nor do they seem to have redundancy in the same sense as human language).

It is in addition currently accepted that no other species (again, with the possible exception of dolphins) has the neurological equipment for language (cf. Lenneberg, 1967, pp. 52 ff.). It does not appear that language is approximated even by higher primates, nor that it developed by accretion of separate traits some of which are evinced by such primates (cf. Lenneberg, 1967, pp. 227-239). It seems certain that no other animal besides man ever demonstrated any true linguistic behavior, for most definitions of the term. Lenneberg proposes a discontinuous theory of language evolution, which presupposes that only man underwent the development which resulted in linguistic capability.

Finally, in regard to latent capacity for linguistic behavior in extant species, it is not at all certain that an approximation to linguistic behavior is a meaningful concept. Without being excessively two-valued, one might wish to assert that, for any given communication system, either it is a language or else it is not, and that it cannot be almost a language. It is probably not reasonable in most instances, either, to speak of the capacity for a language system as a separate entity from the language itself, as though this capacity could be dormant without having produced the resultant system as yet; the most cogent demonstration of lack of capacity to develop a language in any given animal species is in fact the lack of such a language. Were the capacity present, then the language would have developed. This is not to discount the possibility of some such capacity evolving, although it does seem somewhat unlikely, but rather merely to note that if at a given time there is no evidence within a species of a true language, then there is likewise no evidence of dormant or embryonic linguistic capacity.

BIBLIOGRAPHY

Abbott, E. A.,
 1952 *Flatland* (New York: Dover).
Ardrey, R.,
 1966 *The Territorial Imperative* (New York: Atheneum).
Bach, E., and R. T. Harms (eds.),
 1968 *Universals in Linguistic Theory* (New York: Holt, Rinehart and Winston).
Bandura, A.,
 1969 *Principles of Behavior Modification* (New York: Holt, Rinehart and Winston).
Bar-Hillel, Y.,
 1964 *Language and Information* (Reading, Mass.: Addison-Wesley).
Bayley, N.,
 1955 "On the Growth of Intelligence", *Amer. Psychologist* 10, 805-18.
Bettelheim, B.,
 1967 *The Empty Fortress* (New York: Free Press).
Bloomfield, L.,
 1933 *Language* (New York: Holt, Rinehart and Winston).
Blum, G. S.,
 1961 *A Model of the Mind* (New York: Wiley).
Bolinger, D.,
 1965 "The Atomization of Meaning", *Lang.* 41 (4), 555-73.
Bradac, J.,
 Forthcoming "On the Causes of Telegraphic Speech", in S. H. Houston, *A Work-Book in Sociobehavioral Linguistics.*
Braine, M. D. S.,
 1963 "On Learning the Grammatical Order of Words", *Psych. Review* 70, 323-48.
 1965 "On the Basis of Phrase Structure: A Reply to Bever, Fodor, and Weksel", *Psych. Review* 72, 483-92.
Bright, J. O., and W. Bright,
 1965 "Semantic Structures in Northwestern California and the Sapir-Whorf Hypothesis", *Amer. Anthropologist* 67, 5, 2 (Special Publ.), 249-58.
Brown, R.,
 1958 "How Shall a Thing be Called?", *Psych. Review* 65, 14-21.

Brown, R., and U. Bellugi,
    1964   "Three Processes in the Child's Acquisition of Syntax", *Harvard Ed. Rev.* 34 (2), 133-51.
Brown, R., and C. Fraser,
    1961   "The Acquisition of Syntax" (Paper read at the Second ONR-New York Univ. Conference on Verbal Learning, New York), June.
Campbell, D. T.,
    1966   "Ostensive Instances and Entitativity in Language Learning" (Mimeo., Center for Advanced Study in the Behavioral Sciences).
Carmichael, L., H. P. Hogan, and A. A. Walter,
    1932   "An Experimental Study of the Effect of Language on the Reproduction of Visually Perceived Form", *J. Exp. Psych.* 15, 73-86.
Carroll, J. B.,
    1964   *Language and Thought* (Englewood Cliffs, N. J.: Prentice-Hall).
Chase, R. A.,
    1966   "Evolutionary Aspects of Language Development and Function", in F. Smith and G. A. Miller (eds.), *The Genesis of Language* (Cambridge, Mass.: MIT Press), pp. 253-68.
Cherry, C.,
    1957   *On Human Communication* (Cambridge, Mass.: MIT Press).
Chomsky, N.,
    1962   *Syntactic Structures* (The Hague: Mouton).
    1964   A Review of B. F. Skinner's *Verbal Behavior*, in J. A. Fodor and J. J. Katz (eds.), *The Structure of Language* (Englewood Cliffs, N. J.: Prentice-Hall), pp. 547-78 (reprinted from *Lang.*, 1959, 35 [1], 26-58).
    1964a "Formal Discussion of 'The Development of Grammar in Child Language'" (paper delivered by W. Miller and S. Ervin), in U. Bellugi and R. Brown (eds.), *The Acquisition of Language* (= *Monogr. Soc. Res. Child Devel.* 29 [1]), 35-39.
    1965   *Aspects of the Theory of Syntax* (Cambridge, Mass.: MIT Press).
    1966 (1966a)   *Cartesian Linguistics* (New York: Harper and Row).
    1966   *Current Issues in Linguistic Theory* (The Hague: Mouton).
    1967   "The Formal Nature of Language", in E. H. Lenneberg, *Biological Foundations of Language* (New York: Wiley), pp. 397-442.
    1967 (1967a)   "General Properties of Language", in C. H. Millikan and F. L. Darley (eds.), *Brain Mechanisms Underlying Speech and Language* (New York: Grune and Stratton), pp. 73-81.
    1968   *Language and Mind* (New York: Harcourt, Brace).
    1968 (1968a)   "Language and the Mind", *Psych. Today* 1, 9, 47-68.
Chomsky, N., and M. Halle,
    1968   *The Sound Pattern of English* (New York: Harper and Row).
Cofer, C. N., and J. P. Foley Jr.,
    1942   "Mediated Generalization and the Interpretation of Verbal Behavior: I. Prolegomena", *Psych. Review* 49, 6 (Nov.), 513-40.
Cook, W. A.,
    1969   *Introduction to Tagmemic Analysis* (New York: Holt, Rinehart and Winston).

Cowgill, W.,
1963 "A Search for Universals in Indo-European Diachronic Morphology", in J. H. Greenberg (ed.), *Universals of Language* (Cambridge, Mass.: MIT Press), pp. 91-113.
Darley, F. L.,
1964 *Diagnosis and Appraisal of Communication Disorders* (Englewood Cliffs, N. J.: Prentice-Hall).
Deese, J.,
1965 *The Structure of Associations in Language and Thought* (Baltimore: Johns Hopkins Press).
Diamond, A. S.,
1965 *The History and Origin of Language* (New York: Citadel).
Diller, K.,
1967 " 'Compound' and 'Co-ordinate' Bilingualism: A Conceptual Artifact" (Paper read at the 42nd Annual Meeting of the Linguistic Society of America, Chicago).
Dixon, T. R., and D. L. Horton (eds.),
1968 *Verbal Behavior and General Behavior Theory* (Englewood Cliffs, N. J.: Prentice-Hall).
Elkind, D.,
1965 "The Development of Quantitative Thinking: A Systematic Replication of Piaget's Studies", in I. J. Gordon (ed.), *Human Development* (Glenview, Ill.: Scott, Foresman), pp. 61-66.
Epstein, I.,
1915 *La pensée et la polyglossie* (Paris, n. p.).
Ervin-Tripp, S. M.,
1961 "Changes With Age in the Verbal Determinants of Word-Association", *Am. J. Psych.* 74, 3, 361-72.
Fantz, R. L.,
1958 "Pattern Vision in Young Infants", *Psych. Record* 8, 43-47.
Ferster, C. B.,
1968 "The Autistic Child", *Psych. Today* 2, 6, 34-61.
Ferguson, C. A.,
1963 "Assumptions About Nasals: A Sample Study in Phonological Universals", in J. H. Greenberg (ed.), *Universals of Language* (Cambridge, Mass.: MIT Press), 42-47.
Fodor, J. A.,
1965 "Could Meaning Be an r_m?", *J. Vbl. Lng. Vbl. Behav.* 4, 73-81.
1966 "How to Learn to Talk: Some Simple Ways", in F. Smith and G. Miller (eds.), *The Genesis of Language* (Cambridge, Mass.: MIT Press), pp. 105-22.
Fodor, J. A., and T. G. Bever,
1965 "The Psychological Reality of Linguistic Segments", *J. Vbl. Lng. Vbl. Behav.* 4, 414-20.
Fraser, C.,
1966 "Discussion of 'The Creation of Language' " (paper delivered by D. McNeill), in J. Lyons and R. J. Wales (eds.), *Psycholinguistics Papers* (Edinburgh: Edinburgh Univ. Press), pp. 115-26.

Fraser, C., U. Bellugi, and R. Brown,
  1963   "Control of Grammar in Imitation, Comprehension and Produc-
          tion", *J. Vbl. Lng. Vbl. Behav.* 2, 121-35.
Fry, D. B.,
  1966   "The Development of the Phonological System in the Normal
          and the Deaf Child", in F. Smith and G. Miller (eds.), *The
          Genesis of Language* (Cambridge, Mass.: MIT Press), pp. 187-206.
Garrett, M., and J. A. Fodor,
  1968   "Psychological Theories and Linguistic Constructs", in T. R.
          Dixon and D. L. Horton (eds.), *Verbal Behavior and General
          Behavior Theory* (Englewood Cliffs, N. J.: Prentice-Hall), pp.
          451-77.
Gelb, I. J.,
  1952   *A Study of Writing* (Chicago: Univ. of Chicago Press).
Goldman-Eisler, F.,
  1961   "The Distribution of Pause Durations in Speech", *Lang. and
          Spch.* 4, 4, 220-31.
  1968   *Psycholinguistics* (London: Academic Press).
Granich, L.,
  1952   *Aphasia: A Guide to Retraining* (New York: Grune and Stratton).
Greenberg, J. H. (ed.),
  1963   *Universals of Language* (Cambridge, Mass.: MIT Press).
  1966   *Language Universals* (The Hague: Mouton).
Haas, M. R.,
  1964   "Men's and Women's Speech in Koasati", in D. Hymes (ed.),
          Language in Culture and Society (New York: Harper and Row),
          pp. 228-33.
Hall, E. T.,
  1961   *The Silent Language* (Greenwich, Conn.: Premier [Fawcett]).
  1967   *The Hidden Dimension* (Long Island, N. Y.: Doubleday).
Harlow, H. F.,
  1965   "The Heterosexual Affectional System in Monkeys", in I. Gordon
          (ed.), *Human Development* (Glenview, Ill.: Scott, Foresman),
          pp. 150-60 (reprinted from *Amer. Psychologist*, 1962, 17, 1-9).
  1965   "The Nature of Love", in I. Gordon (ed.), *Human Development*
          (Glenview, Ill.: Scott, Foresman), pp. 140-49 (reprinted from
          Amer. Psychologist, 1958, 13, 673-85).
Hayakawa, S. I.,
  1964   *Language in Thought and Action* (New York: Harcourt, Brace
          and World).
Hebb, D. O.,
  1958   *A Textbook of Psychology* (Philadelphia: Saunders) (rev. ed. 1966).
Herdan, G.,
  1960   *Type-Token Mathematics* (The Hague: Mouton).
Herman, D. T., R. H. Lawless, and R. W. Marshall,
  1957   "Variables in the Effect of Language on the Reproduction of
          Visually Perceived Forms", *Percept. Motor Skills* 7, 171-86.

Herman, L., and M. S. Herman,
1943 "Manual of Foreign Dialects" (Chicago: Ziff-Davis).
Hilgard, E. R.,
1956 *Theories of Learning* (New York: Appleton-Century-Crofts).
Hill, W. F.,
1963 *Learning* (San Francisco: Chandler).
Hockett, C. F.,
1960 "The Origin of Speech", *Sci. Amer.* 203 (3), 89-96.
1963 "The Problem of Universals in Language", in J. H. Greenberg (ed.),
Universals of Language (Cambridge, Mass.: MIT Press), pp. 1-22.
1968 *The State of the Art* (The Hague: Mouton).
Hoijer, H. (ed.),
1954 *Language in Culture* (Chicago: Univ. of Chicago Press).
Hoijer, H.,
1964 "Cultural Implications of Some Navaho Linguistic Categories",
in D. Hymes (ed.), *Language in Culture and Society* (New York:
Harper and Row), pp. 142-53.
Holland, J. G., and B. F. Skinner,
1961 *The Analysis of Behavior* (New York: McGraw Hill).
Houston, S. H.,
1967 "Inquiry Into the Structure of Mentation Processes", *Psych.
Reports* 21 (2), 649-59.
1969 "A Sociolinguistic Consideration of the Black English of Chil-
dren in Northern Florida", *Lang.* 45, 3 (Sept.), 599-607.
Forthcoming "An Expansion of Osgood's Mediated Stimulus-Response
Paradigm of Lexicon Acquisition".
Houston, S. H., and C. Kamm,
Forthcoming "Performance in Sentence Imitation Tasks Cannot Be
Explained by Association Theory".
Huxley, J. and L. Koch,
1964 *Animal language* (New York: Grosset and Dunlap).
Jakobson, R.,
1961 "Aphasia as a Linguistic Problem", in S. Saporta (ed.), *Psycho-
linguistics* (New York: Holt, Rinehart and Winston), pp. 419-26.
Jenkins, J. J., and D. S. Palermo,
1964 "Mediation Processes and the Acquisition of Linguistic Structure",
in U. Bellugi and R. Brown (eds.), *The Acquisition of Language.
Monogr. Soc. Res. Child Devel.* 29 (1), 141-49.
Jensen, A. R.,
1967 "Social Class and Verbal Learning", in J. P. DeCecco (ed.), *The
Psychology of Language, Thought and Instruction* (New York:
Holt, Rinehart and Winston), pp. 103-17.
Jones, L. V., and J. M. Wepman,
1965 "Language: A Perspective from the Study of Aphasia", in S.
Rosenberg (ed.), *Directions in Psycholinguistics* (New York: Mac-
millan), pp. 237-54.
Kalmus, H.,
1966 "Ontogenetic, Genetical and Phylogenetic Parallels Between Ani-

mal Communication and Prelinguistic Child Behavior", in F.
Smith and G. Miller (eds.), *The Genesis of Language* (Cambridge,
Mass.: MIT Press), pp. 273-85.

Katz, J. J., and J. A. Fodor,
1964 "The Structure of a Semantic Theory", in J. A. Fodor and J. J.
Katz (eds.), *The Structure of Language* (Englewood Cliffs, N. J.:
Prentice-Hall), pp. 479-518 (reprinted from *Lang.*, 1963, 39, 170-
210).

Kessen, W.,
1965 "Research in the Psychological Development of Infants: An
Overview", in I. Gordon (ed.), *Human Development* (Glenview,
Ill.: Scott, Foresman), pp. 83-90.

Klima, E. S., and U. Bellugi,
1966 "Syntactic Regularities in the Speech of Children", in J. Lyons
and R. J. Wales (eds.), *Psycholinguistics Papers* (Edinburgh:
Edinburgh Univ. Press), pp. 183-208.

Koffka, K.,
1959 *The Growth of the Mind* (Paterson, N. J.: Littlefield, Adams).

Köhler, W.,
1917 *Intelligenzprüfungen an Anthropoiden: I* (Berlin: Königl. Aka-
demie der Wissenschaft).
1925 *The Mentality of Apes* (New York: Harcourt, Brace).
1947 *Gestalt Psychology* (New York: Mentor).

Krogh, A.,
1955 "The Language of the Bees", in D. Flanagan (ed.), *Twentieth-
Century Bestiary* (New York: Simon and Schuster), pp. 47-53.

La Barre, W.,
1964 "Paralinguistics, Kinesics and Cultural Anthropology", in T. A.
Sebeok, A. S. Hayes, and M. C. Bateson (eds.), *Approaches to
Semiotics* (The Hague: Mouton), pp. 191-220.

Lado, R.,
1957 *Linguistics Across Cultures* (Ann Arbor: Univ. of Michigan Press).
1961 *Language Testing* (New York: McGraw Hill).
1964 *Language Teaching* (New York: McGraw Hill).

Lambert, W. E., and S. Fillenbaum,
1961 "A Pilot Study of Aphasia Among Bilinguals", in S. Saporta (ed.),
Psycholinguistics (New York: Holt, Rinehart and Winston), pp.
455-59.

Lambert, W. E., J. Havelka, and C. Crosby,
1958 "The Influence of Language-Acquisition Contexts on Bilingualism", *J. Abnorm. Soc. Psych.* 56, 239-44.

Lambert, W. E., and M. S. Preston,
1967 "The Interdependencies of the Bilingual's Two Languages", in
K. Salzinger and S. Salzinger (eds.), *Research in Verbal Behavior
and Some Neurophysiological Implications* (New York: Academic
Press), pp. 115-19.

Lashley, K. S.,
1960 "The Problem of Serial Order in Behavior", in F. A. Bach,

D. O. Hebb, C. T. Morgan, and H. W. Nissen (eds.), *The Neuropsychology of Lashley* (New York: McGraw Hill), pp. 506-28.

Leach, E.,
1964 "Anthropological Aspects of Language: Animal Categories and Verbal Abuse", in E. Lenneberg (ed.), *New Directions in the Study of Language* (Cambridge, Mass.: MIT Press), pp. 23-63.

Lenneberg, E. H.,
1961 "Color Naming, Color Recognition, Color Discrimination: A Re-Appraisal", *Percept. Motor Skills* 12, 375-82.
1962 "Understanding Language Without the Ability to Speak: A Case Report", *J. Abnorm. Soc. Psych.* 65, 419-25.
1964 "A Biological Perspective of Language", in E. H. Lenneberg (ed.), *New Directions in the Study of Language* (Cambridge, Mass.: MIT Press), pp. 65-88.
1964 (1964a) "The Capacity for Language Acquisition", in J. A. Fodor and J. J. Katz (eds.), *The Structure of Language* (Englewood Cliffs, N. J.: Prentice-Hall), pp. 579-603.
1967 *Biological Foundations of Language* (New York: Wiley).

Lent, J. R.,
1968 "Mimosa Cottage: Experiment in Hope", *Psych. Today* 2, 1, 51-58.

Leopold, W. F.,
1939-47 *Speech Development of a Bilingual Child: A Linguist's Record* (Evanston: Northwestern Univ. Press), 4 vols.

Lilly, J. C.,
1962 *Man and Dolphin* (New York: Pyramid).
1967 *The Mind of the Dolphin* (New York: Avon).

Lorenz, K. Z.,
1952 *King Solomon's Ring* (New York: Time, Inc.).

Lyons, J.,
1968 *Introduction to Theoretical Linguistics* (Cambridge, Eng.: Cambridge Univ. Press).

Mahl, G. F., and G. Schulze,
1964 "Psychological Research in the Extralinguistic Area", in T. A. Sebeok, A. S. Hayes, and M. C. Bateson (eds.), *Approaches to Semiotics* (The Hague: Mouton), pp. 51-124.

Maier, N. R. F.,
1930 "Reasoning in Humans: I. On Direction", *J. Comp. Psych.* 10, 115-43.

McNeill, D.,
1966 (1966a) "The Creation of Language", in J. Lyons, and R. J. Wales (eds.), *Psycholinguistics Papers* (Edinburgh: Edinburgh Univ. Press), pp. 99-126.
1966 "Developmental Psycholinguistics", in F. Smith and G. Miller (eds.), *The Genesis of Language* (Cambridge, Mass.: MIT Press), pp. 15-84.
1968 "On Theories of Language Acquisition", in T. R. Dixon and D. L. Horton (eds.), *Verbal Behavior and General Behavior Theory* (Englewood Cliffs, N. J.: Prentice-Hall), pp. 406-20.

Menyuk, P.,
1969 *Sentences Children Use* (Cambridge, Mass.: MIT Press).
Miller, G. A.,
1962 "Some Psychological Studies of Grammar", *Amer. Psychologist* 17, 748-62.
Miller, G. A., E. Galanter, and K. H. Pribram,
1960 *Plans and the Structure of Behavior* (New York: Holt, Rinehart and Winston).
Morris, C. W.,
1938 "Foundations of the Theory of Signs", *Internat'l Encyclopedia of Unified Science* 1, 2 (Univ. of Chicago Press).
Mowrer, O. H.,
1960 *Learning Theory and the Symbolic Processes* (New York, Wiley).
Odbert, H. S., T. F. Karwoski, and A. B. Eckerson,
1942 "Studies in Synesthetic Thinking: I. Musical and Verbal Associations of Color and Mood", *J. Gen. Psych.* 26, 153-73.
Olmsted, D. L.,
1969 "The Effect of Position in the Utterance on Acquisition of Phones by Children" (Paper delivered to the 44th Annual Meeting of the Linguistic Society of America, San Francisco).
Osgood, C. E.,
1963 "Language Universals and Psycholinguistics", in J. H. Greenberg (ed.), *Universals of Language* (Cambridge, Mass.: MIT Press), pp. 236-54.
1963 (1963a) "On Understanding and Creating Sentences", *Amer. Psychologist* 18, 735-51.
1964 "Semantic Differential Techniques in the Comparative Study of Cultures", *Amer. Anthropologist* 66, 3, 171-200.
1968 "Toward a Wedding of Insufficiences", in T. R. Dixon and D. L. Horton (eds.), *Verbal Behavior and General Behavior Theory* (Englewood Cliffs, N. J.: Prentice-Hall, pp. 495-519.
Osgood, C. E., and T. A. Sebeok,
1965 *Psycholinguistics* (Bloomington, Ind.: Indiana Univ. Press).
Osgood, C. E., and G. J. Suci,
1955 "Factor Analysis of Meaning", *J. Exp. Psych.* 50, 325-38.
Osgood, C. E., G. J. Suci, and P. H. Tannenbaum,
1957 *The Measurement of Meaning* (Urbana, Ill.: Univ. of Illinois Press).
Packard, V.,
1950 *The Human Side of Animals* (New York: Pocket Books).
Pavlov, I.,
1960 *Conditioned Reflexes* (New York: Dover) (1st ed. 1927).
Pedersen, H.,
1931 *The Discovery of Language* (Bloomington, Ind.: Ind. Univ. Press).
Peters, P. S., Jr.,
1969 "On the Complexity of Language Processing by the Brain", in K. N. Leibovic (ed.), *Information Processing in the Nervous System* (New York: Springer-Verlag), pp. 51-82.

Phillips, L. W.,
1958 "Mediated Verbal Similarity as a Determinant of the Generalization of a Conditioned GSR", *J. Exp. Psych.* 55, 56-62.
Piaget, J.,
1952 *The Origins of Intelligence in Children* (New York: Norton).
1954 *The Construction of Reality in the Child* (New York: Basic Books).
1955 *The Language and Thought of the Child* (Cleveland: Meridian).
1967 *The Child's Conception of the World* (Totowa, N. J.: Littlefield, Adams).
Piaget, J., and B. Inhelder,
1958 *The Growth of Logical Thinking from Childhood to Adolescence* (New York: Basic Books).
Pines, M.,
1966 *Revolution in Learning* (New York: Harper and Row).
Pinto, O.,
1952 *Spy Catcher* (New York: Berkley).
Premack, D., and A. Schwartz,
1966 "Preparations for Discussing Behaviorism with Chimpanzee", in F. Smith and G. Miller (eds.), *The Genesis of Language* (Cambridge, Mass.: MIT Press), pp. 295-335.
Pryor, K.,
1969 "Behavior Modification: The Porpoise Caper", *Psych. Today* 3, 7 (Dec.), 46-64.
Rivers, W. M.,
1964 *The Psychologist and the Foreign Language Teacher* (Chicago: Univ. of Chicago Press).
1968 *Teaching Foreign-Language Skills* (Chicago: Univ. of Chicago Press).
Robins, R. H.,
1951 *Ancient and Medieval Grammatical Theory in Europe* (London: Bell).
1967 *A Short History of Linguistics* (Bloomington, Ind.: Indiana Univ. Press).
Rossi, G. F., and G. Rosadini,
1967 "Experimental Analysis of Cerebral Dominance in Man", in C. H. Millikan and F. L. Darley (eds.), *Brain Mechanisms Underlying Speech and Language* (New York: Grune and Stratton), pp. 167-75.
Russell, W. R., and M. Espir,
1961 *Traumatic Aphasia* (London: Oxford Univ. Press).
Sapir, E.,
1921 *Language* (New York: Harvest [Harcourt, Brace]).
1929 "The Status of Linguistics as a Science", *Lang.* 5, 207-14.
1949 *Culture, Language and Personality* (ed. D. G. Mandelbaum) Berkeley: Univ. of California Press).
Scherer, G. A. C., and M. Wertheimer,
1964 *A Psycholinguistic Experiment in Foreign Language Teaching* (New York: McGraw Hill).

Schuell, H.,and J. J. Jenkins,
1961   "The Nature of Language Deficit in Aphasia", in S. Saporta (ed.), *Psycholinguistics* (New York: Holt, Rinehart and Winston), pp. 427-47.
Skinner, B. F.,
1938   *The Behavior of Organisms* (New York: Appleton-Century-Crofts).
1953   *Science and Human Behavior* (New York: Macmillan).
1957   *Verbal Behavior* (New York: Appleton-Century-Crofts).
Slobin, D. I.,
1966   "The Acquisition of Russian as a Native Language", in F. Smith and G. Miller (eds.), *The Genesis of Language* (Cambridge, Mass.: MIT Press), pp. 129-48.
1968   "Imitation and grammatical development in children", in N. S. Endler, L. R. Boulter and H. Osser (eds.), *Contemporary Issues in Developmental Psychology* (New York: Holt, Rinehart and Winston), pp. 437-43.
Spier, L., A. I. Hallowell, and S. S. Newman (eds.),
1941   *Language, Culture and Personality* (Menasha, Wisc.: Sapir Memorial Publ. Fund).
Staats, A. W., and C. K. Staats,
1964   *Complex Human Behavior* (New York: Holt, Rinehart and Winston).
Steiner, G.,
1969   "The Tongues of Man", *The New Yorker* 45, 39 (Nov. 15), 217-36.
Taube, M.,
1961   *Computers and Common Sense* (New York: McGraw Hill).
Thorndike, E. L.,
1898   "Animal Intelligence: An Experimental Study of the Associative Processes in Animals", *Psych. Rev. Monogr. Suppl.* 2, 8.
1913   *The Psychology of Learning* (New York: Teachers' College).
Ullmann, L. P., and L. Krasner (eds.),
1966   *Case Studies in Behavior Modification* (New York: Holt, Rinehart and Winston).
Vernon, M. D.,
1962   *The Psychology of Perception* (Baltimore: Penguin).
Vygotsky, L. S.,
1962   *Thought and Language* (Cambridge, Mass.: MIT Press).
Watson, J. B.,
1930   *Behaviorism* (Chicago: Univ. of Chicago Press) (1st ed. 1924).
Weaver, W.,
1963   "Recent Contributions to the Mathematical Theory of Communication", in C. E. Shannon and W. Weaver, *The Mathematical Theory of Communication* (Urbana, Ill.: Univ. of Illinois Press), pp. 94-117.
Weinreich, U.,
1964   *Languages in Contact* (The Hague: Mouton).
Weisberg, P.,
1963   "Social and Nonsocial Conditioning of Infant Vocalizations",

Child Devel. 34, 377-88.
Weisenberg, T., and K. McBride,
  1935 *Aphasia, a Clinical and Psychological Study* (New York: Com-
         monwealth Fund).
Wertheimer, M.,
  1923 "Untersuchungen zur Lehre von der Gestalt, II", *Psych. Forsch.*
         4, 301-50.
  1938 "Laws of Organization in Perceptual Forms", in W. D. Ellis (ed.),
         A Source Book of Gestalt Psychology (New York: Harcourt,
         Brace), pp. 71-88.
  1945 *Productive Thinking* (New York: Harper).
Wiener, N.,
  1954 *The Human Use of Human Beings* (New York: Doubleday
         [Anchor]).
Whorf, B. L.,
  1964 *Language, Thought and Reality* (ed. J. B. Carroll) (Cambridge,
         Mass.: MIT Press).
Zimmerman, D. W.,
  1958 "An unsuccessful attempt, based on the autism theory of language
         learning, to teach dogs to bark instrumentally" (Unpublished
         research).

INDEX

Abbott, E. A., 49
Abstract nouns, acquisition of, 74
Acalculia, 258, 263
Alexia, 260
Agrammatism, 258-259
Agraphia, 262-263
  letter formation difficulty in, 262
  word-revisualization difficulty in, 263
  written word formation difficulty in, 262-263
Algorithms, 48, 48n.
American Indian languages, 190, 192-194, 212, 248
Analogy, 39, 167, 246
Animal communication, 17, 85, 88, 93-94, 107, 200, 241-249, 260ff.
  dialects in, 249
Animal training, 23-24, 26, 88, 88n., 269
Anomia, 259-260
Anxiety, role in paralinguistics, 231, 232-233
Apes, 32ff., 200
Aphasia, 17, 154, 179, 211-212, 254ff.
  amnesic, 255, 259
  contiguity disorder in, 254-255
  expressive, 255
  loss of phonetic associations in, 261-262
  motor, 257
  pragmatic, 256-257
  receptive, 255, 260
  semantic, 256
  similarity disorder in, 254-255, 256

  syntactic, 256
  visual recognition difficulty in, 260-261
  word-formation difficulty in, 258
Approach behavior, 84
Apraxia, verbal, 254, 258
Arabic, 206, 235
Aranta, 270
Arbitrariness, linguistic, 241, 245
Ardrey, R., 161, 279
Associative chains, 30, 160
Astronomy, 78n.
Attention span, 243
Audio-Lingual Method, 215, 216, 217
Autism, 151-153, 157-158, 254n.
Autism theory of word learning, 89f., 101
Autoclitic, 51, 61-62, 76-77
Avoidance behavior, 82, 84

Babbling, 91, 178, 200
Bach, E., 15
Bandura, A., 25n.
Bar-Hillel, Y., 134n.
Bastian, J., 275-277
Bateson, G., 248n., 274-275
Bayley, N., 38
Bees, communication of, 242, 245, 246, 248, 269, 270-273
Behavior modification, 25n.
Behaviorism, 18, 19, 30, 40, 46, 138
Bellugi, U., 55, 86, 102, 103, 150, 163f.
Bettelheim, B., 141, 152-153, 157-158
Bever, T. G., 16

298   INDEX